Praise for Arthur Goldwag's

Cults, Conspiracies, and Secret Societies

"The kind of reference that the Internet cannot supplant. . . . Goldwag keeps the facts straight and gives the rumors—no matter how lurid and entertaining—about as much respect as they deserve."   —*The Washington Post*

"Goldwag is a colorful writer who makes good use of his material as he aims to explain, rather than debunk or expose, a fascinating diversity of beliefs."   —*The Boston Globe*

"A great plum pudding of a book packed with nutty theories and fruity factoids. Goldwag navigates his way through the wilder reaches of human belief with great urbanity."
              —Mark Booth, author of *The Secret History of the World: As Laid Down by the Secret Societies*

"Delightful."   —*The Weekly Standard*

"Arthur Goldwag is a shrewd, fair minded, learned and enter-taining tour guide through a world that's simultaneously funny and frightening. Not a page goes by without some 'I-didn't-know-that!' nugget. Given what's going on this ever-more-paranoid society, a book like this one becomes not only titillating but cru-cially important."
              —Steven Waldman, Editor-in-Chief and co-founder of Beliefnet.com

ARTHUR GOLDWAG

×××××××

Cults, Conspiracies, and Secret Societies

Arthur Goldwag is a freelance writer and editor who lives in Brooklyn, New York. He is the author of *The Beliefnet Guide to Kabbalah* and *'Isms and 'Ologies.*

CULTS,
CONSPIRACIES,
and SECRET SOCIETIES

CULTS, CONSPIRACIES, and SECRET SOCIETIES

The Straight Scoop on Freemasons, the Illuminati, Skull
and Bones, Black Helicopters, the New World Order,
and many, many more

ARTHUR GOLDWAG

VINTAGE BOOKS
A Division of Random House, Inc.
New York

FIRST VINTAGE BOOKS EDITION, AUGUST 2009

Copyright © 2009 by Arthur Goldwag

Library of Congress Cataloging-in-Publication Data
Goldwag, Arthur.
Cults, conspiracies, and secret societies : the straight scoop on Freemasons,
the Illuminati, Skull and Bones, Black Helicopters, the New World Order,
and many, many more / Arthur Goldwag.—1st Vintage Books ed.
p.   cm.
ISBN 978-0-307-39067-7
1. Secret Societies.   2. Cults.   3. Conspiracies.   I. Title.
HS125.G65 2009
366—dc22
2009021657

Book design by Debbie Glasserman

www.vintagebooks.com

Printed in the United States of America
10   9

THIS BOOK IS FOR GRACE

Now I have come to believe that the whole world is an enigma, a harmless enigma that is made terrible by our own mad attempt to interpret it as though it had an underlying truth.

—Umberto Eco, *Foucault's Pendulum*

Contents

xxxxxxxxxxxxxxxx

List of Topics

xxxxxxxxxxxxxxxxx

CULTS 1

Area 51, Stealth Blimps, Majestic-12, Alien Abductions, and Divine Revelations   133

SECRET SOCIETIES 215

Introduction

Although I didn't know it at the time, the seeds for this book were planted on the morning of September 11, 2001. I had just dropped my older son off at school and was riding my bike to my office in midtown Manhattan. When I was about halfway across the Brooklyn Bridge, an odd-looking airplane popped into my field of view. There were red and blue stripes running down its flank and the letters AA were painted on its tail, but everything else about it was incongruous. Its scale was wrong, for one thing—it took up more space in the sky than it should have. For another, it was going too fast and in the wrong direction. When a passenger jet flies low over Manhattan, it's usually heading north, toward LaGuardia Airport in Queens. This one was hurtling downtown, toward the World Trade Center.

A week before, from the same vantage, two military planes had caught my eye. For a second I'd had the crazy thought that one of them might crash into one of the Twin Towers, but of course they hadn't even come close—it was just a trick of foreshortening, a fluke of angles and perspective. This time, there was a resounding *BOOM!* as the top of the North Tower was engulfed in a fireball. It looked exactly like what Hollywood had taught me it should when an airplane smashes into a 110-story building, except that the plane had simply vanished—I would have expected to see its tail poking out of the building's skin after the flames dispersed, like a ghastly shiver of bone from a compound fracture, or its twisted fuselage tumbling slowly toward the street. It had left a visible wound in the tower, though, through which I could see an ominous glow. Thousands of tiny lights twinkled prettily in the surrounding air. It was sunlight reflecting off sheets of paper, I would realize later—a blizzard of charred and shredded memos, letters, financial statements, and other detritus of office life would drift onto the streets and rooftops of Brooklyn for the rest of the day.

"Did you see that? Did you see that?" someone bleated hysterically. I must have been in a state of shock, because I hardly even slowed down. I pedaled on stupidly—past City Hall, the Municipal Building, and the Tweed Courthouse, snaking through crowds of ashen-faced office workers stopping in their tracks as they emerged from the subways to gape skyward at the stricken building belching inky black smoke—until all of a sudden the nickel dropped and I heard rather than thought the words: "This was no accident."

It was terrorism, I said to myself. It was war. I had just witnessed the deaths of hundreds, maybe thousands, of people. I turned my bike around and wheeled back toward Brooklyn and my family. I had gone maybe two-thirds of the way across the bridge when I heard the shriek of jet engines and then another explosion. I didn't even turn around to look. "This is what it feels like to be inside of history," I heard myself thinking. I was a passerby on the streets of Sarajevo when the Archduke Ferdinand and his wife, Sophie, were shot; I was a sailor swabbing the deck of the *Arizona* on a December morning in 1941 as the first wave of Japanese dive-bombers flew into sight. My life was no longer my own; I was a character in a story that someone else was writing.

When something momentous happens, everything leading up to and away from the event seems momentous too. Even the most trivial detail seems to glow with significance. People who suffer from paranoid schizophrenia or who are under the influence of hallucinogens see the world that way; it is the hypervigilant perspective that a detective brings to a crime scene and that a mystic assiduously cultivates. It is also the point of view that cults inculcate in their followers and that conspiracy theorists bring to bear on the vicissitudes of everyday life.

Knowing what we know now (and knowing how many things there are that we still *don't* know), film footage of Dealey Plaza from November 22, 1963, seems pregnant with enigmas and ironies—from the oddly expectant expressions on the faces of the onlookers on the grassy knoll in the instants before the shots were fired (*What were they thinking?*), to the play of shadows in the background (*Could that flash up there on the overpass have been a gun barrel gleaming in the sun?*). Each odd excrescence, every random lump in the visual texture seems suspicious. *Why is that man carrying an umbrella on a sunny day? Who is that woman in the babushka? That lady in the bright red dress?*

Mystics believe that multiplicity and change are illusory; that everything is ultimately interconnected, part and parcel of a Transcendental Unity, that our universe is a cosmic One in which all contradictions are resolved. There are no coincidences, no accidents—everything is an integral part of the whole, if only you know how to discern the pattern. The Jewish mystics known as **Kabbalists** believe that Creation is formed out of Hebrew letters, which serve double duty as numbers. Their method of numerical analysis is called *gematria* (the Hebrew word comes from the Greek *geōmetria*, or "geometry"). When Kabbalists practice their deep art of decryption, they believe they are reading the mind of God himself.

Michael Drosnin's bestselling book *The Bible Code* (1997), which used computer algorithms to extract gematrical cryptograms from the Old Testament, was swiftly updated and rereleased in 2002. In the introduction to the second edition,

Drosnin recounts how he climbed to the roof of his Manhattan apartment building on September 11, 2001, to watch the World Trade Center towers fall. When he came downstairs, he ran his Bible software and discovered this astonishing acrostic: "'Twin Towers' was encoded in the 3,000-year-old text. 'Airplane' appeared in exactly the same place. 'It caused to fall, knock down' crossed 'Airplane' and 'Towers.'" Drosnin did not explain why this urgent and seemingly unambiguous warning hadn't made it into the book's first edition, but an event like 9/11 could make a temporary Kabbalist out of anyone.

Caught up in the press and stress of a catastrophe, we grope for a significance that's proportionate to the gravity of the events, seizing on whatever clues we can discern for ourselves, listening uncritically as self-appointed seers and wise men translate the figurative entrails of slaughtered animals into messages and scan the heavens for signs and portents. Even years later, long after the dust has settled, the impulse perseveres. An extremely silly but much-talked-about example: Did you know that if you fold a \$20 bill ($9 + 11 = 20$—get it?) in a certain way, you can create uncannily convincing images of the World Trade Center towers and the Pentagon on fire? Fold it slightly differently (actually, you have to sort of crumple it—it's not all that easy to do) and out of the *0* in one of the *20s*, the *S* in "States," and the first two and the final letters of the word "America" you can form the word "Osama." Spooky, isn't it? Or maybe it's suspicious—after all, those newly designed \$20 bills weren't released until 2003. Was someone in the Treasury Department trying to send us a message? Were they telling us that 9/11 was an inside job?

And then there's that quote from Nostradamus, who uncannily prophesied the events of 9/11. Actually 9/11 is one of the few things that the legendary sixteenth-century French seer *didn't* predict, but there was a lot of excitement on the Internet for a while about the quotation "two brothers torn apart by chaos, while the fortress endures," which it turned out had been written by a college student as a parody of Nostradamus's style, in order to demonstrate how opaque and infinitely adaptable his oracles can be.*

If crises can produce a certain paranoid, pattern-seeking frame of mind akin to the cultic and conspiratorial world-view, they can also engender charismatic, omnicompetent leaders—messianic father figures who take matters in hand and tell us what we need to think and do. New York City's mayor Rudolph Giuliani turned out to be such a one. As September 11, 2001, dawned, most New Yorkers were sick to death of him; thousands looked forward to casting their votes for his would-be successors in that day's primary elections. But by day's end, Giuliani's overbearing operatics—his untidy divorce, his incessantly small-minded bullying—were distant memories. Seizing his moment with Churchillian grace, he had transfigured himself into a tower of strength, an icon of quiet courage and effortless authority.

But to carry out the analogy just a bit further: eventually, like countless dictators and cult leaders before him, Giuliani began to believe his own hype: he succumbed to the temptation of self-deification. Mistaking citywide symptoms of post-traumatic stress for a permanent political realignment, he fatally overreached when he suggested that circumstances might require him to continue in office past the end of his term, even after his successor had been democratically elected. "I think that anybody that thinks they're ready for this job on January 1, given the monumental tasks that lie ahead, doesn't understand this job really well," he said. And with that all-too-characteristic act of self-aggrandizement, he administered the sharp slap across the city's collective face that it so badly needed to restore it to its senses. The rest of the world continued to idealize Giuliani for a few more years,

---

*Neil Marshall, "A Critique of Nostradamus" (1997). "Let us analyse this. . . . There are a lot of two brothers on this world (I think the Number runs among the Billions) and fortress endures what—Besiegement, Famine, etc? What Great Leader? . . . Now let the prophecy rest. . . . Eventually, one of them will fit close enough with [future] events . . . that the prophecy will appear to come true."

but as "America's Mayor" would learn when his presidential campaign came to grief in 2008, his aura did eventually fade.

9/11 not only brought a new roster of would-be gurus and leaders to the fore; it gave us an enemy that most of us knew precious little about—wild-eyed, bearded foreigners with unpronounceable names whose savage scriptures, we were told, enjoined them to kill us without mercy. After the attack on Pearl Harbor, thousands of innocent Japanese Americans were sequestered in camps. Though the backlash against Arab Americans was comparatively restrained in the wake of 9/11, many were summarily detained; countless Arabs who weren't citizens were confined without charges, deported, and even tortured. As Congress passed hasty, ill-considered legislation to protect the homeland against all-too-real adversaries like **Al Qaeda**, the media stoked the nation's anxieties with alarmist tales about sleeper cells of terrorists whose seemingly all-American members ate at Applebee's and watched the same TV shows that we did but were wholeheartedly committed to our destruction. Midwestern county seats scrambled to place sandbags in front of their official buildings, denizens of small agricultural towns reported sightings of suspicious-looking Semites equipped with chemical weapons gear—and that was before envelopes of weaponized anthrax were dispatched to politicians and journalists in the mail, spreading new ripples of panic across the land. In the background and on the fringes, the usual anti-Semitic demagoguery about Mossad and the Israel lobby (who were said to have manipulated events to serve their own devious purposes) could be heard; other conspiracy theorists adapted the circumstances to their own preferred cast of evildoers— Masonically connected, arms-trading billionaires, who brought down the towers to provoke a profitable war.

An event doesn't have to be as terrible as the ones that occurred on 9/11 to have a temporarily distorting psychological effect, just stunning and out of the ordinary. To devolve to the ridiculous for a moment, a beloved sports franchise could win its first championship in decades. Here is blogger Tom Merritt, writing in October 2004, after the Boston Red Sox won their first World Series since 1918, breaking the "curse of the Bambino" (the superstition that the Red Sox were fated never to win a World Series because of their folly in selling Babe Ruth to the Yankees in 1920). Of course Merritt's tongue was planted firmly in his cheek, but he nonetheless provides an illustration of the thought processes I am describing:

> The Red Sox first at bat of the World Series was number 19 (Williams) pitching to number 18 (Damon). . . . In 1918 the Red Sox won 86 games. One for every year they would have to wait until the next championship. Their final World Series loss came in 1986.

In the exhilarating flush of victory, it seemed that the Red Sox had fulfilled a destiny that was preordained. If their many losses were fated, so was their ultimate triumph— their eighty-six years in the wilderness had been inscribed in full in the continuous present tense that is the God's-eye perspective of history. The beginning, middle, and end of the story were plain to see, for those who knew how to decipher it—a mode of thinking that would seem familiar to members of the Kingdom of Yahweh, the **Concerned Christians**, the **Order of the Solar Temple**, or any number of other cults that prophesy destruction and proffer salvation.

If two characters in a novel look so much alike that they seem to be siblings, we can fairly presume that their resemblance has some narrative or thematic significance, because we know that the novel is presided over by an Author God who does nothing arbitrarily.* In the throes of crisis, the

---

*Fiction is more than a metaphor for conspiratorial thinking—many novels provide prime exemplars of its twists and turns. For example, Thomas Pynchon's classic *The Crying of Lot 49* (1965), in which a secret society, Tristero, a weird vestige of an age-old conflict between rival postal systems, plays an outsize role in the present day, or Robert Anton Wilson and Robert Shea's *Illuminatus! Trilogy* (1975), which brings a trippy, underground Comix sensibility to the subject.

world feels like it must have been authored too. Synchronicity presides; there is no such thing as happenstance. With the right promptings, superstition and suspicion can metastasize into a fully blown conspiratorial theology. "I knew something bad was going to happen," someone might say in the wake of a devastating event. "I broke a mirror last week. But even so, I can't understand why the president didn't do anything to protect us. There must have been a failure of intelligence."

"There was no failure," the conspiracist replies. "He was in on it from the start. Remember his father's speech about the **New World Order** on September 11, 1990? That was exactly eleven years ago. Do you realize what building the number eleven looks like? And did you know that the cornerstone of the Pentagon was laid on September 11, 1941—after a **Masonic** ceremony?"

"So the Masons did it?"

"It certainly looks that way."

The fact that those dates are authentic proves nothing. There are only 365 days in the year, after all. But in the wake of extraordinary happenings, all of us are more or less susceptible to this sort of magical thinking.

As the precipitating event recedes into the past, the accompanying hysteria fades; the vast majority of us regain our equilibrium; we begin to accept the possibility of accidents, contingencies, and coincidences again. Most people welcome this return to psychic normalcy, even if it requires them to confront unpalatable truths—such as the fact that the world is a dangerous, unpredictable place and that our leaders are as fallible as any other human beings. But some people choose to live in the compressed, deterministic universe of crisis all the time, the psychic environment where the theories, movements, and organizations I describe in this book are engendered. While others may fear that things are spinning out of control, that no one is in charge, these individuals draw precisely the opposite conclusion.

Doomsday cults like **Aum Shinrikyo** and the **Branch**

Davidians provide refuge for those who dread the universal tribulations of the coming End Times; plus they exert such a degree of control over their followers' lives that they need never endure a minute of uncertainty or ennui again. Conspiracy theorists are more likely to lead cults than to join them, and their orientation is often secular, but they too offer a vision of a world that, however terrible, is always purposive, of a Manichaean universe in which angels and demons are perpetually striving and nothing ever happens without reason or rhyme.

For religious cultists and nonbelieving conspiracy theorists alike, secret societies provide the answer to the question of how things got so out of hand. Bad things happen because wicked powers—demonic or human—want them to. Crepuscular cabals are forever gathering in lodges and temples, plush boardrooms, and secret military bases to plot the next assassination, bank failure, or epidemic. Hardly anyone understands this awful truth; those few who do are subject to ridicule and abuse. And yet it is those blessed few, that "saving remnant," who will ultimately prevail over those dark powers.

It is understandable that cult leaders and conspiracy theorists would accuse their enemies of working through secret societies, since they do that themselves. And though they call their adversaries by many names, they all bear a close familial resemblance to each other. John Robison's 1798 exposé about **Illuminism**, *Proofs of a Conspiracy Against All the Religions and Governments of Europe, Carried on in the Secret Meetings of Free Masons, Illuminati, and Reading Societies*, says pretty much the same thing about Adam Weishaupt's two-hundred-year-old secret society as the *Protocols of the Learned Elders of Zion* would say about the Jews at the turn of the twentieth century, and that the Internet-based ConspiracyArchive.com says about the so-called New World Order today.

But conspiracy theory is not just a foible of those who inhabit the extreme margins of the political and religious spectra. As Barack Obama observed in *The Audacity of Hope* (2006), its traces can be discerned wherever partisanship and factionalism hold sway. "In distilled form," he wrote, "the explanations of both the right and the left have become mirror images of each other. They are stories of conspiracy, of America being hijacked by an evil cabal. Like all good conspiracy theories, both tales contain just enough truth to satisfy those predisposed to believe in them, without admitting any contradictions that might shake up those assumptions."

When I first began to plan this book, I thought of it as a journey into the "dark side" of the subject matter of my earlier book, *'Isms and 'Ologies: All the Movements, Ideologies, and Doctrines That Have Shaped Our World*. If religious isms too often degenerate into dogma, cults usually begin that way. And while many political and philosophical ideologies at least attempt to rise above inchoate intuitions and unexamined prejudices and put things on an intellectually coherent footing, too often cults and conspiracy theories are specifically designed to keep us in blinkers and chains. I hoped to get across not just what cultists and conspiracists believe in, but why; to pick apart the strands of facticity and factitiousness, of known truths, myths, misunderstandings, and outright lies from which their ideologies and doctrines are woven. I wanted to write a book that approached this superlatively nutty realm with a spirit of respect where it is warranted, but always with a due regard for the facts. My task, as I saw it, was not so much to debunk or to expose as to explain.

Many cults and secret societies, and many of the conspiracies attributed to them, turn out to be exactly as they are advertised. I cover a lot of them in these pages. Ineffectual as it was, the **Weather Underground** did advocate the violent overthrow of capitalism; Al Qaeda truly regards the West with the same implacable loathing as its ancestors did the Crusaders; not everyone who questions the Warren Commission's explanation of the **Kennedy assassination** is insane. But I confess that the ones that interest me the most—and to which I devote the most attention—tend to be those (many of them inextricably intertwined) that abide on or beyond the fringes.

A few words about the organization of this book: Not all of its entries and essays fit neatly into the three overarching categories—"Cults," "Conspiracies," and "Secret Societies"—that I have assigned them to. Some belong under more than one heading; some may not quite fit into any of them. Not every subject appears under its own rubric—many of the essays cover a wider range of topics than their titles suggest. For example, while writing about the mythical **black helicopters** that so obsessed members of the so-called patriot movement in the 1980s, I wandered as far afield as the **Ananias** societies, or liars' clubs, that cropped up all over the United States toward the end of the nineteenth century; any number of topics required a lengthy digression on Freemasonry. If you are looking to read about a particular group or theory or event, try the list of topics if you can't find it where you think it belongs, or if its short entry doesn't seem to do it justice. That said, honesty compels me to add this caveat: though I cover a lot of ground, I haven't attempted to cover everything. The presiding spirit of this book is exploratory rather than encyclopedic; I am more interested in finding underlying commonalities and connections between groups and theories than in itemizing and delineating the fine distinctions between them.

I've tried to be fair-minded, but the very words "cults," "conspiracy theories," and "secret societies" are value-laden and intrinsically pejorative. Sometimes the distinctions between a cult and a denomination, a conspiracy and a political movement, a "secret society" and a "minority culture" are simply matters of convention and usage. For a deliberately provocative example, take the ritual of Communion. The Sacred Supper is a sacrament of the Roman Catholic Church and a symbolic practice of many Protestant denominations, but it could easily strike an anthropologist from

Mars as a sublimated vestige of anthropophagy (cannibalism, for the unsqueamish). Why do we consider glossolalia (speaking in tongues) to be a stranger practice, and ritual tattooing to be stranger still? Why do we take some things to be normative and declare others beyond the pale? Some of the scandals that our government has tried but failed to keep under wraps—the CIA's Project MK-ULTRA, for example (in which, starting in the early 1950s and continuing through the 1960s, unsuspecting human guinea pigs were dosed with dangerous hallucinogenics as part of a concerted effort to perfect the techniques of "mind control") or the systematic torture of detainees that was carried out at Iraq's Abu Ghraib prison starting in 2004 with the sanction of senior U.S. officials—are as bad as or worse than the fantastical crimes that conspiracy theorists accuse it of.

One last observation: Inevitably, I spent quite a bit of time in cyberspace as I wrote this book. Nearly every conspiracy theorist worth their salt has launched their own Web site, as have most cults. It's remarkably easy, too, to locate digitized versions of obscure, esoteric texts on the Internet, since so many of them are in the public domain. The World Wide Web is not just an enormous library; it offers a unique correlative of the conspiratorial worldview. Once you log on, you discover that everything is connected, whether deliberately, by overt links, or serendipitously, by Google's and other search engines' algorithms. The orientation is horizontal rather than vertical—the old hierarchical categories that scholars used to rely on to assess the reliability of sources no longer apply.

In predigital times, it was considered fair play to judge a book by its cover. A hardcover from a big New York City publisher or a university press was deemed more credible than a paperback from a fly-by-night firm, printed in smeary ink on brittle brown paper. But the Internet has leveled the playing field. Thanks to the ubiquity of cheap and easy-to-use desktop publishing programs, egalitarianism rules; most

Web pages look superficially professional, whether they are produced by an extravagantly capitalized online subsidiary of a national magazine or by borderline psychotic high school kids in their parents' basements. And nothing in cyberspace ever goes away. Just as the **Knights Templar** and the Bavarian Illuminati are still blamed for all manner of malfeasances, long after their movements have ceased to exist or matter in any meaningful way, dead Web sites, long-debunked rumors, and garbled quotations abide on the Net forever. And interactivity can be a sword that cuts both ways. While open sources like Wikipedia are veritable fonts of specialized knowledge, contributors with agendas can easily censor, twist, enhance, and otherwise distort its articles. The subject matter of this book, intrinsically controversial as it is, especially invites such treatment. While I have exercised extreme caution in the use of online resources, I am excruciatingly aware of the hazards and temptations that await even the most skeptical and judicious of researchers.

And finally, the Internet offers its users the great boon of anonymity. Small-town Klansmen wouldn't have been able to terrorize their neighbors without fear of reprisal if they hadn't been hooded and robed. The Internet invites anyone who wishes to inflame, libel, and incite, or simply to say really uncivil things to their intellectual adversaries, to do just that pseudonymously, without any fear of the consequences. Many posters take full advantage of the opportunity, and the intensity of their animus can be disquieting, to say the least.

What can I tell you? It's a little bit scary out there.

CULTS

What Makes a Cult Cultish?

The dictionary defines "cult" as a system of worship, but the word is usually used to denote a religious movement that is out of the mainstream. Christianity, for example, began as a cultic offshoot of Judaism, enjoying a similar status to the Essenes, the desert-dwelling ascetics who preserved the Dead Sea Scrolls, or the Samaritans, who not only belonged to a different ethnicity than the ancient Hebrews, but also didn't worship in the Temple in Jerusalem or acknowledge any but the first five books of the Bible. If a cult gains enough adherents, cultural currency, money, and other appurtenances of respectability, it generally becomes either a recognized denomination of the orthodoxy that spawned it or a full-fledged religion in its own right.

When members of one of those orthodoxies use the word "cult," more often than not they are using it pejoratively, to undercut a disreputably heterodox challenge to their own authority. Many evangelical Christians, for example, dismiss even such large, established movements as the Jehovah's Witnesses, the Church of Christ Scientist, and the Latter-Day Saints as cults, refusing to grant them the status of legitimate Christian denominations. On May 11, 2007, televangelist Bill Keller sent the following message about then–presidential hopeful Mitt Romney, the former governor of Massachusetts and a practicing Mormon, to the millions of subscribers to his daily Internet devotional, "LivePrayer":

> Romney winning the White House will lead millions of people into the Mormon cult. Those who follow the false teachings of this cult, believe in the false Jesus of the Mormon cult and reject faith in the one true Jesus of the Bible, will die and spend eternity in hell.

Although my tone may be snarky at times, I strive to be agnostic when it comes to the tenets and doctrines of the movements I describe in these pages. Though I have occasionally given in to the temptation to write about a group merely because its ideas are entertainingly strange (à la **Koreshanity**), I am much more interested in the power relations between the leadership of a group and its members than I am in its doctrines. For the most part, when I characterize a group as a cult I am using the word as a social scientist or a psychologist would, to denote a coercive or totalizing relationship between a dominating leader and his or her unhealthily dependent followers. What makes a cult cultish is not so much what it espouses, but how much authority its leaders grant themselves—and how slavishly devoted to them its followers are.

On February 25, 2009, the Supreme Court issued its judgment in Pleasant Grove City, Utah *v.* Summum. Summum is a tiny sect founded in 1975 by Claude Nowell (1944–2008)—aka Corky King, Corky Ra, and Summum Bonum Amon Ra—whose members, among other things, mummify their pets and themselves after they die. A statue of the Ten Commandments stands in one of Pleasant Grove's public parks. Summum members wanted to erect a monument of their own commemorating their Seven Aphorisms* (according to Now-

---

*For those afflicted with an irresistible need to know, here are the Seven Aphorisms of Summum:

I.   The Principle of Psychokinesis. *SUMMUM is MIND, thought; the universe is a mental creation.*

II.   The Principle of Correspondence. *As above, so below; as below, so above.*

ell's teachings, the aphorisms were inscribed on the tablets Moses smashed after his first descent from Mount Sinai; he received the Ten Commandments during his second ascent). Not surprisingly, Pleasant Grove did not wish to accommodate them, and the Supreme Court agreed that the city does not need to. Obviously Summum is more than a little weird by conventional standards—though Nowell claimed to have channeled his revelations from otherworldly beings, the theology he developed appears to be a hodgepodge of **Masonic** mysteries, Christian Gnosticism, and kitsch Egyptology—but it is not abusive or controlling and hence it does not fall under my rubric of "cult." Neither do the many iterations of Theosophy, Anthroposophy, Wicca, neo-paganism, Swedenborgianism, and many other occult, esoteric, and New Age movements that the Evangelicalist Web site Cultwatch devotes so much of its attention to.

Robert Lifton, the distinguished psychologist and author of such well-known books as *The Nazi Doctors: Medical Killing and the Psychology of Genocide* (1986) and *Thought Reform and the Psychology of Totalism: A Study of "Brainwashing" in China* (1961), defined cults in a 1981 article in the *Harvard Mental Health Letter* as an "aspect of a worldwide epidemic of ideological totalism, or fundamentalism." Cults, he continued, can be identified by three characteristics: 1) a charismatic leader "who increasingly becomes an object of worship"; 2) a process of "coercive persuasion or thought reform" (brainwashing, in other words); and 3) economic,

---

III.   The Principle of Vibration. *Nothing rests; everything moves; everything vibrates.*

IV.   The Principle of Opposition. *Everything is dual; everything has an opposing point; everything has its pair of opposites; like and unlike are the same; opposites are identical in nature, but different in degree; extremes bond; all truths are but partial truths; all paradoxes may be reconciled.*

V.   The Principle of Rhythm. *Everything flows out and in; everything has its season; all things rise and fall; the pendulum swing expresses itself in everything; the measure of the swing to the right is the measure of the swing to the left; rhythm compensates.*

VI.   The Principle of Cause and Effect. *Every cause has its effect; every effect has its cause; everything happens according to Law; Chance is just a name for Law not recognized; there are many fields of causation, but nothing escapes the Law of Destiny.*

VII.   The Principle of Gender. *Gender is in everything; everything has its masculine and feminine principles; Gender manifests on all levels.*

sexual, or psychological exploitation of the rank-and-file members by the cult's leadership. The chief tool of "coercive persuasion," Lifton writes, is "milieu control; the control of all communication within a given environment."

Scientology has been accused of exploiting its acolytes and threatening its apostates, as has the **Unification Church** (its mass celebrations of arranged weddings, presided over by its founder and leader, Sun Myung Moon, epitomize the infringements of privacy and personal autonomy that so often go hand in glove with cult membership). Stephen Hassan, an ex-Moonie and an "exit counselor" for former cult members, defines a cult as a:

> Pyramid-structured, authoritarian group or relationship where deception, recruitment, and mind control are used to keep people dependent and obedient. A cult can be a very small group or it can contain a whole country. The emphasis of mind control is what I call the BITE model: the control of behavior, information, thoughts, and emotions.

The Latter-Day Saints may be big enough and mainstream enough today to qualify as a religion, but many of the unaffiliated polygamous sects that style themselves as fundamentalist Mormons fit Lifton's and Hassan's definitions of a cult to a T, in that their leaders assume Godlike powers at the expense of their followers' autonomy and individuality. Alma Dayer LeBaron (1886–1951) led his polygamous followers to Mexico in the 1920s when he started his breakaway sect, the Church of the Lamb of God; over the next eighty years his sons Ervil, Joel, and Verlan fought bloodily over the succession, as did the fratricidal generation that followed theirs. While they carried on the family business of writing visionary screeds and murdering anyone who challenged their authority, they put their child brides and neglected children to work stealing cars, dealing drugs, and fencing stolen goods. Warren Jeffs, who succeeded his father,

Rulon Jeffs (1909–2002), as President and Prophet, Seer and Revelator of the Fundamentalist Church of Jesus Christ of Latter-Day Saints, has been convicted of "accomplice rape" for forcing minors into marriage.

Of course renegade Mormons don't have a monopoly on this sort of egregious behavior. A Hasidic rebbe who demands that his disciples submit every aspect of their personal and financial lives for his approval can justly be accused of cultism. The Armenian-Greek mystic G.I. Gurdjieff (1866?–1945) wrote books, composed music, and choreographed dances; his Fourth Way, an eclectic spiritual discipline which seeks to awaken the body, mind, and emotions, continues today under the auspices of the international Gurdjieff Society. But in his lifetime, he led a cult of personality; he was notoriously cruel and demanding to his students, who unreservedly gave themselves up to his power. His charisma was said to be so intense that he could cause a woman to have an orgasm just by looking at her across a room. 1 Mind Ministries, a tiny group led by a woman who calls herself Queen Antoinette, made headlines during the summer of 2008 when it was discovered that the one-year-old child of a member had been starved to death because he refused to say "amen."

A cult needn't be religious, either. The dancer Olgivanna Hinzenberg, one of Gurdjieff's disciples, married the architect Frank Lloyd Wright (1867–1959). Wright's Taliesin school of architecture, where young architectural students performed virtual slave labor for the chance to learn from the master, had intensely cultish aspects to it. As Hassan notes, a whole country can devolve into cultishness—one need only think of Hitler's infamous Nuremberg rallies, Maoism at the height of China's Cultural Revolution, or the cult of personality surrounding Kim Jong Il, North Korea's "Dear Leader." A global, multilevel marketing concern like Amway, whose entrepreneurial leaders relentlessly pressure its salesmen to comport with their wider philosophy, to conform to their

standards of success, to purchase only their approved products, and to associate only with their fellow Amway representatives, is no less cultic in some essential respects than the
True Russian Orthodox Church, led by a schizophrenic
named Pyotr Kuznetsov, whose thirty-some-odd members
holed up in a cave in the Penza region of Central Russia in
late 2007 to await the end of the world.

Then there are the cults of personality that grew up
around supposed flying saucer contactees. George Adamski
(1891–1965) was a self-proclaimed teacher of Tibetan wisdom and a would-be science fiction writer until he announced
that he had been contacted by a Venusian named Orthon
who told him about the dangers of nuclear war. Later he was
taken for a ride in a flying saucer—adventures he recounted
in his books *Flying Saucers Have Landed* (1953) and *Inside
the Spaceships* (1955). Billy Meier is an ex-farmer from Switzerland who says he has been in communion with astronauts
from the Pleiades star cluster since he was five years old.
Thanks to their instruction, Meier says, he has achieved "the
highest degree of spiritual evolution of any human being on
earth." Though neither man had mass followings or required
their disciples to worship them, the "nonprofit" foundations
that they founded handsomely supported their various
endeavors.

Mystical practice—whether in Buddhism, Hinduism,
Sufism, **Kabbalism**, or the ecstatic Christianity of Meister
Eckehart, Saint John of the Cross, and Teresa of Avila—is
the pursuit of egolessness. Yoga and meditation are one
means of dissolving the barriers of everyday consciousness
and opening oneself up to a transcendent mode of experience; another is to temporarily surrender oneself up to an
authoritarian teacher. The ninth-century Zen master Lin Chi
is said to have beaten his disciples, even thrown one out of a
second-story window, to shock them out of their worldly
complacency. Reshad Feild's classic *The Last Barrier: A
Journey into the Essence of Sufi Teachings* (1977) vividly

describes how his teacher assaulted his worldly assumptions. One of his less-resilient fellow questers was driven insane. Of course all gurus are not so overbearing. Some hold out the paradisical prospect of limitless sex; still others terrify their followers with prophecies of a coming catastrophe that only they can save them from.

Religious movements, like businesses, require a constantly refreshed stream of customers in order to grow or merely keep pace with their natural rate of attrition. Recruitment and fund-raising are critical activities for cults, often carried out by the members themselves, who tirelessly distribute pamphlets on street corners, proselytize friends, family, and colleagues, and even use their bodies as lures (as female members of the **Children of God** were instructed to do in the 1960s and 1970s—a practice that their founder called "Flirty Fishing"). I have experienced some of this persuasion for myself and know how formidable it can be. For someone seeking to fill a void in his or her life, especially someone who is cut off from family and friends, it can be well-nigh irresistible.

When I was in my early twenties, one of my coworkers belonged to Arica, a syncretic movement founded by a Bolivian mystic named Oscar Ichazo, which brings together aspects of Gurdjieff's Fourth Way, Tai chi chuan, and ideas and practices associated with Esalen and the human potential movement, and wraps them up in a high-gloss package. As we got to know each other, he pressed me to accompany him to one of Arica's weekend retreats—strongly intimating that, if nothing else, I could meet attractive and accessible women there. When I finally broke down and did, I was immediately struck by three things: 1) that nearly every minute of the weekend was rigidly scripted—the session leaders had neither time nor toleration for questions or intellectual give-and-take; 2) that, rather than expounding or elaborating ideas, the teachers orchestrated experiences, through physical exercises and guided meditations, which were specifically designed to whet one's appetite for more; 3) that none of the women attending paid the slightest bit of attention to me.

Nothing bad happened; nobody tried to brainwash me or steal my money. But somewhere around the halfway point, I distinctly remember feeling a twinge of resentment when I realized that nobody wanted to engage me or persuade me or establish a relationship with me—instead they were trying to break down my resistance, to lull me into a state of susceptibility, to rope me in. I wasn't exactly in danger, but I felt obscurely threatened. I understood that to receive enlightenment on someone else's terms required an act of surrender that I wasn't prepared to make.

Clearly the path to enlightenment can be a perilous one for masters and disciples alike, with figurative and all-too-literal robbers, rapists, and murderers lurking behind every tree. The too-compliant initiate can be reduced to zombiehood; an unscrupulous or undisciplined master can easily yield to the temptation to take carnal or material advantage of the power they wield—or succumb to the delusion that they themselves are the Messiah or even God. It is a story that will be told again and again in the pages that follow.

Aetherius Society (see **Area 51** in Conspiracies)

Amma the Hugging Saint, or Mata Amritanandamayai
(see **Indian Gurus**)

Assassins
Storied Muslim cult which held sway in remote areas of Persia and Iraq and made inroads into Syria for a period in the
eleventh and twelfth centuries. Like the **Druze**, the Assassins
were an outgrowth of Ismailism, a schismatic movement
within the already-schismatic Shiism. Like the Shiites, the
Ismailis believe that the succession passes from Muhammad
through Ali and Fatimid, but they disagree about the identity
of the Seventh Imam. While Twelvers, the majority of Shiites, believe he was Musa al-Kadhim (746–799), Ismailis say
he was Isma'il ibn Jafar (721–755). The Ismailis themselves
would schism in 1094 over another dispute about the succession of the caliphate. After the death of the Eighteenth
Imam, Mustansir, in 1094, some supported his younger son
Musta'li (d. 1101); some supported his elder brother Nizār
(ca. 1044–1095).

Hassan-i Sabbāh (1034–1124) would become the leader
of the Nizārites. A widely traveled, well-connected Persian—
the great poet and astronomer Omar Khayyam (1048–1122)
was one of his schoolmates—Sabbāh was forced into exile
after he was accused of embezzling from the Shah. As cere-
bral as he was ruthless, he attended Al-Azhar University in
Cairo, where he studied Ismailite philosophy. The Ismailites'
esoteric teachings are highly syncretic, combining aspects of
Neoplatonism, Manichaean dualism, and Gnosticism. At
their heart is the notion that the conflict between good and
evil begins within the nature of God, and that the world is a
product of divine emanations that contain both light and
darkness. Only a select group of students was admitted to

Ismailism's inner circle—according to some accounts, initiation was accomplished through nine degrees of knowledge (a system that anticipated secret societies like the **Masons**). Initiates to the ninth and innermost degree or circle were taught that the teachings of the Koran were merely allegorical, useful for maintaining order among the ignorant, but not literally true. A famous phrase attributed to Hassan epitomizes the radically antinomian consequences of this belief: "nothing is true, everything is permitted"—a notion that would carry down to the twentieth century as Aleister Crowley's "Do what thou wilt."

Upon his return to Persia, Hassan-i Sabbāh established himself in the mountaintop fortress of Alamūt, from whence he unleashed a reign of terror throughout the Islamic world—not only on his Sunni and Musta'lite adversaries, but on their mutual enemies, the Christian Crusaders. Though Sabbāh rarely emerged from his study for the thirty-five remaining years of his life, his soldiers, known as Assassins, implacably carried out his orders. Assassin operatives were infiltrated into their enemies' cities and organizations to form what in today's parlance would be called sleeper cells. Universally feared for their preternatural ability to penetrate the most elaborate security arrangements, their skill with daggers, and their eerie equanimity in the face of torture and death, they foreshadowed the advent of today's Middle Eastern suicide bombers by almost a thousand years.

Legend has it that Hassan brainwashed his followers, not just with his radical teachings, which—very much in the manner of contemporary cults—substituted an ethos of personal loyalty to their Godlike master for traditional religious piety, but by convincing them through outright chicanery that their obedience would be rewarded in heaven. The Venetian explorer Marco Polo (not, to be sure, the most reliable of witnesses—he was born in 1254, 130 years after Hassan died; the Assassins were long out of power by the time he began his travels) recounted an oft-told story about

Hassan. When his young recruits were intoxicated by hashish, Hassan would convey to them a luxurious pleasure garden.

> Upon awakening from this state of lethargy ... each perceived himself surrounded by lovely damsels, singing, playing, and attracting his regards by the most fascinating caresses, serving him also with delicious viands and exquisite wines, until, intoxicated with excess of enjoyment, amidst actual rivers of milk and wine, he believed himself assuredly in paradise, and felt an unwillingness to relinquish its delights. When four or five days had thus been passed, they were thrown once more into a state of somnolency and carried out of the garden. ... The chief thereupon addressing them said, "We have the assurance of our Prophet that he who defends his lord shall inherit paradise, and if you show yourselves devoted to the obedience of my orders, that happy lot awaits you." Animated to enthusiasm by words of this nature all deemed themselves happy to receive the commands of their master, and were forward to die in his service.

Another medieval account of the Assassins (this one from the twenty-fourth chapter of *A Choice Book for Discovering the Secrets of the Art of Imposture* by Sheikh Abd-ur-Rahman Ben Ebubekr Al-Jeriri of Damascus) describes still another example of Hassan's trickery. Promising a follower rewards for his participation and swearing him to secrecy, he would bury him up to his neck in sand and pour blood around him. Then he would bring a group of young soldiers in and address the seemingly severed head.

> "Which wouldest thou prefer," said the master, "to return to the world and thy friends, or to dwell in paradise?" "What need have I," replied the head, "to return to the world after having seen my pavilion in paradise, and the hoories, and all that God has prepared for me? Comrades, salute my family,

and take care not to disobey this prophet, who is the lord of
the prophets in the state of time, as God has said unto me.
Farewell." These words strengthened the faith of the others;
but when they were gone the master took the man up out of
the hole, and cut off his head in right earnest. It was by such
means as this that he made himself obeyed by his people.

There are many reasons to take these stories with a grain
of salt. Written for an audience that already regarded Hassan as a monster and an infidel, they are clearly sensationalized. Hassan, it has been pointed out, eschewed intoxicants;
in fact he is said to have had his own son put to death for
drinking wine. Still, it's not difficult to imagine how he might
have made exceptions. The CIA agents who administered
LSD to test subjects while carrying out the MK-ULTRA
program in the 1950s and 1960s also undoubtedly disap-
proved of recreational drugs. And there can be no doubt
about either Hassan's brutality or his megalomania.

Whether the Assassins were cannabis users or not, their
name is widely believed to be derived from *hashshashin*, the
Arabic word for "hash smoker." Charles William Heckethorn, in *Secret Societies of All Ages and Countries* (1897),
offers two other possible etymologies—one, suggested by
"the Jew Benjamin, who wrote in 1173," is the word *asasa*,
"to lay snares"; another is the "Arab word *hass*, meaning 'to
destroy, kill.'" A fourth possible source is Hassan's name.

The Assassin cult outlived its founder by many years. In
1191, Assassins killed Conrad of Montferrat, the king of
Jerusalem, striking fear into the very heart of Europe.
Henry, Count of Champagne, who married Conrad's widow,
visited an Assassin stronghold in Syria, and watched in
astonishment as young *fedayeen* hurled themselves off its
towers at a nod from their commander, Rashīd ad-Dīn as-
Sinān, also known as the Old Man of the Mountain. But by
the midthirteenth century, caught between invading Mongol
armies and the defensive forces of the Mamluks, the Assas-

sins were overwhelmed and dispersed. The Nizārite sect survives to this day, albeit with a greatly altered belief system, under the leadership of its Forty-ninth Imam, the Aga Khan.

Aum Shinrikyo

A syncretic religion that mixed elements of Buddhism, Hinduism, and apocalyptic Christianity, Aum Shinrikyo was founded in Tokyo in 1987 by a thirty-two-year-old blind acupuncturist and yoga teacher who called himself Shoko Asahara and claimed to be the reincarnation of the god Shiva (his parents had named him Chizuo Matsumoto). Aum Shinrikyo was that rare doomsday cult that, unwilling to risk the embarrassment of predicting an apocalypse that failed to materialize on schedule, took matters into its own hands.

The religion's name comes from the Sanskrit syllable *om* (which represents the cosmos); *Shinrikyo* translates roughly as "True Principle Teachings." Asahara's writings reference a panoply of esoteric Buddhist and Yogic traditions as well as the prophecies of Nostradamus and Isaac Asimov's science fiction classic *The Foundation Trilogy*; he also drew liberally on an olio of writings about the **Masons**, the Jews, and the British royal family—crackpot conspiratorial fare of the sort that so many demagogic cult leaders find irresistible. A pamphlet he published in 1995 blamed the Jews for the Khmer Rouge's massacres in Cambodia, the genocide in Rwanda, and ethnic cleansing in Bosnia, and went on to describe a Jewish "'world shadow government' that murders untold numbers of people and, while hiding behind sonorous phrases and high sounding principles, plans to brainwash and control the rest."

Asahara had unwittingly described his own religion, which initially promised to guide its members through ascending stages of enlightenment via strenuous feats of Yogic meditation, but soon became an extension of his grandiose, paranoid, and murderous personality. Asahara encouraged a cult of personality, claiming that he had the ability to levitate and read minds; he sold his used bathwater to his followers so they could drink it, and his hair clippings so they could steep them in hot water and make tea. In 1990, he campaigned for a seat in parliament (and lost by a landslide). As Asahara became increasingly unhinged, troublesome cult members were murdered. So was Tsutsumi Sakamoto, a lawyer who was spearheading a major lawsuit against Aum Shinrikyo. Sakamoto's wife and child were murdered as well.

By then Asahara was identifying himself with Christ as well as Shiva. Prophesying that World War III would begin in the mid-1990s with an American attack on Japan, he formulated a plan in which Aum Shinrikyo would emerge from the ensuing chaos to inherit the world. In 1993, in a book called *Shivering Predictions*, he foretold the coming catastrophe:

> From now until the year 2000, a series of violent phenomena filled with fear that are too difficult to describe will occur. Japan will turn into waste land as a result of a nuclear weapons' attack. This will occur from 1996 through January 1998. An alliance centering on the United States will attack Japan. In large cities in Japan, only one-tenth of the population will be able to survive. Nine out of ten people will die.

Fabulously wealthy from its members' contributions, as well as its far-flung publishing, real estate, and other business ventures (many of them illegal), Aum Shinrikyo recruited ex-military men and scientists and stockpiled conventional, chemical, and biological weapons, among them Ebola, anthrax, cholera, Q fever, and botulin, which Asahara planned to use to hasten the advent of Armageddon. Botulin and anthrax were sprayed from vehicles and office buildings in Tokyo to little effect; sarin gas was released in Matsumoto in June 1994, killing seven, and then again in March 1995 on the Tokyo subways. Thousands were injured and twelve died during this second sarin attack; massive raids on Aum

Shinrikyo facilities followed, resulting in some two hundred arrests. A number of subsequent attempts to release cyanide into the subway system were successfully thwarted. Twelve members of Aum Shinrikyo have been condemned to death, including Asahara, who was captured in May 1995.

The cult lives on today in a much smaller form as Aleph. Riven by disputes about Asahara's status within the religion, a splinter group called Hikari no Wa, or "Ring of Light," broke away from Aleph in 2007. Bankruptcy proceedings against Aum Shinrikyo were formally concluded in March 2008, with a plan to distribute 1.5 billion yen to its victims— about 40 percent of its legal obligations. The Japanese government has agreed to make up a portion of the shortfall.

Branch Davidians

The Branch Davidians are an outgrowth of the Shepherd's Rod, a breakaway sect of the Seventh-Day Adventists founded by the Bulgarian-born Victor Houteff (1885–1955) in 1929. In 1993 their leader, David Koresh (1959–1993), and more than seventy of his followers died during a confrontation with the United States government.

Houteff had been "disfellowshipped" by the SDA church because of his heterodox ideas, especially his interpretation of Revelation 14:1: "And I looked, and, lo, a Lamb stood on the mount Sion, and with him a hundred forty and four thousand, having his Father's name written in their foreheads." Houteff contended that those 144,000 were purified Seventh-Day Adventists, who were destined to inhabit the restored Kingdom of David in Jerusalem. In 1935, Houteff and eleven followers moved to a complex outside of Waco, Texas, which they called Mount Carmel, to prepare for the coming End Times.

Seven years later the Mount Carmelites, now sixty strong, were living self-sufficiently and printing and mailing tracts around the world. When America entered World War II, the mainstream Seventh-Day Adventist movement's continuing refusal to recognize the Shepherd's Rod threatened to deprive its members of their conscientious objector status; accordingly Houteff and his followers formally reconstituted themselves as an independent church. In 1955, when Houteff died, the Davidian Seventh-Day Adventists, as they now called themselves, claimed to have a worldwide membership of ten thousand. Soon after Houteff's widow, Florence, assumed the reins of the movement, she received a revelation that Judgment Day would occur on April 22, 1959. Her announcement set the stage for a recapitulation of the Millerite disappointment of 1843, from which the Seventh-Day Adventist movement had originally sprung.

A tent city sprang up as nine hundred members converged on Waco to await the end, which of course did not occur. The humiliated Houteff formally dissolved her church a few years later, leaving the way free for an apostate Davidian named Benjamin Roden to purchase seventy-seven acres of its abandoned complex and begin a revived movement of his own that he called the "Branch Davidians," a reference to his saying, "Get off the dead rod and onto the living branch," which referred both to Houteff's Shepherd's Rod and Numbers 17:8: "Behold, the rod of Aaron for the house of Levi had sprouted and put forth buds." (The saying alludes to other biblical passages as well: the Messianic figure called the Branch in Zechariah 3:8, "Hear now, O Joshua the high priest, thou and thy fellows that sit before thee; for they are men which are a sign: for, behold, I will bring forth my servant the Branch"; and Isaiah 11:1, "A shoot will come up from the stump of Jesse, from his roots a Branch will bear fruit."

When Roden died in 1978, his wife, Lois, assumed the leadership of the Branch Davidians. Like Houteff's wife before her, she was given to prophesying. Lois's chief disciple and chosen successor was Vernon Wayne Howell, a twenty-something former rock guitarist who was rumored to be her lover. But Lois's son George, who had hoped to lead the church himself, soon forced his rival into exile. Howell and his teenage bride traveled to Israel, where he changed his name to David Koresh.* When Lois died, Koresh, who had started his own church on a complex in Palestine, Texas, after he came back from Israel, returned to Waco to settle the issue of succession once and for all. His rival, George Roden, challenged him to a contest to see which of them could raise the dead (a corpse was dug up from the complex's cemetery for the purpose). Gunplay ensued and Koresh was arrested for attempted murder (the trial ended with a hung jury); a few years later Roden was committed to a mental hospital after he killed one of Koresh's followers with an ax. When authorities seized Roden's Waco compound and put it up for sale to pay its back taxes, Koresh and his followers were able to buy it.

David Koresh, as witnessed by his name change, believed that he had a messianic role to play—he proclaimed that he himself was the lamb of God destined to open the seventh seal spoken of in Revelation. The Davidians, who made much of their income by selling firearms and military memorabilia (such as hand grenade hulls mounted on plaques) at gun shows, owned a small arsenal of weapons; Koresh stirred up his followers' paranoia by prophesying that Armageddon would begin with an attack on the complex that he had begun to call "Ranch Apocalypse." He was also widely reputed to have granted himself spousal privileges with all the females in his church—including girls younger than fourteen years old (Texas's legal age of consent). "Equipped with both a creamy charm and a cold-blooded willingness to manipulate those drawn to him," *Time* magazine would write after his death, "Koresh was a type well known to students of cult practices: the charismatic leader with a pathological edge."

On February 28, 1993, agents from the Bureau of Alcohol, Tobacco, and Firearms launched a raid against the Davidian

---

Koresh is the Hebrew pronunciation of "Cyrus," the Persian emperor who released the Jews from their exile in Babylon; he is the only non-Hebrew in the Old Testament to be given the appellation of "anointed one" or "Messiah," in Isaiah 45:1.

compound, ostensibly to execute a search warrant. The warrant was narrow and legalistic (it merely permitted them to
search for evidence of tax violations on the sale of automatic
weapons), but there is reason to believe that the ATF, which
had suffered considerable adverse publicity in recent months,
calculated that a violent confrontation with a gun-crazed,
child-abusing doomsday cult would play well in the media
(its none-too-cryptic code name for the operation was
"Showtime"). The operation unfolded like a publicist's worst
nightmare. First, four ATF agents and six Davidians were
killed in an entirely avoidable firefight. Then, after a fifty-
one-day siege, the FBI broke the stalemate with a tear gas
assault, ostensibly because of its humanitarian concern for
the children in the compound. Seventy-plus Davidians died,
twenty-one of them children, when the compound's wooden
buildings burst into flames. Though an extensive investigation led by former U.S. senator John Danforth exonerated
the FBI and ATF of criminal wrongdoing, few defended
their conduct of the siege. For many ultra (and not-so-ultra)
conservatives, the tragedy provided a textbook example of
American police power run amok. Soon after the events, the
libertarian Texas congressman Ron Paul (a presidential candidate in 2008) wrote:

> In its dealings with the community of believers at Mount
> Carmel, the central government abandoned the moral prom-
> ise of a free society, and, as all tyrannies eventually do,
> ignored its own standards of law and ethics. . . . A govern-
> ment that governs by fear alone eventually finds itself unable
> to govern at all.

Bruderhof
Now known as Church Communities International, the
Bruderhof movement was founded by Eberhard Arnold
(1883–1935) in Germany in 1920 on the model of the
Anabaptist Hutterite Brethren. The original members lived

together in a self-sufficient farming community in which, as in Acts 2:44, "all that believed were together and had all things in common." The Bruderhof were pacifists; when the Nazis came to power, they moved to the Cotswold region of England. Facing mandatory repatriation to Germany when war broke out and denied visas to the United States or Canada, they moved to Paraguay, where the community swelled to about seven hundred members. After the war, satellite communities were reestablished in England and Germany; a small detachment moved to the United States in the early 1950s and joined a traditional Hutterite community in North Dakota. Relations between the two groups became strained almost immediately and the Bruderhof were excommunicated. A year later, the first independent North American Bruderhof community, Woodcrest, was founded in Rifton, New York.

A major rift occurred in 1961, when Heinrich Arnold, the founder's middle son, decided to close the South American and European communities; many longtime members were purged. This "Great Crisis," writes Julius Rubin, author of *The Other Side of Joy: Religious Melancholy Among the Bruderhof* (2000), "became the watershed that transformed the Bruderhof."

The movement owns several businesses, among them Community Playthings, which supplies wooden furniture for classrooms, and Rifton Equipment, which manufactures rehabilitative devices for the handicapped. Though manifestly progressive in its educational and social views (the Bruderhof have led protests against the death penalty and championed the cause of Mumia Abu-Jamal), the group guards its public image fiercely (as Rubin learned when it tried to block publication of his book). Its leadership, which has a decidedly authoritarian tinge, remains in the Arnold family (the current elder is Johann Christoph Arnold); obedience and conformity are strictly enforced. Though Bruderhof children are encouraged to spend at least a year living in the outer world before they commit to the movement (on the model of the Amish), once they join it, they surrender much of their freedom. Rubin's description of the inner dynamics of the church brings Lifton's criteria for cults to mind:

> Those persons whose ideas or individual consciences endanger doctrinal orthodoxy; those who stand against the leadership and threaten unity; those who cannot or will not repent and reform from sinful thoughts and conduct, must be punished with increasingly severe forms of church discipline. . . . The threat of exclusion proves a powerful and dreaded method of social control in the Bruderhof.

Today some twenty-five hundred Bruderhof live in communities in New York, Pennsylvania, Connecticut, England, and Australia, varying in size from as large as three hundred to as small as a dozen members. Though church members live as families, they work within the community and cook and share at least some meals communally; children attend Bruderhof schools. A significant community of apostates and estranged families of the faithful also exists, whose members are forbidden to contact their loved ones. KIT (Keeping in Touch) and COBI (Children of the Bruderhof International) are support and advocacy groups founded by ex-members. The Bruderhof has used every legal means at its disposal to frustrate them.

The Children of God (see **The Family International**)

Christian Identity
Racist theology of the Church of Jesus Christ Christian, the Aryan Nations, Kingdom Identity Ministries, the White Aryan Resistance (WAR), and White Separatist Banner. A descendant of British Israelitism—the belief, first propounded by the seaman and would-be Messiah Richard Brothers (1757–1824), that the Anglo-Saxon people are the true Israelites—Christian Identity looks forward to a racial Apoca-

lypse in which the "Zionist Occupation Government" of the United States is overthrown and the dark races and the Edomite impostors who pretend to be the Jews are exterminated. Gerald L.K. Smith (1898–1976), the founder of the America First Party and the Christian Nationalist Crusade; Dr. Wesley Swift (1913–1970), the founder of the Church of Jesus Christ Christian; and Swift's protégé Richard Butler (1938–2004), who founded the Aryan Nations, were some of its leading expositors. (See also **Ku Klux Klan** in Secret Societies.)

Church of the Last Testament

Led by a Red Army veteran, former metalworker, and traffic cop who was born in Krasnodar, Russia, in 1961 as Sergei Torop but who began to preach as Vissarion after he had the revelation that he was the reincarnation of Jesus Christ, the Church of the Last Testament claims to have some ten thousand members worldwide. Its core are the four thousand faithful who live near their leader in a remote Siberian settlement called Tiberkul. It is probably no coincidence that Vissarion's revelation came at the same time that the Soviet Union began to implode, in 1991.

Vissarion (his name means "He who gives new life") has published four volumes of his teachings. The Vissarionites quote his aphorisms by heart and decorate their cottages with his likeness. As it happens, he looks almost exactly like a sentimental depiction of Jesus, with shoulder-length hair and a neatly trimmed beard. At the heart of his teachings is the one "Great Mystery—that the Creator of the universe and your Heavenly Father are not one and the same Source." Vissarionism purports to unite the principles of the great religions of the East and the West. God is at once the abstract, impersonal ground of being, but also exists in a personal form, as the font of all goodness and the means by which the faithful can achieve personal salvation.

Vissarionism is not a theology, however—it is a cult of personality. "I am the living word of God the Father," Vissarion declares. "Everything that God wants to say, he says through me." His followers use a calendar that begins with his birth date; they celebrate his birthday every year instead of Christmas. Vissarion's commune is "governed by arcane rituals, laws, symbols, prayers, hymns," writes Ian Traynor of the *Guardian*.

> A strict code of conduct is enforced: no vices are permitted. Veganism is compulsory for all. . . . Monetary exchange is banned within the commune, and only reluctantly allowed with the outside world.

Russian authorities had expressed concern that Vissarion would lead his followers in a mass suicide at the turn of the millennium, but their apprehensions turned out to be unfounded. "To do what I'm called to do, I need to have a human body," Vissarion told Kevin Sullivan of the *Washington Post*. "This is the first time I have been needed in 2,000 years. This is a critical point. Only when mankind becomes one family on Earth will the doors to the universe become open to them."

Concerned Christians

A Christian millennialist cult that began its short life as an outgrowth of a bimonthly newsletter published by a former marketing executive named Monte Kim Miller, who was purportedly concerned about the dangers of cults. *Report from Concerned Christians* began by targeting New Age beliefs like alternative medicine, neo-paganism, and the Harmonic Convergence of 1987,* but soon turned its sights on Roman Catholicism and the charismatic Word-Faith movement (a pentecostalist variation of New Thought, which has influenced many faith healers and preachers of the so-called Pros-

---

*An event based partially on the Mayan calendar, partially on an actual alignment of planets, which was thought to have immense mystic significance. Many New Agers have since turned their attention to the winter solstice of 2012, when, according to the Mayan calendar, the current cycle of history will come to an end and a new cycle will begin—an event, some say, that may be marked by violent climate change, an asteroid impact, and possibly the return of ancient astronauts.

perity Gospel). Starting around 1988, Miller widened his line of attack to include the Southern Baptists, the Assemblies of God, and seventeen other denominations. By 1989, Miller had irrevocably embarked on his own journey into cultism, when he claimed that he was in direct communication with God, declared that patriotism and Christianity are fundamentally incompatible, and insisted that his followers completely divorce themselves from mainstream society. Taking the Pledge of Allegiance, he said, was a form of "spiritual adultery"; even the fundamentalists in the Christian Right, he said, were "helping to build Babylon."

By 1997, Miller's radio show was off the air and he had declared bankruptcy (despite pressuring his followers to make very substantial donations); soon afterward, he prophesied that the Apocalypse would begin on October 10, 1998, when Denver would be destroyed by an earthquake. Identifying himself as one of the two witnesses of Revelation 11, he predicted that he would be killed and resurrected in Jerusalem before the turn of the millennium. Then, on September 30, 1998, Miller and more than seventy of his followers disappeared. Three months later, Miller and fourteen of his followers (six of them children) reemerged in Israel, where they were detained by the police for allegedly conspiring to "carry out violent and extreme acts in the streets of Jerusalem at the end of 1999" in order to hasten the second coming of Christ. Although no weapons were found, Israeli authorities alleged that the Concerned Christians had been planning to provoke a gun battle with police near the Church of the Holy Sepulchre (an Arab group later accused them of planning to blow up the Al-Aqsa Mosque as well). Miller and his followers were deported back to Denver, but they disappeared again soon afterward. The Concerned Christians Web site would post its last update in 2002.

The Mesa, Arizona–based Concerned Christians is a ministry that seeks to convert Mormons to evangelical Protestantism. It is entirely unrelated to Kim Miller's group.

Divine Light Mission (see Indian Gurus)

Druze

Neither a cult nor a secret society but with elements of both, the Druze (or Druse) are an ethnic/religious community that grew out of an Islamic heresy; their religious practices remain esoteric and secretive to this day. "The Druses of Lebanon . . . might indeed be described as the **Freemasons** of the East," Nesta Webster wrote in her *Secret Societies and Subversive Movements* (1921). "Their outer organization closely resembles that of the Craft Degrees in Western Masonry, yet such is their power of secrecy that few if any Europeans have ever succeeded in discovering the secret doctrines."

The Druze originated in Egypt in the eleventh century but live primarily in the mountainous regions of Lebanon, Syria, Jordan, and Israel today (scattered Druze communities can also be found in Australia, Europe, Africa, and North and South America). The word "Druze" most likely derives from the name of one of their two most prominent founding preachers, a Persian named Muhammad ibn Ismail al-Darazi (which is curious because the Druze regard al-Darazi, who died in 1019, as a disreputable figure; the Druze call themselves the *muwahhidun*, or "believers in oneness"). The Druze consider Al-Darazi's rival Hamza ibn Ali ibn Ahmad (985–?), another Persian, to be their true founder.

An outgrowth of Ismaili Shiism, the Druze believe that al-Hakim bi-Amr Allah (985–1021), the sixth Egyptian Fatimid Caliph, was an incarnation of God. Though the Druze regard Muhammad as a major prophet and derive many of their laws from the Koran, they do not regard him as the "last prophet"; nor do they pray five times a day, fast during the month of Ramadan, or make a hajj to Mecca. They don't proselytize, either. Having suffered intense persecution in the years after al-Hakim's mysterious disappearance (some believe he was assassinated by his sister; the

Druze believe he will return from his "occultation" at the end of history to preside over a golden age), the gates of the Druze religion were officially closed in 1043. The only way one can become a Druze is to be born of two Druze parents (the penalty for intermarriage is excommunication). Though strictly endogamous, the Druze (unlike many Muslims) are not polygamous, and Druze women are permitted to initiate divorces (in general, Druze laws regarding women are much more liberal than in sharia).

At the heart of Druze ethical teachings are seven imperatives:

1. The necessity to be honest at all times
2. To take care of one another
3. To eschew idolatry
4. To avoid the devil and abstain from evil acts
5. To acknowledge the oneness and uniqueness of God
6. To accept God's deeds, no matter what they are
7. To accept one's fate

"Not a ritual ceremonial faith in essence, but rather a neo-Platonic philosophy," according to Nissim Dana's *The Druze in the Middle East* (2003), Druze theology is expounded in the 111 epistles of its early leaders that comprise, along with a body of commentaries, the *Kutub al-Hikma* (or *The Book of Wisdom*). The Druze believe in reincarnation and that al-Hakim is a divine emanation. Most of the rest of their beliefs are closely held secrets, not only from the outer world, but from the vast majority of their own communities. The *Kutub al-Hikma* is hand-copied rather than printed; only the *uqqal*, or "the wise" (as opposed to the *jubbal*, or "the simple"— about 80 percent of the Druze), are permitted to study its teachings. Should a *jahil* (a member of the *jubbal*) aspire to join the *uqqal*, they must prove themselves through a course of assiduous study. Many of these privileged wise ones are women; they worship with men (albeit separated by a barrier) during their Thursday night meetings. The most respected members of the *uqqal* are called the *ajawid*, or "the good." It is from their ranks that the Druze's spiritual and political leaders—their sheikhs—are chosen.

Elan Vital (see **Indian Gurus**)

est

Latin for "it is," *est* is also the acronym for Erhard Seminars Training, the phenomenally successful transformational program of the 1970s, which applied a concentrated distillate of ideas from New Thought, Zen, the Human Potential Movement, and existential philosophy to alter its participants' "ability to experience living" so that life's problems "clear up just in the process of life itself." Est claimed to render its graduates more confident, happy, focused, centered, and, most importantly, free of guilt and self-doubt. "You are perfect exactly the way you are," its founder Werner Erhard taught. Premised as it was on self-absorption, metaphysical arrogance, and antinomian ethics, and fueled by relentless hucksterism, est epitomized the "culture of narcissism," as Christopher Lasch called it, that epitomized the era.

In two grueling weekends, est's paying participants were run through a brutally demanding regime of primal group therapy, administered by coaches who used methods of indoctrination and reeducation that are most often associated with the commissars of Mao's Cultural Revolution. In his decidedly unsympathetic biography of Erhard, *Outrageous Betrayal* (1993), Steven Pressman captures an est trainer in action: "IN THIS TRAINING" he bellows to a packed hotel ballroom, "YOU'RE GOING TO FIND OUT YOU'VE BEEN ACTING LIKE ASSHOLES. ALL YOUR FUCKING CLEVERNESS AND SELF-DECEPTION HAVE GOTTEN YOU NOWHERE!" Est promised to strip away the cultural, behavioral, intellectual, and experiential accretions that get in the way of living in the moment, hindering life's optimal flow. As Erhard's Zen teacher Alan Watts (1915–1973) famously put it, "Things are as they are. Looking out into the universe at night, we make no comparisons between right and wrong stars, nor between well and badly arranged constellations." In Erhard's words, "Happiness is a function of accepting what is."

Werner Erhard came into the world as John Paul Rosenberg in Norristown, Pennsylvania, in 1935. A car salesman, he was married with four children when he abruptly left his family at age twenty-five and headed west with a new partner (they would have three children together before their marriage also ended in divorce in 1988). Erhard sold correspondence courses, book continuity programs, and encyclopedias door-to-door, eventually settling in San Francisco, where he would rise in the corporate ranks of *Parents* magazine and the Grolier Society. Already steeped in the self-help gospels of Dale Carnegie (1888–1955) and Norman Vincent Peale (1898–1993) and the applied mind science of Napoleon Hill's *Think and Grow Rich* (1937), Erhard immersed himself in Maxwell Maltz's (1899–1975) Psycho-Cybernetics, Fritz Perls's (1893–1970) Gestalt therapy, and the humanistic psychology of Abraham Maslow (1908–1970) and Carl Rogers (1902–1987). He dabbled in **Scientology**, which influenced him both as an applied psychology and as a business model, studied Zen, took Mind Dynamics seminars, and participated in encounter groups at the Esalen Institute.

The first est seminar was held in 1971; the last took place in 1984, when the program was rebranded for the decade of greed as the staider, more corporate "the Forum." In 1991, after twenty years and seven hundred thousand customers, Erhard retired and sold his intellectual property to his brother Harry Rosenberg. Investigated by the IRS and hounded by lawsuits from his children and ex-employees alleging abuse and exploitation, he left the country soon after. Though Erhard remains an elusive figure, his legacy continues to flourish at his brother's Landmark Education

Forum, which offers courses, seminars, and programs in 125 cities in twenty-four countries, on how to improve relationships, enhance self-confidence, increase productivity, and achieve lasting happiness.

Though neither est nor Landmark Education could be described as religious cults, they institutionalized a lot of the methods that cults use to exercise their power over their followers and gain access to their money. Erhard's and Rosenberg's clients pledge their loyalty to a program instead of to a personal guru. As in Scientology, once "a body is in the shop," it gets shuffled along to more and more expensive activities.

Faithism (see **Oahspe**, below, and **Area 51** in Conspiracies)

The Family International

Starting in 1968, in Huntington Beach, California, David Brandt Berg (1919–1994), a radio and television minister whose parents had been traveling evangelists and faith healers (and whose Jewish forebears on his maternal side had converted to Christianity in the eighteenth century, joining the Dunkard Brethren, a pietist, separatist Protestant sect), began to preach to hippies. His church went by a number of names in its early days, including Teens for Christ, Revolutionaries for Jesus, the Jesus Children, and the Jesus Movement, though by the early 1970s, when it became an organized international movement, its official name was the Children of God. Tom Wolfe described the phenomenon in his epochal 1976 *New York* magazine article, "The Me Decade":

> At the outset practically all the Jesus People were young acid heads, i.e., LSD users, who had sworn off drugs (except, occasionally, in "organic form," meaning marijuana and peyote) but still wanted the ecstatic spiritualism of the psychedelic or hippie life. This they found in Fundamentalist evangelical holy-rolling Christianity.

In 1977, in the course of a reorganization in which some three hundred church leaders were dismissed (the internal name for this traumatic event was the Reorganization Nationalization Revolution, or RNA), Berg changed his movement's name to The Family of Love. In 1982, it was shortened to The Family; in 2004, it changed its name again, to The Family International, which is what it goes by today.

Berg's followers lived in communes and regarded Berg (whom they called Father David, Moses David, Mo, or "Dad") as a prophet. As his movement spread, he communicated with its far-flung outposts via "Mo Letters"—rambling epistles that he illustrated comic book–style. Pentecostalist and premillennialist in his theological beliefs, Berg's teachings on sex departed radically from his fellow fundamentalists'. Berg's golden rule was what he called "Jesus's Law of Love":

If a person's actions are motivated by unselfish, sacrificial love—the love of God for our fellow man—and are not intentionally hurtful to others, such actions are in accordance with Scripture and are thus lawful in the eyes of God.

A corollary to the Law of Love is the "belief that heterosexual relations, when practiced as God ordained, designed, and intended between consenting adults of legal age, is a pure and natural wonder of God's creation, and permissible according to Scripture." In other words, Christian belief encourages rather than stands in the way of a bounteous sexual life, in or out of marriage, committed or otherwise. Here is how Berg put it in one of his Mo Letters:

The Devil hates sex! . . . True sex, honest sex, Godly sex. . . . If you hate sex you are one of the Devil's crowd! If you think it's evil, then God and love are evil, for He created it! Come on, let's love and enjoy it like God does! He loves it!

Berg himself cast his first wife aside for his secretary Karen Zerby, who inherited the leadership of the movement after he died (she legally changed her name to Karen Rianna Smith in 1997; some of the other names she's gone by are Maria David, Maria Berg, Maria Fontaine, Mama Maria, and Queen Maria).

Flirty Fishing, or FFing (as in, "You shall be fishers of men"), was one of the movement's approved missionary techniques. Women were encouraged to pick up men in bars so they could proselytize them, acting, in Berg's words, as "God's whores." Flirty Fishing and sex with nonmembers would be banned in the early 1980s, largely as a response to AIDS. Even more controversial was the high incidence of incest and child abuse in the movement's communes (sexual relations with children would become an excommunicable offense in 1986). Ironically, The Family's most notorious juvenile victim would be Berg's stepson Ricky Rodriguez, also known as Davidito, who was born to his second wife in 1975 in Tenerife, the product of her FFing relationship with a hotel employee named Carlos. Ricky was the centerpiece of "The Story of Davidito," a 729-page illustrated child-rearing manual that the church published in 1982. While it didn't promote incest per se, its descriptions of Ricky's guilt-free upbringing are often troubling. Here is one example, written when Ricky was seventeen months old:

> Sex!: Little David stood watching through the pool fence as a couple made love in the water. He imitated every motion by wiggling his bottom and his right hand up and down, then went into the house to show Mommy the story of how to goose a girl!

In 2005, the thirty-year-old Rodriguez, long since estranged from his mother and her church, sought out Angela Smith, one of his former caregivers, and stabbed her to death. He committed suicide shortly afterward, leaving behind a videotaped confession in which he spoke of "a need for revenge. It's a need for justice, because I can't go on like this."

Today, The Family International claims some eight thousand members, who live in more than seven hundred communal houses in approximately one hundred countries. It describes itself as "a Christian fellowship dedicated to sharing God's Word and love with others. Our mission is to comfort, aid, and minister to those in need, endeavoring to follow the example of Jesus."

Growing in Grace (Creciendo en Gracia)

Antinomian religious movement led by José Luis de Jesús Miranda, an ex-convict and former drug addict who claims to be the "Man Jesus Christ," returned to earth to deliver the gospel of "uncircumcision." Born in Puerto Rico in 1946, José de Jesús, as he calls himself, was visited by angels in 1973. In 1986 he founded his church in Puerto Rico; its headquarters were moved to Miami, Florida, two years later. Today there are some three hundred Growing in Grace churches in thirty countries, mostly in Latin America.

Growing in Grace is organized around six basic tenets:

1. Sin does not exist, it was removed
2. The Devil does not exist, he was destroyed
3. There are two Gospels, the Gospels of Circumcision and Uncircumcision
4. There is One Ministry
5. The Church is Already Perfect
6. All religious systems are wrong

In a nutshell, de Jesús teaches that the law—and with it the notion of sin—was nullified by Jesus's resurrection. The Gospel of the Bible was written for the circumcised Jews; the Gospel that de Jesús teaches (based largely on scriptural quotation) is for the uncircumcised—for those who are already saved in Christ and predestined for Grace. "All churches that base their doctrines on the apostles of the circumcision (the law) and the rudimentary doctrine of Jesus of Nazareth are APOSTATES and find themselves in spiritual ADULTERY," he declares. The letters SSS, which stand for *Salvo, siempre salvo* ("Saved, always saved"), are one of Growing in Grace's most visible symbols.

De Jesús smokes and drinks ("Jesus drank wine because he didn't have Dewar's," he quips) and has been married and divorced twice. He regards celibacy as an affront, "a demonic doctrine"—physical pleasure and material comforts are not distractions from the life of the spirit but positive goods. "I don't deal with 'walk this way, dress this way, don't drink, don't smoke,'" he says. "Christianity doesn't prohibit anything." That said, de Jesús doesn't get drunk, abhors drugs, and recognizes the legitimacy of civil laws. Provocatively, he calls himself the Antichrist (to distinguish himself from the lesser Jesus of Nazareth). De Jesús had the number 666—the so-called number of the beast—tattooed on his arm. He calls it "the number of prosperity," and prosperity is very much to the point.

De Jesús's followers do not pray, but they *do* tithe to his church, on the understanding that if they share their money with the Man Jesus Christ, he will repay them many times over—and it is this promise, along with de Jesús's personal charisma, that drives his church. De Jesús's statement on "bling" is revealing:

> Why would it surprise you that upon his return God wears "bling," and lives in a good home, and drives a good car? Money is not evil; the love of money is the root of all evil. The Apostle José Luis de Jesús Miranda has given everything that he has and more many times over for the ministry and for the mission of spreading the true gospel. He has sown and for that he reaps. He also has enriched the lives of millions with the true gospel that he preaches, and therefore the angelic covering that serves him prospers his life.

De Jesús's very contentious second divorce shone an unwelcome light into his personal finances, which are inextricably intertwined with those of his church.

Heaven's Gate

Billed as "the cult of cults" by its cofounder Marshall Herff Applewhite (1931–1997), Heaven's Gate exploded into public consciousness in the winter of 1997, when Applewhite and thirty-nine of his disciples, after taking a few moments to record farewell videos, quit their fleshly "containers" to ascend to the Level Above Human and return to their home planet near the star Sirius. The vehicle that they believed would carry them there was hidden in the tail of the Hale-Bopp comet; their exit was accomplished with the help of phenobarbital mixed with vodka.

The son of a Presbyterian minister who attended a seminary himself, rose to the rank of sergeant in the army, sang in operas with Plácido Domingo, and taught music at the college level, Applewhite began his bizarre journey in a mental hospital in Houston in the early 1970s. He had recently been fired from the University of St. Thomas in Houston (allegedly for carrying on a homosexual relationship with a student) and was estranged from his wife and children. One of his nurses, a forty-four-year-old married mother of four named Bonnie Lu Trusdale Nettles (1927–1985), was also an astrologist and Theosophist. The two became friends and in time a platonic couple; one day, on the banks of the Rogue River in Oregon, they shared a simultaneous revelation— that they were the two witnesses foretold in Revelation 11:3: "And I will give power to my two witnesses, and they will prophesy for 1,260 days, clothed in sackcloth." After these two witnesses are killed, the chapter continues, they will come back to life and ascend to heaven in a cloud.

Applewhite and Nettles would promote themselves to an even higher status as they developed their theology over the next decade—Do, as Applewhite now called himself, was

Present Representative, or the successor to Jesus; Ti, aka Nettles, was his Heavenly Father. They named their religion HIM, for Human Individual Metamorphosis. Traveling around America (except during an interlude when Apple-white was incarcerated for credit card fraud), they spread a gospel that combined elements of millennialism (civilization was about to recycled, "spaded under in order that the planet might be refurbished"), Gnosticism (traditional reli-gion is a Luciferian tool to keep humans in thrall), and sci-ence fiction (the Luciferians are "space alien races opposed to the next level"). Bo and Peep (as they also called themselves) had become incarnated so they could teach earthlings how to "slough off" their mammalian attributes and rise to the next evolutionary level. "The final act of metamorphosis or sepa-ration from the human kingdom," Applewhite wrote, is:

> The "disconnect" or separation from the human physical con-
> tainer or body in order to be released from the human envi-
> ronment and enter the "next" world or physical environment
> of the Next Level. This will be done under the supervision of
> Members of the Next Level in a clinical procedure. We will
> rendezvous in the "clouds" (a giant mothership) for our brief-
> ing and journey to the Kingdom of the Literal Heavens.

Surprising numbers of people severed their worldly ties and followed the "UFO Two." In 1975 they caused a national stir when they harvested twenty new disciples at a meeting at a motel in Waldport, Oregon, all of whom disappeared shortly afterward. (As it turned out, they'd traveled to east-ern Colorado to rendezvous with a flying saucer, which failed to materialize as scheduled.) Walter Cronkite reported the story on the CBS *Evening News*; the incident would inspire a TV movie starring John Forsythe called *Mysterious Two*.

Nettles died of cancer in 1985 but continued to provide telepathic guidance to Applewhite, who went underground with the group's remaining followers. In 1993, he reemerged and began to proselytize again. At first he called his revived movement Total Overcomers Anonymous; then he changed its name to the more euphonious Heaven's Gate. In 1997, Applewhite and about forty followers were living under strict monastic discipline in a rented mansion in Rancho Santa Fe, supporting themselves as Web designers. They dressed androgynously in identical baggy clothes, sheared their hair close to the scalp, and abstained from sex. Some male members (including Applewhite) had themselves castrated. When rumors began to circulate that a spaceship was concealed in the tail of the approaching Hale-Bopp comet, a banner appeared on the home page of the Heaven's Gate Web site: RED ALERT. HALE-BOPP BRINGS CLOSURE TO HEAVEN'S GATE.

Apparently Applewhite suffered from extreme guilt about his sexuality as well as from narcissistic delusions; very likely he was schizophrenic—it's no wonder that he took his own life. But why did the members of Heaven's Gate go along with him so willingly? Most of them were marginal cases when they joined the cult; their initial susceptibility to Applewhite and his highly unusual message suggests as much. And though by all accounts Applewhite was a low-key tyrant—he wasn't violent or overtly abusive; when members wanted to leave his movement, he didn't force them to stay—the regime he imposed on his disciples was nonetheless coercively totalistic. When you belonged to Heaven's Gate, as one ex-member put it, you had to follow "a procedure for every conscious moment of life." "We wanted our brains washed," another ex-member (whose wife remained with Applewhite to the bitter end) told a news reporter. "There's a lot of joy in it."

Los Hermanos Penitentes

A highly secretive syncretic Christian sect, also sometimes known as the Confraternity of Our Father, Jesus the Nazarene, that still exists in parts of the Spanish-speaking Southwest and in Mexico. Primarily comprised of Genízaros, the descendants of non-Pueblo Indians (mostly Navajo) who had been enslaved by the Spanish, the Penitente communities were cut off from the traditional Catholic Church for most of the nineteenth century because of their low social status and isolation. *Hermanos mayores*, or "elder brothers," ruled over independent communities that met in *moradas*, or abodes. Self-mortification, a carryover from the teachings of seventeenth- and eighteenth-century Franciscan missionaries, is at the heart of their rituals, which symbolically represent the emergence from darkness to light, the passage from death to rebirth. This description of a Penitente ceremony comes from *The Catholic Encyclopedia* (1911):

> Fifty years ago the Hermanos Penitentes would issue from their *morada* (in some places, as Taos, N.M., three hundred strong), stripped to the waist and scourging themselves, led by the *acompanadores* (escorts), and preceded by a few Penitentes dragging heavy crosses (*maderos*); the procession was accompanied by a throng, singing Christian hymns. A wooden wagon (*el carro de la muerte*) bore a figure representing death and pointing forward an arrow with stretched bow. This procession went through the streets to the church, where the Penitentes prayed, continued their scourgings, returned in procession to the *morada*. Other modes of self-castigation were often resorted to; on Good Friday it was the custom to bind one of the brethren to a cross, as in a crucifixion.

Hermetic Order of the Golden Dawn

England's leading occult society around the turn of the last century, the Hermetic Order of the Golden Dawn was founded by three **Freemasons**, Dr. William Robert Woodman (1828–1891), Dr. William Wynn Westcott (1848–1925)—who was also active in Theosophy—and Samuel Liddell Mathers (1854–1918).

Organized on a lodge basis with three degrees of membership, the order incorporated the full gamut of Masonic and neo-**Rosicrucian** mysticism. Its practices, which included spell casting, tarot, yoga, astrology, and channeling, were inspired by Qabalah (the *Q* distinguishes occult from Jewish **Kabbalah**), Hermeticism, alchemy, *grimoires* (magic texts) like the thirteenth-century *Sefer Raziel HaMalakh*, and the Enochian magic of John Dee (1527–1609).* Famous members of the group included the poet William Butler Yeats (1865–1939), Maud Gonne (1866–1953), and Arthur Machen (1863–1947).

The Order of the Golden Dawn was also where Aleister Crowley (1875–1947) got his start. His parents named him Edward Alexander and raised him in the conservative, evangelical Plymouth Brethren Church. Crowley later wrote that his mother called him The Beast because of his scandalous irreverence; as an adult he assiduously cultivated his reputation as "the wickedest man in the world."

Crowley left the Golden Dawn at odds with virtually all its members; he went on to develop his own philosophic system, which he called Thelema, after the abbey in Rabelais's *Gargantua et Pantagruel* (see **Hellfire Club** in Secret Societies), whose motto was "Do what thou wilt"—an exhortation that became a positive commandment in Crowley's *The Book of the Law*, a collection of aphorisms he channeled in 1904, in which he declared, "Do what thou wilt is the whole of the law." Crowley wasn't just issuing an invitation to hedonism, though he didn't preclude it. In his commentaries and later books, he elaborated on his notion of "True Will" as the fulfillment of one's ultimate, highest nature. "True Will should spring, a fountain of Light, from within, and flow unchecked, seething with Love, into the Ocean of Life," he wrote in *Little Essays Towards Truth* (1938). As with the left-handed Tantra, Thelemic practices include meditation and yoga and mindfulness, but they also extended to liberatory sexual

---

*Spells and invocations written in the Angelic, or Enochian, language that was used by Adam to communicate with God before the Fall and that were channeled to Dee by the medium Edward Kelley (1555–1597). Methuselah's father, Enoch, was said to be the only mortal besides Adam to speak it.

transgressions (including rape) and consciousness-altering drugs. Crowley, who published the novel *Diary of a Drug Fiend* in 1922, was a heroin addict, a practicing bisexual, and an adept at sex magick (the *k* is used to distinguish authentic ritual magic from mere stage trickery).

After he left the Golden Dawn, Crowley would become deeply involved with two lodge societies, the A∴A∴, also known as the Silver Star and the *Arcanum Arcanorum*, and Ordo Templi Orientis, or OTO (Order of the Oriental Templars). OTO had been founded as an "Academia Masonica" by the Austrian chemist and high-degree Mason Carl Kellner (1851–1905) and the German neo-Illuminatus Theodor Reuss (1855–1923), but Crowley remade it in his own image when he took it over, starting around 1912. OTO's manifesto (written by Crowley) modestly describes its mission:

> The aims of the O.T.O. can only be understood fully by its highest initiates; but it may be said openly that it teaches Hermetic Science or Occult Knowledge, the Pure and Holy Magick of Light, the Secrets of Mystic attainment, Yoga of all forms, Gnana Yoga, Raja Yoga, Bhakta Yoga and Hatha Yoga, and all other branches of the secret Wisdom of the Ancients. . . . [I]ts brain has resolved all the problems of philosophy and of life. . . . Moreover, it possesses a Secret capable of realizing the world-old dream of the Brotherhood of Man.

OTO did not survive World War II as an international organization; by 1946, only one lodge remained. Conspiracists who believe that the **Illuminati** control the U.S. space program take pointed notice of the fact that OTO's Agapé Lodge 2, which was located in Pasadena, California, was headed for a time by Jack Parsons (1914–1952), one of the founders of the Jet Propulsion Laboratory at the California Institute of Technology.* Though there have been fierce

---

*Strange but true: Parsons and **Scientology** founder L. Ron Hubbard were "frenemies" for a time in the 1940s (Hubbard's second wife was Parsons's ex-mistress).

arguments about succession and legitimacy, OTO has since been revived. Crowley's Gnostic Mass is celebrated at forty-five lodges in twenty-five states in America; there are also lodges in England and Australia.

House of Yahweh

"A barbed-wire kingdom of brimstone prophecies and abject poverty fifteen miles southeast of Abilene," *The Dallas Morning News* wrote on May 16, 2008, The House of Yahweh is led by seventy-three-year-old Yisrayl Hawkins, who has described himself as "a Jew whose family was severely persecuted and forced to flee from Europe to the United States. He was raised without synagogue, but was strictly taught by his Jewish parents, both of whom trace their lineage to the tribe of Levi." When this passage from his authorized biography was read to one of Hawkins's brothers, Robert Draper reported in the *Texas Monthly* in July 1997, he sighed before saying, "Bill's my brother, but he ain't got both oars in the water, if you know what I mean. Our daddy was a Dutchman, our mother was three-quarters Cherokee, and we don't have a drop of Jewish blood in us." Hawkins's given name was "Buffalo Bill." A former rockabilly musician, he also served as an Abilene police officer until 1977, when he was caught carrying beer in his patrol car.

The House of Yahweh claims some thirty thousand members worldwide; Hawkins transmits his teachings via satellite television, books, newsletters, and the Internet. No stranger to controversy, Hawkins was arrested early in 2008 for promoting bigamy (he is rumored to have as many as thirty wives) and violating child labor laws; as of this writing, he is still awaiting trial. In late 2008, church elder Yedidiyah Hawkins* was convicted of bigamy and sexual assault and sentenced to thirty years in prison.

*Like many House of Yahweh members, he legally changed his last name to Hawkins and his first name to one beginning with a *Y* as a sign of his discipleship.

Hawkins's beliefs are strongly influenced by Herbert W. Armstrong (1892–1986), who preached a hybrid of Sabbatarianism, British Israelitism, and Messianic Judaism, teaching his followers that Christianity not only did not abrogate Old Testament law, but that all 613 commandments should still be followed. An anti-Trinitarian, Hawkins teaches that Christ was born a man and only became divine when he was baptized. Hawkins identifies himself and his late brother Jacob, who founded the first version of the House of Yahweh after living in a kibbutz in Israel, as the two witnesses from Revelation 11:3 (he is not the first doomsday cult leader to focus on this passage). In recent years, he has claimed a prophetic status that is equal to or greater than Christ's. In preparation for the coming End Times, he is working to rebuild the Temple in Israel.

Hawkins has prophesied the precise date of doomsday on several occasions—unfortunately for his credibility, and fortunately for the rest of us, he has been wrong each time. Followers in Kenya built fallout shelters in anticipation of the holocaust he prophesied for September 12, 2006; most of them dropped out of the movement when the day passed without incident. On June 6, 2008, Hawkins appeared on the network television news show *20/20* and announced that a nuclear war would begin in less than a week. For what it's worth, he has also claimed that sexually transmitted diseases contribute to global warming.

Indian Gurus

Guru is the Hindu, Buddhist, and Sikh term for a spiritual guide (in Sanskrit, the word literally means "weighty" or "venerable"). In some Indian traditions, the guru is considered the living embodiment of the truth and is venerated as a deity—the student not only grants the guru unconditional devotion, but turns over his or her possessions and becomes the guru's servant.

As the saying goes, power corrupts. A number of Indian

gurus rose to world prominence during the so-called Age of Aquarius in the 1960s and 1970s, some of them acquiring incredible wealth, fame, and power along the way. Many of them proved themselves to be the possessors of all-too-human appetites. Bhagwan Shree Rajneesh (1931–1990), for example, became notorious for his ostentatious display of wealth (he collected jewelry and designer watches; at one point he owned more than ninety Rolls-Royces), drug abuse, and advocacy of a sexually permissive lifestyle—and especially for the criminal activities of his cohorts at Rajneeshpuram, the eponymous commune he founded in Oregon.

Born Chandra Mohan Jain, he established a substantial reputation as a philosopher, social critic, and religious thinker in India. By 1974, when he opened the Acharya Rajneesh Ashram in Pune, he was calling himself Bhagwan Shree Rajneesh (which translates roughly as "God Master Moon"). There he taught his own brand of Tantric yoga and meditation, incorporating aspects of Zen Buddhism, Gnosticism, pre-Socratic philosophy, and therapeutic innovations from the Human Potential Movement. Plus, he encouraged his acolytes to explore their sexuality. "We had a feast of fucking," his former bodyguard Hugh Milne recalled, "the likes of which had probably not been seen since the days of Roman bacchanalia." Within a few years, some six hundred satellite ashrams had opened around the world, attended by some two hundred thousand devotees, or, as Rajneesh called them, neo-Sannyas.

A *sannyasi* is a Hindu monk; the word is derived from the Sanskrit for "renounce." But as Rajneesh explained:

> Sannyas means courage more than anything else, because it is a declaration of your individuality, a declaration of freedom, a declaration that you will not be any more part of the mob madness, the mob psychology. It is a declaration that you are becoming universal; you will not belong to any country, to any church, to any race, to any religion.

Rajneesh's neo-Sannyas expressed their independence and individuality by dressing in identical orange robes and hanging a portrait of their guru around their necks on a beaded necklace. In rejecting the madness of the modern world, they had delivered themselves into the power of a megalomaniac.

Rajneesh suffered from chronic fatigue syndrome, which he self-medicated with staggering quantities of nitrous oxide and valium. In 1981, he traveled to America on a medical visa, though he was also evading a bill for back taxes that the Indian government had issued after revoking his movement's tax exemption. After a short sojourn in New Jersey, he moved to a 64,000-acre property near Antelope, Oregon, that his movement had purchased for five million dollars (nearly thirty times its assessed value). In short order the former Big Muddy Ranch was transformed into Rajneeshpuram, a thriving town of five thousand–plus residents, with its own power station, airstrip, police force, and fire department. Rajneesh took a vow of silence, devoting his days to his spiritual development and the pursuit of Rolls-Royces and other expensive toys and leaving the day-to-day care of his movement in the hands of his overbearing assistant, Ma Anand Sheela. The Queen, as she called herself, issued apocalyptic prophecies in Rajneesh's name, fought bitterly with the locals, and governed the commune with an iron hand. Just four years later, Rajneesh was in custody for violating immigration laws; much worse, Ma Anand Sheela and her associates were accused (not just by the American authorities but by Rajneesh himself, who complained that she'd turned Rajneeshpuram into a "fascist concentration camp") of a whole docket of serious crimes, from illegal wiretapping to attempted murder and bioterrorism. Members of Rajneesh's commune had infected ten salad bars in nearby Dalles, Oregon, with salmonella, sickening more than 750 people, in an attempt to manipulate a school board election by incapacitating the electorate. Other high officials at

Rajneeshpuram had conspired to assassinate Oregon's U.S. attorney.

Rajneesh pleaded no contest to his immigration rap, paid a fine, and agreed to leave the United States. Twenty-one countries denied him a visa before he returned to India, where, deeply humbled by his American experience, he changed his name to Osho (an echo of "oceanic experience," William James's poetic term for mystical consciousness; Osho is also a Japanese term for a Zen master) and resumed his eccentric, syncretic teachings. Remarkably, his efforts to rebrand himself were completely successful. Though he died in 1990, the steady stream of posthumous Osho books, as well as scores of audiotaped lectures and even corporate seminars (administered by Osho trainees) shows no signs of abating. *Being in Love: How to Love with Awareness and Relate Without Fear* was published in 2008; its cover identifies Osho, in the present tense, as an author who is "known for his revolutionary contribution to the science of inner transformation."

Rajneesh claimed that he was a victim of the puritanical prejudices of Ronald Reagan's backward-looking America; many of his defenders have pointed out that his cult's legal troubles coincided with a rash of rumors that it was stockpiling weapons, foreshadowing the line of attack that the government would deploy against the **Branch Davidians** in Waco, Texas. But Rajneesh's narcissism and his cult's paranoid penchant for violence were all too real. Having risen far above the petty concerns of the world, Rajneesh looked down on it with a serene sense of ironic detachment that was indistinguishable from contempt. "Rajneesh/Osho is the worst thing that ever happened to spirituality in the West," wrote his ex-follower Julian Lee. "Osho was basically a kind of pimp who used the base desires of average people, along with their beautiful hunger for real spirituality, to build a financial empire and a following of worshippers who would do whatever he asked."

Bhagwan Rajneesh wasn't the first guru whose carnal

desires got the better of him. The Beatles' song "Sexy Sadie" was originally titled "Maharishi"; John Lennon wrote it after he learned that the ostensibly celibate Maharishi Mahesh Yogi (1917–2008), the founder of the Transcendental Meditation movement and for a time the Beatles' spiritual mentor, had made a pass at Mia Farrow. And then there is Sathya Sai Baba, India's most famous living guru. Born Sathyanarayana Raju in 1926, he took his name from the Sufi/Hindu saint Sai Baba of Shirdi, whom he claims to be the reincarnation of. Thousands gather at his ashram in Puttaparthi to experience "darshan," when he briefly mingles with his followers and sometimes performs miracles, which range from carnival tricks like pulling jewelry out of the air to raising the dead. Since 1970, when an ex-follower named Tal Brooke published an exposé entitled *Lord of the Air*, Baba has been suspected not just of charlatanry but of pederasty— dozens of boys and young men have accused him of molesting them.

Swami Satchidananda (born as C. K. Ramaswamy Gounder in 1914; the name Satchidananda means "Existence, knowledge, bliss") arrived in America in the 1960s, just in time to deliver an invocation at the Woodstock music festival. In short order he amassed a personal fortune and a celebrity following as the founder of Integral Yoga. The hallmark of a guru, he said, is "complete mastery over his or her body and mind, purity of heart, and total freedom from the bondage of the senses." But he too was dogged by accusations of sexual improprieties until his death in 2002.

Amma the Hugging Saint, or Sri Mata Amritanandamayi Devi (her name means "Mother of immortal bliss"), offers a decidedly noncarnal sort of love to her millions of followers— nor has she been discredited or disgraced. Born to a humble family of fishermen in the village of Parayakadavu in 1953, she left school at age nine; as a teenager she took a vow of celibacy and devoted herself to a life of contemplation. Believed to be an avatar of the goddess Kali, she lives in her ashram in Amritapuri with ten thousand followers. On her world tours, she dispenses hugs and nondenominational lectures about the power of love, "felt not only towards one's own children, but all people, animals and plants, rocks and rivers—a love extended to all of nature, all beings." Though she is suspiciously adept at raising money, she is famously charitable as well; her organization runs hospitals, schools, and orphanages; distributes disaster relief; and plants trees, to name only a few of its humanitarian activities.

Amma stands in stark contrast to Prem Rawat, who achieved massive but fleeting celebrity in the early 1970s when he was barely an adolescent. The son of Guru Maharaj Ji, who taught a quartet of meditational techniques called "Knowledge," Rawat inherited his father's organization (the Divine Light Mission), his name, and his mass following upon his death in 1966. In 1970, when he was just twelve years old, Rawat addressed a crowd of one million in Delhi, declaring:

> I will establish peace in this world. Just give me the reins and let me rule and I will rule in such a way that even Rama, Hariscandra, Krishna and other kings could not have ruled like that! . . . If with a true heart you give me the reins of your life, place them in my hands, you will be saved.

By 1972, the Divine Light Mission was headquartered in Denver, Colorado; ashrams were opening up throughout the United States, England, Australia, Japan, and other countries. In 1973, Rawat announced that the "most holy and significant event in human history" would soon occur when 144,000 devotees—including beings from other planets—would gather in Houston's Astrodome to pay him homage. The event fizzled when only fifteen thousand—all of them earthlings—showed up. Rawat married a flight attendant when he was all of sixteen years old; his scandalized mother revoked his inheritance and bestowed it on his eldest brother.

By then, the movement was hemorrhaging members. Even so, it continued to throw off enough money for Rawat to amass a vast personal fortune. Though nowhere near as famous as he was, he continues to teach "Knowledge" under the auspices of Elan Vital (Divine Light Mission's new name) and the Prem Rawat Foundation.

Hosts of ex-members have come forward over the years to recount horror stories about their years in the cult. Mahatma Jagdeo, one of Rawat's senior advisers, was accused of raping both young men and women; Rawat himself has been widely criticized for his indulgence in drugs, alcohol, and sex and for his grotesque materialism. "Consumerism is like a disease with him," writes Bob Mishler, a former president of Divine Light Mission's American organization. "He no sooner has the object of his desire, whether it's a new Maserati or Rolls-Royce . . . [than] he's thinking about the next thing: it's got to be a helicopter, it's got to be a Grumman Gulfstream II, it's got to be this or that."

International Peace Mission Movement (see **Peoples Temple**)

ISKCON, or International Society for Krishna Consciousness
The largest and best-known movement in the Gaudiya Vaishnava tradition that was founded by Chaitanya Mahaprabhu (1486–1533) five hundred years ago, the International Society for Krishna Consciousness was the creation of a seventy-year-old ex–pharmaceuticals salesman who was born in Calcutta in 1896 as Abhay Charan De. A disciple of Srila Bhaktisiddhanta Sarasvati Thakur Prabhupada (1874–1937), A. C. Bhaktivedanta Swami Prabhupada, as he would become known, had been involved with Bhakti yoga since the 1930s. He began publishing the magazine *Back to Godhead* in 1944, translated the *Bhagavad Gita* into English, and wrote extensive commentaries on the Vedas. In 1950 he renounced his family and in 1959 he became a sannyasi (the highest order of religious ascetic). He traveled to America in 1965, where he

lived as a mendicant in New York City's East Village, attracting the first members of what swiftly blossomed into an international movement.

Krishna Consciousness is essentially monotheistic in that it teaches that the god Krishna is Supreme; its goal is not dissolution but devotion—ISKCON maintains that every soul is unique, and promises its followers personal immortality rather than a merger with a Cosmic Allsoul. By cultivating bodily purity—eating a vegetarian diet, remaining sober, drug-free, and sexually chaste (except for procreative purposes)—and by chanting the Krishna mantra 1,728 times a day and performing other rituals, one changes the quality of one's consciousness and achieves bliss. Especially important are evangelical activities, known as *sankirtan.*

In the 1970s, the Hare Krishnas, with their shaved heads and topknots (called *sikha*), their body paint (*tilaki*), their saffron robes (*dhotis*) and saris, were ubiquitous, chanting and offering flowers and copies of their guru's books for sale, especially in airports and bus stations. Allen Ginsberg became a follower; Beatle George Harrison's star power drove a recording of the "Hare Krishna" chant onto the pop music charts:

> *hare Krishna hare Krishna,*
> *Krishna Krishna, hare hare,*
> *hare Rama, hare Rama,*
> *Rama Rama, hare hare*

(Harrison would reprise the chant a few years later on his own hit single, "My Sweet Lord.")

After Prabhupada died in 1977, a series of controversies erupted over the succession of authority as well as some knotty theological issues. Perhaps because they had come out of the counterculture, a number of the movement's first generation of gurus would be implicated in scandals (criminal, sexual, and pharmaceutical). There were legal difficulties too. In 1983 a jury awarded Robin George and her mother the staggering sum of $32.5 million. George had sued ISKCON in 1977, claiming that she had been kidnapped, brainwashed, and unlawfully imprisoned as a teenager; the suit also claimed that ISKCON had been partially responsible for her father's premature death, which had been hastened by stress. After making its way through a lengthy appeals process, the award was reduced to $4 million. The suit was ultimately settled in 1994 for an undisclosed sum that is believed to be considerably smaller. Another damaging case was International Society for Krishna Consciousness, Inc. *v.* Lee, which reached the Supreme Court in 1992, in which the right of airports and bus stations to ban soliciting was upheld, with significant consequences for the movement's ability to raise funds. Even more devastating to ISKCON were the allegations of widespread sexual abuse of children in the movement's schools and ashrams, which began to be heard in the 1990s, followed by a rash of individual lawsuits and a large class action lawsuit. In 2005, the movement set aside $9.5 million to divide among the 450 claimants and declared bankruptcy to protect itself from further litigation.

Though much less visible in America than it was, ISKCON claims some 260,000 members today, ten thousand of them full-time residents of temples. Worldwide, the movement runs 350 centers, sixty rural communities, fifty schools, and sixty vegetarian restaurants.

Ismailism (see Assassins)

Jesuits

Not a cult at all, "Jesuits" is the informal name for Roman Catholic priests belonging to the Society of Jesus, a religious order founded by the Spanish soldier and cleric Ignatius of Loyola (1491–1556) in 1540. Loyola wrote the *Spiritual*

Exercises, a program for "examining one's conscience, of meditating, of contemplating, of praying vocally and mentally, and of performing other spiritual actions," while recovering from wounds he received at the Battle of Panteluna in 1521. As with "Puritan" and "Quaker," "Jesuit" was originally a pejorative label—the Jesuits have been stepping on toes since they came into existence—but they swiftly adopted it as a badge of honor.

Rigorously disciplined and ascetic, profoundly educated, and skilled in dialectics, Loyola's "foot soldiers of the Pope" undertook missionary work and opened schools throughout the world. Because of their work in the Counter-Reformation, in which they challenged Protestantism while simultaneously pressing for reform within the Roman Church, they made many enemies on both sides. Between 1773 and 1814, the Society of Jesus was suppressed by order of the Pope. Today, with close to twenty thousand priests serving in more than one hundred countries on six continents, it is the largest religious order in the Roman Catholic Church; it is also one of its most progressive. Much to the Vatican's displeasure, Jesuits were at the forefront of Liberation Theology in Latin America. In 2006 "a small but representative group of members of the Society of Jesus" issued a strong protest when Condoleezza Rice, "one of the principal architects and representatives of the Bush administration's illegal and immoral invasion and occupation of Iraq," as they called her, was awarded an honorary doctorate at Boston College. "Faith *and* justice," reads one of the decrees published after the Society of Jesus's Thirty-fifth General Congregation, held in early 2008:

> It is never one without the other. Human beings need food, shelter, love, relationship, truth, meaning, promise, hope. Human beings need a future in which they can take hold of their full dignity; indeed they need an absolute future, a great hope that exceeds every particular hope.

But the Jesuits are not included in this book because of their liberal politics or because of their ongoing struggles with their own institutional authorities. Almost since the Jesuits' inception, non-Catholics have accused them of being not just a religious order, but a cult, a conspiracy, a sinister secret society.

In 1614, the *Monita Secreta Societatis Jesu* (or *The Secret Instructions of the Society of Jesus*) was published in Kraców, Poland. While it was supposedly written by Claudio Acquaviva (1543–1615), the Fifth General of the Society, as a Machiavellian instruction manual on the arts of dissimulation and manipulation in the pursuit of money and power, most scholars believe that it was forged by its "editor," an ex-Jesuit named Jerome Zahorowski. Especially chilling are its closing lines, which bear strong stylistic similarities to the ***Protocols of the Learned Elders of Zion***:

> We must be careful to change our politics, conforming to the times, and excite the princes, friends of ours, to mutually make terrible wars that everywhere the mediation of the society will be implored. . . . In fine, that the Society afterwards can yet count upon the favor and authority of the princes, procuring that those who do not love us shall fear us.

In 1678 the Englishman Titus Oates (1649–1705) claimed to have infiltrated the Jesuits and discovered a "Popish Plot" to assassinate Charles II. Before his accusations were revealed as the fraud they were, laws were passed forbidding Catholics to serve in Parliament and a number of innocent men were executed. Eleven years later, in a book called *Foxes and Firebrands*, Robert Ware published another forgery: the "Oath of Secrecy devised by the Roman Clergy, as it remaineth on Record at Paris, amongst the Society of Jesus," or as it is better known today, the "Extreme Oath of the Jesuits" or "The Knights of Columbus Oath," which remains a staple on the Internet today. It is quite long, but a single hair-raising paragraph will suffice to convey its tone:

I furthermore promise and declare that I will . . . make and wage relentless war, secretly or openly, against all heretics, Protestants and Liberals, as I am directed to do, to extirpate and exterminate them from the face of the whole earth; and that I will spare neither age, sex, or condition; and that I will hang, waste, boil, flay, strangle and bury alive these infamous heretics, rip up the stomachs and wombs of their women and crush their infants' heads against the walls, in order to annihilate forever their execrable race. That when the same cannot be done openly, I will secretly use the poisoned cup, the strangulating cord, the steel of the poniard or the leaden bullet, regardless of the honor, rank, dignity, or authority of the person or persons, whatever may be their condition in life, either public or private, as I at any time may be directed so to do by any agent of the Pope or Superior of the Brotherhood of the Holy Faith, of the Society of Jesus.

A staple of anti-Catholic Know-Nothing literature in nineteenth-century America, a version of the oath was even read into the Congressional Record in 1913—not because Congress was investigating Jesuit perfidies, but because a Catholic candidate for a closely contested congressional seat claimed that his opponent had inflamed prejudice against him by circulating it within his district.

Kabbalah

The catchall name for the Jewish mystical tradition that began in Biblical times, flowered in Provence and the Rhine Valley in the twelfth century, matured in Spain and, after the Explusion of 1492, in Palestine, and then, as a major influence on Hasidism, became a mass movement throughout Eastern Europe in the eighteenth century. Kabbalism today is both a subject of academic attention—the towering German Jewish scholar Gershom Scholem (1897–1982) was the first to give it serious scrutiny; Joseph Dan and Moshe Idel at Hebrew University in Jerusalem and Daniel Matt, Arthur

Green, and Elliot Wolfson in the United States have all published important studies in recent years—and a mode of Jewish religious practice. The Hebrew word *kabbalah* means "receiving"; it is so called because 1) as an esoteric tradition, Kabbalah's wisdom and secrets were passed down from teachers to a few carefully selected students; and 2) a basic premise of Kabbalah is that the revelation at Sinai is eternally ongoing, a perpetual receiving for those initiates who know how to translate the divine message inscribed in the Torah and other sacred texts into human language.

Kabbalah teaches that God manifests Himself in the world through the *Sefirot*, a series of ten emanations from the Godhead, which in its highest form is *Ein Sof* (the changeless infinite) and in its most materialized is the *Shekhinah* (the feminized personification of the divine presence). Through meditation, Kabbalists can ascend through the *Sefirot* to merge with the Eternal.

A theosophy (a mystical revelation) rather than a systematic theology, Kabbalah's oldest text, the *Sefer Yezirah* (or *Book of Creation*) declares that the ultimate constituents of creation—its atoms and molecules, as it were—are Hebrew letters (and also numbers—the Hebrew alphabet does double duty). Kabbalists consider themselves to be the equivalent of nuclear physicists, not only on the level of their understanding, but because of the power they potentially wield. By decoding and manipulating sacred names, they can perform miraculous feats, from teleportation all the way up to the creation of life. (The story of the Golem, a clay monster that was brought to life in the ghetto of Prague when the Hebrew word for "life" was inscribed on its forehead, is a Kabbalistic tale—it is the ur-source for Mary Shelley's *Frankenstein* (1818) and the Arnold Schwarzenegger *Terminator* movies.) Reincarnation is a major component of Kabbalistic thinking, as is its vision of the world as a flawed, incomplete creation, which requires human intervention before it can be redeemed. Kabbalah's most important text is the *Zohar*, or *Book of Splendor*, which tradition ascribes to Shimon bar Yochai, a second-century sage, but which most historians believe was written by Moses ben Shem Tov de León in Spain in the late 1200s.

Many students of Kabbalah regard their teachers with cultic devotion; a significant number of history's greatest Kabbalists have believed themselves to be the Messiah. Shabbetai Zevi (1626–1676) and Jacob Frank (1726–1791) were self-styled Messiahs who came out of the cauldron of Kabbalah only to end in heresy and out-and-out apostasy—Zevi as a convert to Islam; Frank to Catholicism. Both of them were antinomians. Zevi (who almost certainly suffered from a bipolar disorder) committed such public sacrileges as pronouncing the forbidden name of God out loud and wedding a Torah to a religious ceremony; Frank pursued a program of transgressive sex, including incest and orgies, to hasten the advent of the messianic age, when all would be permitted. Many Hasidic rebbes have exercised a level of control over their followers' daily lives that could fairly be called coercive; Rabbi Menachem Mendel Schneerson (1902–1994), the grand rebbe of the Lubavitcher movement, was widely criticized by many orthodox rabbis for encouraging the personality cult that grew up around him. Many Lubavitchers still believe that he is the Messiah.

Kabbalah enjoyed considerable mainstream visibility around the turn of the millennium when a number of A-list celebrities—Madonna, Demi Moore, Ashton Kutcher—joined the Kabbalah Centre International, the creation of Rav Philip Berg. Born Feivel Gruberger in Brooklyn in 1929, the onetime insurance agent studied with the renowned Israeli Kabbalist Yehuda Brandwein, his first wife's uncle. With his second wife, Karen, and their two sons, Yehuda and Michael, Berg built the Kabbalah Centres into a far-reaching business empire, opening schools all over the world and selling truckloads of merchandise—books, audiocassettes, red string bracelets (to ward off the evil eye), and even blessed water. Berg's innovation was to

dumb down and mass-produce Kabbalah, eliminating the traditional requirements of deep study and mentally challenging
meditations, offering it instead as a "spiritual technology" that
"promises nothing less than a world wholly free of chaos,
destruction and death." Not only that, he threw open the doors
of the Kabbalah Centre to everyone: "Christians, Muslims,
Hindus, Jews, and all humanity. After all, everyone is entitled
to happiness and a fulfilling and productive life free of chaos."
The Kabbalah Centre sells expensive Hebrew texts, but it tells
its customers that they needn't take the trouble to learn how to
read them, because merely looking at the characters ("scan-
ning them") can be spiritually efficacious. Many Jewish leaders
have deplored Berg's version of Kabbalah as snake oil for the
soul; anticult activist Rick Ross goes a step further. "In my
opinion," he told WCBS TV news, "the Kabbalah Centre can
be seen as a cult. If the family doesn't go along with the loved
one's involvement with the Kabbalah Centre, they may break
up a family, they may break up a marriage."

Kabbalah plays a role in a number of secret societies as well.
Having absorbed elements of Hermeticism, Neoplatonism, and
Gnosticism throughout its own long history, both in the Middle
East and in Europe (the Kabbalists of Provence were neighbors
of the neo-Gnostic Cathars or Albigensians), Kabbalah began
to make inroads into the Christian world starting as early as the
fifteenth century, when the Platonic philosopher Giovanni Pico
della Mirandola (1463–1494) declared that "no science can
better convince us of the divinity of Jesus Christ than magic
and the Kabbalah." Christian variants of Kabbalah, like those
of Jakob Boehme (1875–1609), are usually termed "Cabala";
the Kabbalah of occultists and alchemists like John Dee
and Heinrich Cornelius Agrippa of Nettesheim (1486–1535),
the author of the encyclopedic *De Occulta Philosophia*, is
spelled "Qabala." Qabala was absorbed into **Masonry** via
Rosicrucianism in the eighteenth century and played a
significant role in Theosophy, the **Hermetic Order of the Golden
Dawn**, and other occult groups in the nineteenth century.

Conspiracy theorists have long taken a dim view of Kabbalah's penchant for secrecy and sorcery; they have been intensely aware of the influence it exerted on esoteric Masonry. And yet, ironically enough, the methods of Kabbalistic interpretation—the deconstructive hermeneutics of deep textual exegesis, the unpacking and decrypting of embedded mathematical ciphers or gematria—are those of the conspiracy theorists as well, who subject the texts they study to the same sort of obsessively microscopic scrutiny. Unfortunately, many of those texts—the ***Protocols of the Learned Elders of Zion***, the anti-Christian passages of the Talmud, the Luciferian tracts of the Masons, the blood-curdling Extreme Oath of the Jesuits—are completely apocryphal, either pseudepigraphia (works that are falsely attributed to historical or Biblical characters) or out-and-out hoaxes and libels.

As a brief illustration of how incestuous things can get in the realm of cults, conspiracies, and secret societies, here is Rabbi Ariel Bar Tzadok, an orthodox Jewish Kabbalist, subjecting the Great Seal of the United States (which has already been analyzed to a fare-thee-well by conspiracists who see in it evidence that **Illuminists** and Masons secretly control the Republic) to a Kabbalistic interpretation: "Thirteen," he explains, "is the numerical value for the Hebrew word 'Ehad' which means 'one' as in Deut. 6:4, the verse that declares the eternal pledge of the Jewish people, '*Hear O Israel, the L-rd our G-d, the L-rd is One (Ehad).*'" He continues: "With the number 26 concealed in the right talon and the number 13 in the left, it appears as if there is a secret 'Jewish' message concealed in the Great Seal, that '*the L-rd (26) is One (13).*'"

Compare the rabbi's methodology, if you would, to the conspiracy theorist Robert Howard's, who in the following brief excerpt from one of his Web pages, collects and marshals a mass of numerological evidence against George W. Bush, who he believes is at the center of an occult Masonic plot involving the royal family:

We have President George Bush Jr. who is 13th cousin of Britain's Queen Mother, and of her daughter Queen Elizabeth and is a 13th cousin once removed of the heir to the throne, Prince Charles. Officially becoming the 43rd President on December 13th of a nation who had originally 13 colonies.

In *Secret Societies and Subversive Movements* (1921), Nesta Webster sums up the conspiracist attitude toward Kabbalah with a quotation from Sixtus of Sienna (1520–1569), a Jew who became first a Franciscan and then a Dominican.

One must know that the Cabala is double; that one is true, the other false. The true and pious one is that which . . . elucidates the secret mysteries of the holy law according to the principle of anagogy (i.e. figurative interpretation). This Cabala therefore the Church has never condemned. The false and impious Cabala is a certain mendacious kind of Jewish tradition, full of innumerable vanities and falsehoods, differing but little from necromancy. This kind of superstition, therefore, improperly called Cabala, the Church within the last few years has deservedly condemned.

In other words, what's legitimate in Kabbalah (its mode of interpretation) is not Jewish, but was merely borrowed from ancient traditions. What's Jewish is singularly evil.

Kingdom of Yahweh (see MOVE)

Koreshanity and Other Hollow Earth Theories
Religio-political-pseudoscientific cult founded by Dr. Cyrus Read Teed (1839–1908) which, despite its name, bears no relationship whatsoever to David Koresh's Branch Davidians of Waco, Texas. *Koresh* is the Hebrew rendering of "Cyrus," as in Cyrus the Great, the Persian emperor who redeemed the Israelites from their Babylonian exile, and of

whom God said, according to Isaiah 44:28, "He is my shepherd, He shall fulfill all my purposes!" Vernon Wayne Howell changed his name to David Koresh when he received his religious vocation. Cyrus Teed was given his name by his parents; he Hebraized it in 1891, twenty-two years after he had the vision that provided the basis of the religion of Koreshanity.

A distant cousin of Joseph Smith (1805–1844), the founder of the Latter-Day Saints, Teed came of age in the "burned-over" district of upstate New York that was so susceptible to religious enthusiasm in the first half of the nineteenth century. As a soldier in the Union Army during the Civil War, he suffered such a severe case of sunstroke that he was hospitalized for months with neurological symptoms (this could be pertinent to an assessment of his mental health in later years). After his discharge, Teed finished his medical studies in New York City and joined his uncle's practice in Utica, New York. Just one year later, in 1869, he electrocuted himself while conducting an alchemical experiment. A beautiful woman appeared to him in a vision and revealed a cosmic secret: that we don't live on the surface of the earth but inside it—that the entire universe is contained inside the globe, or, as Teed would put it in his magnum opus, *The Cellular Cosmology* (1922), published, oddly enough, some fourteen years after his death:

> The alchemico-organic (physical) world or universe is a shell composed of seven metallic, five mineral, and five geologic strata, with an inner habitable surface of land and water.

From this inverted geography, he derived a geodesic theology:

> The true interpretation of the alchemico-organic cosmos is the revelation of the mysteries of Deity; for as the outward and most material structure is but the expressed thought of the voluntary and involuntary mental cause producing it, so

a knowledge of this expressed and manifest language reveals the history of human origin and destiny.

Teed was not the first to conceive of a hollow earth. In 1692, the great English astronomer and mathematician Sir Edmond Halley (1656–1742) submitted a paper to the Royal Society entitled "An Account of the Cause of the Change of the Variation of the Magnetical Needle with an Hypothesis of the Structure of the Internal Parts of the Earth," which proposed that the interior of the planet was comprised of two hollow, concentric spheres and a solid inner core. A century later, the American John Cleves Symmes (1780–1829) lectured widely about his theory that the earth's interior contained four nesting spheres, which could be accessed via large openings at the poles (the interior of each sphere was accessible in the same way). The idea was further promoted in a book by the Ohio politican James McBride (1788–1859) and immortalized in Edgar Allan Poe's *Narrative of Arthur Gordon Pym of Nantucket* (1838). William F. Lyon published the intriguingly titled *The Hollow Globe, or, The World's Agitator and Reconciler* in 1873, a work that combined science, mediumship, and Manifest Destiny, arguing that mankind would ascend to its next evolutionary level when we take possession of the world's inner spaces. The occultist Alexandre Saint-Yves d'Alveydre (1842–1909) wrote extensively about Agartha, the underground caverns beneath the Himalayas that are the dwelling place of the Ascended Masters. And of course there is Jules Verne's *Journey to the Center of the Earth* (1864), not to mention the camp classic horror movie *The Mole People* (1956), which explicitly references Symmes and Teed. Sir Edward Bulwer-Lytton's *Vril: The Power of the Coming Race* (1871) is the story of a subterranean superrace, refugees of an ancient deluge who have harnessed the powers of "vril," the ultimate energy. "I should call it electricity," *Vril*'s narrator explains, except that it comprehends in its manifold branches other forces of nature. These subterranean philosophers assert that, by one operation of vril, which Faraday would perhaps call "atmospheric magnetism," they can influence the variations of temperature—in plain words, the weather; that by other operations, akin to those ascribed to mesmerism, electro-biology, odic force, &c., but applied scientifically through vril conductors, they can exercise influence over minds, and bodies animal and vegetable, to an extent not surpassed in the romances of our mystics.

These and many other theories are described in detail in David Standish's encyclopedic *Hollow Earth: The Long and Curious History of Imagining Strange Lands, Fantastical Creatures, Advanced Civilizations, and Marvelous Machines Below the Earth's Surface* (2006).

But if Teed wasn't the first (or the last) to posit a hollow earth (a notion that Hitler was purportedly fascinated by), he was the only one to derive a full-blown religion from it. For all of its weirdness and counterintuitiveness, Koreshanity is disquietingly detailed and internally consistent. Some of its assertions about the influence of gravity on light and the identity of matter and energy sound almost proto-Einsteinian. Both Teed's radical skepticism toward sensory experience and his conviction that his knowledge had been personally transmitted to him (to say nothing of Teed's conviction that God is a hermaphrodite) provide a case in point for Harold Bloom's famous assertion that the American religion is a "democratized Gnosticism."

Science and religion both ask us to put our faith in the "evidence of things not seen." Christianity, for example, demands that we accept revealed truths about miracles, resurrection, and a triune yet mysteriously indivisible deity; science asks us to disregard our physical senses (which tell us that the world is flat, for example, or that we reside on the outside, not the inside of our planet) when they contradict the laws of physics. Quantum mechanics has introduced us to a realm of existence in which Newtonian physics don't apply, where all that we can know with any certainty are probabilities instead of concrete causes and effects.

Teed attempted to reconcile science and religion within his own wholly speculative (some might call it a "crackpot") schema. Under Teed's supervision, his follower Professor Ulysses Morrow carried out extensive experiments on the beaches of Florida, in which specially designed surveyors' instruments (giant T squares called rectilineators) were deployed to determine if the earth's surface was concave or convex. Strangely enough, the results supported Teed's thesis (probably due to a flaw in the design of the rectilineator)—although, because of something known as inversion geometry, it's virtually impossible to prove whether we live on the inside or outside of a sphere using mathematics alone.

Teed did a lot of wandering in the years after his illumination. He lived in a utopian commune and with Shakers (the communal Protestant religious movement that was founded in the mideighteenth century as the United Society of Believers in Christ's Second Appearing). Teed opened and closed a number of medical practices; he ran the family mop business into the ground; he published and edited a daily newspaper called *Herald of the Messenger of the New Covenant of the New Jerusalem.* Eventually his wife and son left him. There was a scandal in Syracuse when he was accused of passing himself off as Jesus Christ; there was a series of women with whom he forged chaste but suspiciously close connections. Then, in 1886, he lectured at the convention of the National Association of Mental Science in Chicago, where he found his audience. In the next few years, Teed changed his name to Koreshan and began to write his many books. In due course, he attracted some four thousand followers; in 1894, they purchased land on the Estero River near Fort Myers, Florida, and began to build their New Jerusalem.

Koreshan's New Jerusalem grew into a utopian commune that was prosperous, socialistic, clean, and ecologically minded, much like the Shaker community he had lived in. Also like the Shakers, the Koreshans were celibate. None of the Koreshans were wage slaves; their industry—they manufactured mattresses, hats, and baskets, sold "Risin' Bread" from their bakery, and put on plays and concerts in their Art Hall—benefited all. Women (and most of the Koreshans were educated women) enjoyed absolute equality. Unfortunately, as would happen with Bhagwan Rajneesh in Oregon in the 1980s (see **Indian Gurus**), political relations with the locals became increasingly strained when the Koreshans decided to incorporate themselves as the town of Estero so they could receive road taxes. Matters came to a head in 1906 when Teed was severely injured in a street brawl that broke out in Fort Myers. Despite having argued, in *The Immortal Manhood: The Laws and Processes of Its Attainment in the Flesh* (1902), that "there be operative mental laws through which the bodies of men should consume by an electromagnetic combustion, which could obviate the unnatural processes of corruption called death," Teed went into a decline and died two years later. The Koreshans not only expected their leader to be resurrected; they had been promised that they too would become immortal upon his return. They waited as long as they could before burying him. Though most of the community dispersed after this disappointment, a small core of faithful remained in Estero for almost fifty years.

What accounts for Koreshanity's weird appeal? Perhaps it was its unabashed quixotism, its determination to believe in something so contrary to both common sense and scientific orthodoxy. In *Fads and Fallacies in the Name of Science* (1957), Martin Gardner suggests that the notion of a hollow earth evokes the comforting sensation of a return to the womb. As Teed put it:

[T]he universe is the great ovum of integral incubation. . . . Humanity as a whole is incubated within the great cell or ovum of universal life and not . . . on the outside of an uneconomic adjustment and compilation of matter, as men throughout the world of boasted civilization have been blindly taught.

Maharaj Ji (see Indian Gurus)

Charles Manson's "Family"
The murders were singularly cruel and ghastly: the victims had been bound and tortured; their bodies were mutilated; bizarre slogans were daubed on the walls in blood. Some of them (the very pregnant movie star Sharon Tate, who was married to the director Roman Polanski; Abigail Folger, the coffee heiress; the celebrity hairstylist Jay Sebring) were famous and glamorous; none of them had done anything to deserve their fates. And their killers—a ragtag band of zombielike hippies who were dominated by a sinister Svengali, an ex-con and would-be rock star named Charles Manson— seemed the very personification of the dark side of the Age of Aquarius. The year was 1969. And for those who regarded flower power, free love, rock 'n' roll, and psychedelic drugs as the four horsemen of the Apocalypse, Charles Manson was nothing less than the Antichrist.

According to his prosecutors, Manson preached an End Times gospel, which he had gleaned from the Beatles' *White Album* and the Book of Revelation. John, Paul, George, and Ringo were the first four angels of Chapter 8; Manson was the fifth angel of Chapter 9, who blew the trumpet. The song "Helter Skelter" prophesied a race war that black people would win—but due to their innate inferiority, they would prove incapable of governing themselves. When that happened, Manson and his Family would emerge from their refuge in a cavern beneath Death Valley and take their places as society's new leaders. By then, Manson taught, their tribe would number 144,000, as in Revelation 14:3's "the hundred and forty and four thousand, which were redeemed from the earth." (The Jehovah's Witnesses make much of this passage too.)

It was in order to hasten this race war (much as **Aum Shinrikyo** sought to jump-start its own anticipated Armageddon with sarin gas attacks) that Manson ordered his followers to decorate their crime scenes with graffiti ("Death to Pigs"; "Rise") that he hoped would be mistaken for the slogans of black militants. He had them plant Rosemary LaBianca's wallet in a gas station in a black neighborhood in the expectation that a local customer would find it and use her credit cards, attracting the attention of the police.

Manson and members of his Family would be tried for eight murders at three different locations. As well as the three victims already mentioned at the Polanski-Tate residence, Folger's boyfriend Wojciech Frykowski, and Steve Earl Parent, a friend of the mansion's caretaker, lost their lives. UCLA graduate student Gary Allen Hinman was killed in his house on Old Topanga Canyon Road outside Los Angeles; and Leno and Rosemary LaBianca were slaughtered in their home in the Los Feliz district of Los Angeles. A ninth victim was Donald Shea, an employee of the desert ranch where Manson's Family lived, whom Manson suspected of snitching. A possible tenth victim was Family member Leslie Van Houten's lawyer Ronald Hughes, who objected vehemently when she and two other Family members attempted to exonerate Manson at their trial by incriminating themselves. "I refuse to take part in any proceeding where I am forced to push a client out the window," he'd declared. Hughes's badly decomposed body was found in a canyon in Ventura County, where he had been camping. There may have been others as well—anonymous runaways, hitchhikers, and hippies who were never missed or searched for.

Manson began assembling his Family—most of them teenagers—in 1967 when he was thirty-three years old, after his release from a seven-year stint in prison (he had been in and out of the penal system most of his life for crimes like car theft, pimping, and kiting checks). "At that time," he disingenuously told Nuel Emmons, an old prison acquaintance and the author of *Manson in His Own Words* (1986), "I didn't see myself as wanting to control anyone or be leader. I didn't want to pull a person away from what he or she desired or enjoyed." He went on:

> I simply felt that if I ran across someone at a crossroads in life, I could lend a helping hand. I had a need to be with people who needed love and understanding. Because I had experienced so much shit in my life, I felt my advice could help and strengthen some of those lost children.

But as Manson's circle of runaways, street people, petty criminals, bikers, and druggies enlarged, and as he discovered the extent of the erotic and psychological sway he could exert over them, his power went to his head. "Being the center of attraction," he observed, "the one everyone leans on, the adviser, the authority and the hub that turns the wheel, can sometimes have an adverse effect on a person." He explained:

> You see it every day among wealthy people. It often happens in charitable organizations, in religion, in those who govern, those with physical strength, and those who receive even the slightest bit of authority. Given a little taste of power, personalities often change, and someone who was once humble and righteous becomes a tyrant, so caught up in status that the original good becomes bad.

Manson and his family had some contact with members of Anton LaVey's Church of Satan (see **Satanism**) and possibly with the **Processeans**. Family member Charlie Watson was said to have introduced himself at the Tate residence as "the Devil," saying, "I am here to do the Devil's work"; Susan

Atkins would later speak of Sharon Tate as if she had been a human sacrifice. It's easy to imagine how Satanism would have played into Manson's natural grandiosity, which was also likely enhanced by his dabblings in **Scientology**, his ingestion of hallucinogenics, and his tantalizing brushes with fame.* But Manson's dreams of Beatles-like stardom would all come to nothing. His frustration, he told Emmons, left him feeling "down and sorry for myself . . . the self-pity . . . pretty well shadowed by hate and contempt. Hate for a world that denied. Contempt for people who can't see or understand." The killings began soon afterward.

There is no question that Manson possessed a powerful charisma—there was literally nothing that his followers wouldn't do for him, including acts of astounding cruelty (Susan Atkins confessed that when Sharon Tate pleaded for her life, she looked her in the eye and said, "Look, bitch, I don't care about you. I don't care if you're going to have a baby. You had better be ready. You're going to die and I don't feel anything about it.") Decades after the killings, Manson remains an object of cultic devotion—he receives bales of fan mail in prison and is the subject of countless books and documentaries. But it would be difficult to prove that he systematically "brainwashed" his young disciples. Most of them were heavy drug users and dropouts when they came into his orbit. It didn't take much for him to push them over the edge.

"These children that come at you with knives, they are your children," Manson said during his trial. "You taught them. I didn't teach them. I just tried to help them stand up." His moralizing is shallow and self-serving, and his irony is all too obvious, but the horrors that he helped unleash beggar understanding.

*Manson played music in prison with Alvin Karpis, who had been Public Enemy Number One when he robbed banks with Ma Barker's gang in the 1930s; he would meet Dennis Wilson of the Beach Boys in Los Angeles, who helped him cut a few demo recordings. Unfortunately for Sharon Tate, her house was leased from Doris Day's son, Terry Melcher, a prominent record producer who had also taken a passing interest in Manson. Melcher might have been Manson's intended target.

In his latest revision of his classic *The Family* (2002), Ed Sanders notes the mixed legacy of the hippie movement (which Sanders himself, as a poet and member of the transgressive rock band The Fugs, had participated in):

> Potentially, flower-power was one of the most powerful forces of change ever seen in recent history. . . . It was a noble experiment. It was the politics of Free. . . . There were no rules. But there was a weakness . . . the flower movement was like a valley of thousands of plump white rabbits surrounded by wounded coyotes.

Most of Manson's progeny were as innately coyotelike as he was.

Martinism (see **Synarchy** in Secret Societies)

MOVE

Anarchist, back-to-nature revolutionary collective founded in the early 1970s in the Powelton neighborhood of West Philadelphia by John Africa (1931–1985). Africa died along with ten of his followers, six of them children, when the police bombed the heavily fortified town house that served as MOVE's headquarters, igniting a conflagration that engulfed fifty-three neighboring houses, leaving more than two hundred people homeless.

Africa's given name was Vincent Lopez Leaphart. He was born into a family of ten children. His school would assess him as "orthogenetically backward" (mentally retarded) when he was nine years old; when he dropped out of high school at age sixteen he was said to have achieved a third-grade level of education. Despite that diagnosis—and a pair of arrests for armed robbery and car theft—he was drafted into the military and served in Korea. He married Dorothy Clark in 1961 and worked for a time as an interior decorator in New York City. As their marriage unraveled, his wife became involved with the Kingdom of Yahweh, a Phoenix-based church founded by Dr. Joseph Jeffers, PhD, Doctor of Eschatology, Theology, and Divinity, whose teachings amalgamate pyramids, lost continents, ESP, and astrology with End Times prophecies, reincarnation, vegetarianism, the Rapture, and flying saucers. They divorced in 1968 amid accusations of wife battering.

The next chapter of Leaphart's life began in 1970, when he moved into Philadelphia's Powelton neighborhood near the University of Pennsylvania. Once a dapper interior designer, he now wore his hair in dreadlocks and supported himself as a carpenter/handyman and dog walker. But the mentally challenged child had grown up to be a hyperarticulate, quietly charismatic adult, albeit a marginally literate one. He was taken up by neighborhood activists and became involved in the housing co-op. Donald Glassey, who had just received his master's degree in social work from the University of Pennsylvania, became Leaphart's first disciple, transcribing hundreds of pages of his philosophical musings and compiling them into the manuscript that would later be known as the "the Book" or "the Guidelines," the foundational bible of MOVE. "We don't believe in this reform world system—the government, the military, industry and big business," it declared.

Over the last century, industry has raped the earth of count-less tons of minerals, bled billions of gallons of oil from the ground, and enslaved millions of people to manufacture cars, trucks, planes and trains that further pollute the air with their use. . . . Big business and industry are responsible for the mass production and mass marketing of cigarettes, alcohol, and drugs, which are used to extract further profits from people while keeping them sick and addicted. Politicians are put in place to legalize, endorse, and protect industry and big business, therefore we don't believe in politics at all.

Leaphart and Glassey refused to spray the apartment they
shared for roaches; when the building became infested, the
co-op evicted them. They rented an apartment in a Victorian house across the street and eventually purchased the
building. Over the next year, Leaphart completed his transformation into John Africa, a brooding, dominating, and
increasingly volatile figure, and the commune he presided
over was formally organized as the American Christian
Movement for Life—a name that was quickly shortened to
MOVE. "For many of its members," wrote the *Philadelphia
Inquirer*, MOVE

> offered shelter from the world—a haven for seekers, drug-
> users, lost souls. John Africa played the father figure, advis-
> ing, cajoling, ordering. To win his approval, members had to
> change their diets, swear off junk food and meat, become
> physically fit. Periodically, they were sent on an "activity"
> ordered by John Africa.

MOVE members picketed the zoo and a pet store; television
talk show host Mike Douglas was handcuffed to a chair in
his studio to protest the treatment a renegade chimp had
received when it ran amok on his show (it was shot with a
tranquilizer dart and handcuffed). "We don't see any difference," Glassey told the press, "between putting Jews in
Auschwitz, napalming Vietnam or enslaving black people
and enslaving puppies."

By May 1977, tensions between the growing MOVE family (members all changed their names to Africa when they
joined out of solidarity with their leader) and the Powelton
co-op had reached the breaking point. When the police were
called in, MOVE issued an ominous statement:

> Don't attempt to enter MOVE headquarters or harm MOVE
> people unless you want an international incident. . . . We are
> prepared to hit reservoirs, empty hotels and apartment

houses, close factories, and tie up traffic in major cities of Europe. . . . We are not a bunch of frustrated, middle class college students, irrational radicals or confused terrorists. We are a deeply religious organization totally committed to the principle of our belief as taught to us by our founder, John Africa. We are not looking for trouble. We are just looking to be left alone.

Printed at the bottom of the page were the chemical formulas for nitroglycerin and TNT.

That same day, police arrested Glassey for possession of an illegal firearm and secured his cooperation as an informer. Over the course of the next six months, he led authorities to caches of firearms and explosives, providing them with enough evidence to secure indictments against ten MOVE members. After a year of legal manuevering, the police raided the MOVE compound; officer James Ramp was killed in the fighting. Nine MOVE members would be tried and convicted for his murder, but John Africa eluded capture until 1981, when, along with eight of his followers, he was arrested in Rochester, New York, and brought back to Philadelphia to stand trial. Africa spoke eloquently in his own defense:

I'm fighting for air that you've got to breathe. And I'm fighting for water that you've got to drink. . . . I've been a revolutionary all my life. Since I could understand the word "revolution," I have been a revolutionary, and I remain a revolutionary because, don't you see, "revolutionary" simply means to turn, to generate, to activate. It don't mean it should be evil and kill people and bomb people. It simply means to be right.

To the prosecutors' astonishment, the jury agreed and acquitted him.

Africa and his followers moved to Osage Avenue in the

Cobbs Creek section of Philadelphia, where they built a new compound and began arguing with a new set of neighbors. In 1981, Mumia Abu-Jamal, a prominent African American journalist and activist (and an ex–Black Panther) who had written sympathetically about MOVE, was arrested for murdering Philadelphia police officer Daniel Faulkner; his request that John Africa be allowed to defend him was refused. Convicted and sentenced to death, he has become an international cause célèbre as his appeals work their way through the system.

Meanwhile John Africa had become increasingly demagogic and dictatorial. He subjected his neighbors to nighttime sermons broadcast through loudspeakers, inflicted cruel discipline on current members, and harassed and threatened former ones. On May 13, 1985, MOVE's final standoff with the police came to a terrible end when a satchel of plastic explosives was dropped onto its rooftop bunker.

MOVE still exists, led by Alberta Wicker Africa (John Africa's widow); most of its three dozen members live communally in a double town house on Kingsessing Avenue in Philadelphia. Though quieter (and much wealthier— survivors received significant reparations from the city of Philadelphia) than it once was, MOVE continues to provoke controversy. In 2002, Alberta Wicker Africa's estranged second husband was murdered in the midst of a custody dispute, a crime that remains officially unsolved. Ramona Africa (one of the survivors of the conflagration) gives speeches around the world on behalf of still-imprisoned MOVE members; Pam Africa is prominent in the movement to free Mumia Abu-Jamal. MOVE's Web site remains unabashedly confrontational:

> Is there any question why MOVE people are so bitter, so full of fight and so motivated to keep revolting against this rotten ass system? JOHN AFRICA has opened our eyes and HE keeps us motivated, keeps us full of fight. They can hurt

MOVE because we're alive, we have feelings, but thanks to
JOHN AFRICA they WILL NEVER STOP MOVE!

Nizārites (see Assassins)

Oahspe

The "bible" of Faithism, a nineteenth-century American
spiritualist movement, channeled by a dentist named John
Ballou Newbrough (1828–1891). With its stories of angelic
wars fought in outer space, it anticipated some of the science
fiction elements in **Scientology**—and inspired at least one flying saucer enthusiast in the 1950s, Gloria Lee, who starved
herself to death in 1962 when the U.S. government ignored
her alien-sent messages. (See **Area 51** in Conspiracies for a
fuller account.)

Opus Dei

Although its leaders and the vast majority of its membership
(approximately eighty-five thousand worldwide, about three
thousand in the United States) would adamantly deny that
the Roman Catholic organization Opus Dei (or as it is known
officially, the Prelature of the Holy Cross and Opus Dei) is
either a cult, a secret society, or a conspiracy, its critics, many
of them former members, have accused it of being all three.

Opus Dei (the name means "the Work of God") was
founded by Josemaria Escrivá (1902–1975) in Spain in 1928.
On the occasion of his canonization, Pope John Paul II said
that Escrivá "was chosen by the Lord to proclaim the universal call to holiness and to indicate that everyday life, its cus-
tomary activities, are a path towards holiness. It could be
said that he was the saint of the ordinary." In Escrivá's own
words, Opus Dei's mission is to:

Foster the search for holiness and the carrying out of the
Apostolate by Christians who live in the world, whatever
their state in life or position in society. The Work of God was

born to help those Christians ... to understand that their
life, just as it is, can be an opportunity for meeting Christ:
that it is a way of holiness and apostolate.

Opus Dei's members are active in the world—they are not
monks or nuns—but their spiritual practice is central to all
that they do. A mother of seven who lives in a small town in
upstate New York and owns a small business told the *New
York Times* that

> the determination I have definitely comes from my vocation
> with Opus Dei, because every single day with Opus Dei, you
> wake up and say, "I'm giving 100 percent of my day to you,
> Lord." And if you slack off, that's a boss you don't want to
> answer to.

A "personal prelature" (meaning the church exercises its
authority over its widely dispersed members directly, instead
of through the administrative machinery of the dioceses
where they live), each Opus Dei chapter reports to the
order's leader in Rome, who in turn reports directly to the
Pope. Seventy percent of Opus Dei's members are "supernumeraries," which means they work in the outside world, are
married, and live at home. Celibate, or numerary, members
live in communities at Opus Dei centers; only about 2 percent of Opus Dei's members are priests (the Priestly Society
of the Holy Cross was founded in 1943). Finally, there are
"cooperators," nonmembers who support the movement
with time and money.

Opus Dei has been called a "brainwashing cult" because of
its high-pressure recruiting tactics, especially on college campuses; it imposes an intense discipline on members (which for
numeraries includes corporal mortification with the "cilice,"
a spiked chain wrapped around the leg for several hours a
day, and the "discipline," a whip used for self-scourging while
reciting the Lord's Prayer) and an extraordinary degree of

control over their daily lives. Numeraries' comings and goings are closely monitored, as is their mail; their reading and movie viewing is censored, and they are required to confess weekly to a spiritual adviser, reporting their own and their fellow members' lapses and transgressions. Many former members say they were encouraged to break off ties with their families. All members are urged to make substantial financial contributions to the movement; numeraries donate their entire salaries.

Opus Dei has been called a secret society because it does not reveal the names of its members; it has been called a conspiracy because of its alleged involvement in right-wing politics (it was an ardent supporter of Franco in Spain). Escrivá said, "We are an intravenous injection in the bloodstream of society, so that you, as men and women of God . . . may immunize all men and women from corruption and illuminate every human intellect with Christ's light." According to its critics, Opus Dei injects more than its "spirituality" into the veins of the body politic—it systematically lobbies politicians, runs schools and think tanks whose connections to Opus Dei are not always transparent, and, as an article in the April 2006 edition of *Harper's* magazine put it, infiltrates "its indoctrinated technocrats, politicos and administrators into the highest levels of the state." Supreme Court justice Antonin Scalia has been reputed to have connections to Opus Dei, as have U.S. senator Sam Brownback (R-KS) and former senator Rick Santorum (R-PA).

Dan Brown's megablockbuster novel *The Da Vinci Code* (2003) portrayed Opus Dei in wildly sensationalistic terms as a fabulously wealthy arm of the Vatican that carried out covert activities on its behalf. One of the book's villains, a terrifying albino Opus Dei numerary named Silas, specialized in "wet" work, like assassination, murder, and torture. Opus Dei attempted to persuade Sony pictures to expunge all references to itself in the motion picture adaptation of *The Da Vinci Code*. When Sony refused, it launched an

aggressive, multipronged public relations counteroffensive.
Authorized books were rushed to press, documentaries were
filmed, Web sites were launched, officials were made available for interviews, articles were pitched to magazines, and
fact sheets were distributed to the news media. Opus Dei
even dug up a real member named Silas,* a Nigerian-born
stockbroker who lives in Brooklyn, New York. "I'm not a
monk nor an albino," he told CNN. "I'm married with a wife
and three children." When the reporter asked him what he
thought about Opus Dei's sinister reputation, he replied,
"No murders in my background. All you have to find in my
background is a jolly fellow."

Order of the Solar Temple

The Order of the Solar Temple was founded in Geneva,
Switzerland, in 1984 by a French jeweler and reputed
swindler named Joseph di Mambro (1924–1994) and Luc
Jouret (1947–1994), a homeopathic doctor who was born in
the Belgian Congo. Both men died during the rash of mass
suicides and murders that occurred at various locations in
Canada, Switzerland, and France in 1994, 1995, and 1997, in
which some seventy-four cult members lost their lives.

Di Mambro, who had become involved with the **Rosicrucian** order AMORC (the Ancient and Mystical Order Rosae
Crucis) in the 1950s, had launched his own New Age group in
Geneva called the Golden Way Foundation; he was also
active in Julien Origas's (1920–1983) Renewed Order of the
Solar Temple. After Origas died, the two groups were amal-
gamated under Jouret's charismatic leadership as the International Chivalric Organization of the Solar Tradition. The
name was later shortened to the Solar Temple.

Origas was an ex-Nazi who might have stepped out of the
pages of *Foucault's Pendulum* (1989), Umberto Eco's thriller

---

*Full disclosure: Some years ago I was introduced to Silas Agbim and his wife, Ngozi, at a
social function that had nothing whatever to do with Opus Dei, conspiracies, or cults. I can
personally attest that they seemed like perfectly ordinary people.

about an all-encompassing conspiracy involving neo-Templars and modern-day alchemists. Origas had been influenced by Jacques Breyer (1922–1996), an occultist who claimed to be the reincarnation of Jacques de Molay (ca. 1244–1314), the last Grand Master of the **Knights Templar**. As early as 1952, Breyer had helped organize a group known as the Sovereign Order of the Solar Temple; in 1959 he published a book entitled *Arcanes solaires ou les secrets du temple solaire*, or "Arcane Solar Energies, or the Secrets of the Solar Temple." Breyer owed his belief that remnants of the Knights Templar had secretly survived into modern times (an idea which also plays a role in Dan Brown's mega-bestselling 2003 novel, *The Da Vinci Code*) to the esoteric writings of Bernard-Raymond Fabré-Palaprat (1773–1838), one of the founders of the Gnostic, neo-Catharite Johannite Church. Breyer, Origas, di Mambro, and Jouret were also influenced by the esoteric writings of Aleister Crowley (1875–1947), Madame Blavatsky (1831–1891), the Theosophists, and Alice Bailey (1880–1949).

Though the Solar Temple was never a mass movement (at its peak, it numbered between four hundred and six hundred members), its recruits were educated, wealthy, and extremely generous—by some accounts, they donated almost one hundred million dollars to the organization. Its beliefs remain somewhat obscure. Some of them hearkened back to the medieval Templars and their supposed hermetic antecedents; there was a survivalist element at the beginning too. A global environmental catastrophe was prophesied that would spare a corner of Quebec; shelters were constructed there for the faithful. The notion of Ascended Masters, enlightened beings who have broken free from the cycles of reincarnation but who remain in this plane to assist humans in their development, was adapted from Theosophy. From Alice Bailey's *Initiation: Human and Solar* (1922) came the idea that "the energy of thought, or mind force . . . reaches the solar system from a distant cosmic center via Sirius. Sirius acts as the transmitter, or the focalizing center, whence emanate those influences which produce self-consciousness in man." At some point, Jouret and di Mambro came to believe that they had the power to ascend to Sirius themselves, though not in their earthly containers.

The killings in Canada were clearly murders. A baby was stabbed through the heart with a wooden stake (members later explained that di Mambro believed the infant was the Antichrist). The infant's parents—who had recently left the cult—were brutally and repeatedly knifed. The scores of victims who were discovered at various sites in Switzerland over the next few weeks appeared to have gone to their deaths willingly. Their bodies were dressed in ceremonial vestments and laid out in patterns that suggested crosses and stars. Some of them wrote testimonials before they died, which made it clear that they did not believe they were going to their deaths at all. "From the planes where we will work from now on and by a just law of magnetism," read one of them, "we will be in the position of calling back the last Servants capable of hearing this last message." "With a clear mind," read another, "we leave this earth for a Dimension of Truth and Perfection." But forensic examinations also revealed signs of force; many of the victims had been drugged and shot execution-style. The chalets where the bodies were found had been rigged with incendiary devices. Fire clearly played a critical role in the "transformation" (the historical Templars had been burned at the stake).

In the months before the killings, the Solar Temple had been riven by internal dissent and was under attack from without—a crisis was clearly imminent. Jouret and several Canadian members had been arrested for possession of illegal handguns, and di Mambro's failing health had been worsened by his emotional stress. His daughter—the miraculously conceived Messiah, he claimed—was rebelling; his son had publicly denounced him as a charlatan. Angry ex-members were lining up to sue. Surprisingly, Jouret and di Mambro actually believed in their own teachings; they decided that the time had come to leave the earth for a better place. The Temple's truest believers took their own lives; fearful but faithful souls were assisted. Traitors and apostates were executed.

Jouret's and di Mambro's deaths left authorities with no one to prosecute. Then, in a development that one might think could happen only in an airport novel, the internationally renowned Swiss conductor and composer Michel Tabachnik, whose first wife had been one of the cult's victims, was identified by surviving members as di Mambro's partner and heir apparent, or possibly even his superior, a member of the secret council of elders that was reputed to wield ultimate control over the sect. It was Tabachnik, they said, who announced that the Temple's earthly mission had been completed, laying the groundwork for its grisly finale. Though the maestro insisted he'd severed all connections with the cult in 1992, he was arrested and tried in France for having "published and distributed doctrinal instructions intended to condition individuals . . . and to create a dynamic towards murder." He was acquitted twice, first in 2001 and then in 2006.

Palladism

A sinister devil-worshipping cult that purportedly developed within **Masonry**, directed by Albert Pike (1809–1891), the long-serving Sovereign Grand Commander of the Ancient and Accepted Scottish Rite, Southern Jurisdiction. Pike was the author of the magisterial, eight-hundred-plus-page *Morals and Dogma of the First Three Degrees of the Ancient and Accepted Scottish Rite of Freemasonry*, an epic compendium of Masonic mysteries, which included long disquisitions on **Kabbalah**, Gnosticism, Hermeticism, Zoroastrianism, Buddhism, Pythagoreanism, astrology, and Hinduism. It is only one of the many volumes Pike authored on Masonic and religious arcana, yet it is best known in anti-Masonic circles for a few notorious sentences:

LUCIFER, the *Light-bearer*! Strange and mysterious name to give to the Spirit of Darkness! Lucifer, the Son of the Morning! Is it *he* who bears the *Light*, and with its splendors intolerable blinds feeble, sensual, or selfish Souls? Doubt it not! For traditions are full of Divine Revelations and Inspirations: and Inspiration is not of one Age nor of one Creed. Plato and Philo, also, were inspired.

Pike was a racist and an unregenerate Confederate, no doubt, but he was no Satanist: the quest for light and still "more light" is at the very heart of Freemasonry. Pike was making the rhetorical point that the name Lucifer, which means "light-bearer" or "the morning star" in Latin, is hardly a fitting name for the Devil, who personifies darkness and ignorance rather than the blinding illumination of wisdom and truth. Elsewhere Pike wrote that the "true name of Satan, the Kabalists say, is that of Yahveh reversed; for Satan is not a black god, but the negation of God. The Devil is the personification of Atheism or Idolatry."

But then what is one to make of this seemingly blasphemous passage—as Gnostic as anything believed by the Albigensians—which is also attributed to Pike?

The Masonic Religion should be, by all of us initiates of the higher degrees, maintained in the Purity of the Luciferian doctrine . . . the true and pure philosophical religion is the belief in Lucifer, the equal of Adonay; but Lucifer, God of Light and God of Good, is struggling for humanity against Adonay, the God of Darkness and Evil.

Nothing at all, because Pike didn't write it. It was attributed to him in the writings of Léo Taxil, the pen name of Marie Joseph Gabriel Antoine Jogand-Pagès (1854–1907), an ex–free thinker and convert to Catholicism who purported to have discovered Palladism and exposed it in a series of inflammatory books. But then, in a bizarre press conference that he held in 1897, Taxil admitted that he had made the whole thing up. A lifelong prankster, almost a proto-Dadaist, he had created "the most colossal hoax of modern times," feeding the Catholic Church exactly what it wanted to hear about its enemies the Freemasons in order to set it up for humiliation later on—much as the contemporary guerilla performance artists the Yes Men concoct media hoaxes today to expose the hypocrisy of multinational corporations.*

Peoples Temple

Founded and led by James Warren Jones (1931–1978), the Peoples Temple came into being in Indianapolis, Indiana, around 1954 and ended in Jonestown, Guyana, on November 18, 1978, when Jones, his wife, Marceline, and more than nine hundred members of his church committed suicide.

By all accounts a dreamy, neglected child, Jones was equally drawn to Marxism, Christianity, and the civil rights movement as a young man. Though his church services featured faith healing and speaking in tongues, Jones was no fundamentalist. His pamphlet "The Letter Killeth" offers a catalog of "Errors," "Absurdities," "Atrocities," and "Indecencies" that can be found in the Bible; he preached a progressive gospel that he called "Apostolic Socialism":

I represent divine principle, total equality, a society where people own all things in common. Where there is no rich or poor. Where there are no races. Wherever there is people struggling for justice and righteousness, there I am. And there I am involved.

---

*For example, on December 3, 2004, the twentieth anniversary of the Bhopal disaster (the industrial accident that killed three thousand Indians at once and as many as seventeen thousand over time, and injured hundreds of thousands more) a Yes Man passing himself off as Dow Chemical spokesperson Jude Finisterra announced that his company was prepared to admit its culpability and make substantial amends. Its first step, he said, would be to liquidate its Union Carbide division and invest the entire $12 billion windfall in cleanup and victim compensation. Dow's stock plunged, forcing its management to send out a real spokesperson, who vehemently denied that they intended to do anything at all.

Known as the Community Unity Church for the first few years of its existence, Jones changed his church's name twice in 1955, first to Wings of Deliverance and then to the Peoples Temple Full Gospel Church. In 1959, after affiliating with the Christian Church (the Disciples of Christ), Jones changed its name again, to the Peoples Temple Christian Church Full Gospel. Jones's good works—he started a soup kitchen that distributed twenty-eight hundred meals a month; he worked to desegregate Indianapolis (a cause he carried over to his personal life as well—he and his wife Marceline adopted a Korean War orphan and an African American child)— earned him an appointment as director of the Indianapolis Human Rights Commission in 1961.

One often-overlooked early influence on Jones was the International Peace Mission Movement of the African American preacher who called himself Father Jealous Divine (1880–1965). Father Divine became notorious in the 1930s because of a series of scandals, prosecutions, and lawsuits. His church, which blended elements of New Thought Science of Mind with Booker T. Washington's entrepreneurship movement, offered up an inspiring vision of a prosperous, color-blind, economically self-sufficient, morally continent, debt-free society of small businessmen. Its economic conservatism notwithstanding, the International Peace Mission Movement allied itself with the Communist Party in the early 1930s. "Because your god would not feed the people, I came and am feeding them," Father Divine preached. "Because your god kept such as you segregated and discriminated, I came and am unifying all nations together."

Unfortunately, the International Peace Mission Movement also provided the template for many future American cults. Father Divine enjoyed a more-than-comfortable lifestyle at the expense of his less-than-wealthy disciples; in his overweening grandiosity, he came to believe that he was the living embodiment of God. From Woodmont, his estate in Gladwyne, Pennsylvania, off Philadelphia's Main Line, he issued prophecies, long after his movement began to fade from public consciousness:

> To the most remote parts of the earth, from WOODMONT I have sent forth the LAW . . . as a short wave station that no physical barrier can prohibit, MY LAW of VIRTUE is going forth from WOODMONT to heal the nations.

In 1957, Reverend Jim Jones heard the call. Accompanied by a busload of his church members, he made the pilgrimage.

"When Jimmy come back from seeing Father Divine," Gene Cordell, one of Jones's earliest disciples, recalled in an interview in the *San Francisco Chronicle*, "he was a changed man. Father Divine convinced him he was The Man—that he was God."

A decade and a half later, infuriated that Jones was poaching members from her Peace Mission churches and that he was claiming to be the embodied God, Father Divine's widow cut off relations with the Peoples Temple. "We have entertained Pastor Jones and the Peoples Temple," Mother Divine wrote in 1972. "We were entertaining angels of the 'other fellow' [the devil]! We no longer extend to them any hospitality whatsoever." Like the adage says, it takes one to know one.

In 1965, fearing an imminent nuclear apocalypse, Jones and about 150 of his followers moved to the safe haven of Ukiah, California. By the early 1970s, with his church membership climbing and a radio show and newspaper giving him national exposure, Jones bought property and started up congregations in Los Angeles and San Francisco. By delivering blocs of votes, turning out his followers at rallies, and carefully targeting donations, he purchased himself no small measure of political influence within the Bay Area's liberal political establishment. After George Moscone was elected mayor of San Francisco in 1975, he appointed Jones head of the city's housing commission.

But there were already harbingers of trouble. Ex-members of the Peoples Temple were complaining about physical, sexual, and financial abuses; concerned parents were trying to reclaim their children. In the summer of 1977 a devastating exposé in *New West* magazine detailed episodes of charlatanry (Jones had passed off chicken gizzards wrapped in napkins as "cancers" he'd removed from sick bodies), extortion (members had been pressured to deed their houses to the church; their signatures on blank sheets of paper were used to obtain powers of attorney; old people who had signed over their Social Security checks were languishing in church-owned nursing homes), and beatings. By the time the article appeared, tax investigations were also looming. Jones and about a thousand of his followers pulled up stakes and moved to a tract of land the church purchased in the jungles of Guyana, which they called Jonestown.

In May 1978, Deborah Layton, who had fled Jonestown just a few weeks earlier, issued a sworn affidavit in support of concerned relatives' complaints about Jones and the Peoples Temple. In it she detailed concentration camp–like conditions: Jones, she said, "had assumed a tyrannical hold over temple members." He was "deluded by a paranoid vision of the world. He would not sleep for days at a time and talked compulsively about the conspiracies against him." And she described ominous suicide rehearsals:

At least once a week, Rev. Jones would declare a "white night," or state of emergency. . . . During one "white night," we were informed that our situation had become hopeless and that the only course of action open to us was a mass suicide for the glory of socialism. We were told that we would be tortured by mercenaries if we were taken alive. Everyone, including the children, was told to line up. As we passed through the line, we were given a small glass of red liquid to drink. We were told that the liquid contained poison and that we would die within forty-five minutes. We all did as we were told. When the time came when we should have dropped dead, Rev. Jones explained that the poison was not real and that we had just been through a loyalty test. . . . Life at Jonestown was so miserable and the physical pain of exhaustion was so great that this event was not traumatic for me. I had become indifferent as to whether I lived or died.

Six months later, in November 1978, Congressman Leo Ryan—who had excoriated **Scientology**, the Divine Light Mission, **ISKCON**, and **Unification Church** from the floor of the House of Representatives—embarked on a fact-finding mission to Jonestown, accompanied by reporters and relatives determined to extract their loved ones. It wasn't the first time Ryan had gone into the field. After the Watts Riots, he'd had himself hired as a substitute teacher in the neighborhood; while investigating conditions in California's penal system he'd arranged to have himself arrested and incarcerated at Folsom Prison.*

Jones arranged a Potemkin village reception for the congressman. Preselected residents were made available for interviews, in which they waxed enthusiastic about their lives in Jonestown. But then other residents began to slip notes to members of the delegation, asking them for help. After a series of increasingly acrimonious confrontations with Jones and other Temple authorities, Ryan departed with a group of defectors. As they prepared to board their planes at Port Kaituma airstrip, they were ambushed by members of Jones's security team. Ryan, three journalists, and one of the defectors were killed; ten were wounded, including Ryan's legislative assistant Jackie Speier (who would be elected to the U.S. Congress in 2008).

*In addition to his critique, Ryan ventured a definition of a harmful cult, which is worth quoting at some length: "All of the groups that we are talking about have living leaders who are demonstrably wealthy. The beliefs of all these cults are absolutist and nontolerant of other systems of beliefs. Their systems of governance are totalitarian. A requirement of membership is to obey absolutely without questioning. . . . One of the most important of the common properties of such cults is the presence of a leader who, in one way or another, claims special powers or may even allow himself to be thought of as the Messiah."

A recovered audiotape captured Jones's voice during the Peoples Temple's last hours. Warning his followers that avenging paratroopers were en route to torture their children and seniors, he urged them to "be done with the agony of it":

> Be patient. Death is—I tell you, I don't care how many screams you hear. I don't care how many anguished cries. Death is a million times preferable to ten more days of this life. If you knew what was ahead of you—if you knew what was ahead of you, you'd be glad to be stepping over tonight. . . . Take our life from us. We laid it down. We got tired. We didn't commit suicide, we committed an act of revolutionary suicide protesting the conditions of an inhumane world.

Not long afterward, parents and nurses squirted a mixture of potassium cyanide and potassium chloride into the babies' and toddlers' mouths. Then the grown-ups and older children sipped purple Kool-Aid mixed with poison out of paper cups (this is where the phrase "drinking the Kool-Aid" comes from). Aerial views of the complex revealed the horrifying results. "The large central building was ringed by bright colors," wrote a *Time* magazine correspondent who flew in the next day:

> It looked like a parking lot filled with cars. When the plane dipped lower, the cars turned out to be bodies. Scores and scores of bodies—hundreds of bodies—wearing red dresses, blue T-shirts, green blouses, pink slacks, children's polka-dotted jumpers.

Jones had retained the famous radical lawyer and conspiracy theorist Mark Lane (whose 1966 bestseller, *Rush to Judgment*, was one of the first books to question the Warren Commission's account of the Kennedy assassination). Lane, who called Jonestown "the closest thing on earth like paradise I have ever seen," had been present during Ryan's visit (he and his cocounsel, the renowned civil liberties attorney Charles Garry, hid in the jungle while Jones and his followers killed themselves). In his book *The Strongest Poison* (1979), Lane portrays Jones much as Jones had characterized himself: as an innocent victim of persecution by racists, right-wingers, and dark forces within the government. Lane strongly intimated that agent provocateurs had pressed Jones into carrying out the mass suicide—an atrocity they could have easily prevented.

A new generation of conspiracy theorists takes things a step further, arguing that Jones was a CIA operative himself and that Jonestown was a laboratory for mind control experiments or, even worse, a pilot concentration camp where techniques for conducting genocides against the darker races were perfected. Ryan was manipulated into walking into a death trap because of his hostility to the CIA (the Hughes-Ryan Act prohibited the CIA and the Defense Department from undertaking covert actions without a presidential "finding" certifying their importance to national security; the findings must then be submitted to the appropriate legislative oversight committees). Jones's CIA handlers allowed the minister to kill himself (or they killed him themselves) because he was a loose cannon who had outlived his usefulness. Some have it that Jones escaped alive and the body passed off as his was a ringer's. One theorist suggests that San Francisco city supervisor Harvey Milk and Mayor George Moscone were assassinated less than two weeks later (on November 27, 1978) because they were about to reveal the connections between San Francisco's former housing commissioner and the CIA (Dan White, their killer, was a Manchurian candidate).

Dick Gregory would offer up the gruesome theory that the CIA had murdered the people of Jonestown so they could use their repatriated corpses as containers for the heroin that they were smuggling into the United States (Mark Lane had been Gregory's running mate when he ran for president in

1968; in 1977 they'd collaborated on *Code Name Zorro*, a conspiratorial account of the Martin Luther King assassination, which was reprinted in 1993 as *Murder in Memphis*). One theorist bravely extends the frontiers of the lunatic fringe by arguing that Jones was a crypto Jew who'd organized Jonestown on the principles of a kibbutz. He orchestrated the mass suicide to divert attention from an imminent secret U.S. commando operation against a Soviet missile base deep in the jungles of Guyana.

The whole story may never be known, but it is likely that the most salient fact about Jim Jones has nothing to do with his politics, his religion, or his 1973 arrest for soliciting a male undercover police officer for sex—a story that surprisingly few conspiracy theorists make much of. Jones's emotionally remote, chronically unemployed, alcoholic father spent five years in a psychiatric hospital in the 1920s. His son, like so many other charismatic but narcissistic, grandiose, and paranoid cult leaders, almost certainly suffered from an inherited schizophrenic disorder.

The Process Church of the Final Judgment

A short-lived cult that began in the 1960s as a **Scientology**-derived psychotherapy movement called Compulsions Analysis, passed through a flamboyant satanic phase (possibly influencing Charles Manson), and continues today, albeit in a completely unrecognizable form, as the well-known Best Friends Animal Society, which operates America's largest sanctuary for abandoned pets in Angel Canyon, Utah.

Process was founded by a former British architecture student and cavalry officer who would change his name to Robert De Grimston (his given name was the much more prosaic Robert Sylvester Moore) and Mary Anne MacLean, who became his second wife. MacLean's background was less conventional than her husband's. Abandoned by both parents, she grew up in poverty in Glasgow and immigrated to the United States, where she was briefly engaged to the boxer Sugar Ray Robinson. Back in London, she ran a call girl ring for a while. She met De Grimston at the Institute of Scientology in 1963 and soon afterward they opened up their own shop. The Compulsions Analysis that they practiced was an outgrowth of Alfred Adler's (1870–1937) theory that people were driven by "secret goals" or complexes. The De Grimstons uncovered these compulsions in their patients through a combination of talking therapy and the use of Scientology's E-meters. By 1966, their psychoanalytic practice had transmogrified into a religion and their patients had become their disciples (the well-known author and TV personality Alistair Cooke's daughter and stepdaughter among them). When a follower received a substantial inheritance and donated it to Process, they purchased a mansion in Mayfair and began to publish an eponymous magazine. Mick Jagger appeared on one of *Process*'s early covers; Marianne Faithfull posed for an inside spread. De Grimston published a chapbook whose first and last lines gave the group its catchphrase: *As it is, so be it.* All in all, it was a groovy, Austin Powers–like scene, but with a sinister undertone. Tabloids dubbed the De Grimstons "the Mindbenders of Mayfair."

In the summer of 1967, the De Grimstons, their German shepherd dogs (Mary Anne was already an animal lover and an impassioned antivivisectionist), and a group of Processeans decamped first to Nassau in the Bahamas and then to the Yucatán, where they occupied an abandoned salt refinery and lived a paradisiacal, back-to-nature existence—until Hurricane Inez devastated the region, killing thousands. That was when De Grimston's thinking began to take on an apocalyptic tinge.

The power of Jehovah, Lucifer, and Satan is the dominant power. Conflicted though they may be for the purpose of the Game, upon one matter They are in total agreement . . . and that matter is the fact of the End. The End of the world as we know it; the end of humankind as we know it; the end of

human values as we know them; the end of human endeavors;
human creations; human ambitions. . . . All these shall be
destroyed, to make way for a New Age and a new way of life.

The church's eschatology was reflected in a new, punning
interpretation of its name, which had originally referred to
the auditing process of Scientology. Now it was said to mean
"pro-cessation," or being in favor of the Apocalypse. Aspects
of pleasure-loving Lucifer, punitive, judgmental Jehovah,
and evil Satan can be found in every human being, Process
preached, though only one of them tends to dominate in
most individuals. When Judgment Day comes, only those
who have accepted and reconciled those conflicting tenden-
cies in themselves will be saved.

The De Grimstons largely withdrew from the rank and file
of their movement as Processean churches, whose Sabbath
assemblies featured sitar music and invocations of Christ,
Lucifer, Satan, and Jehovah, were established in Boston,
New Orleans, San Francisco, and Los Angeles. Ed Sanders
tracked the "black-caped, black-garbed, death-worshipping"
Processeans' contacts with Charles Manson and Sirhan
Sirhan in Los Angeles in the first edition of his bestselling
book *The Family*. (After the church filed suit, his publisher
recalled the book, apologized, and then rereleased it with all
references to Process removed. The deleted material can easily be found on the Internet today.) A decade and a half later,
in *The Ultimate Evil* (1987) journalist Maury Terry argued
that the Processeans also influenced the serial killer David
Berkowitz, who had terrorized New York City in the summer
of 1977 as the Son of Sam.

By the mid-1970s, the Omega, as the De Grimstons called
themselves, had gotten a divorce. With Mary Anne at the
reins, the church changed its name to the Foundation Faith
of the Millennium. Mary Anne and her new husband,
Gabriel DePeyer, founded the animal shelter that would
become Best Friends Animal Society in the early 1980s. She

died in 2005; Robert De Grimston, who had founded and dissolved a few churches of his own in the late seventies, is rumored to have become a corporate consultant in New York City, but he has not been heard from in decades.

Raëlians

"The world's only atheistic religion," the Raëlian movement was founded in 1974 by Claude Vorilhon, who was at the time a former race car driver, a would-be singer-songwriter, an automotive journalist, and the editor of the magazine *Auto Pop*. In 1973, when he had been twenty-seven years old, Vorilhon had been strolling in the crater of an extinct volcano in Auvergne, France, when a four-foot-tall, green-skinned entity with long dark hair emerged from a silver UFO and entrusted him with a message: that human beings were created in alien laboratories some twenty-five thousand years ago and planted on earth. It would be the first of many meetings, in the course of which Vorilhon learned the story of the Elohim (our alien creators, whose name was mistakenly applied to God by the authors of the Bible) and of humanity's ultimate destiny, which is to achieve an "intergalactic level of civilization." He was also assigned a specific set of tasks:

> You, Claude Vorilhon, you will spread the truth under your present name, which you will replace progressively with RAEL, which means literally "light of God" and if we translate it more accurately, "light of the Elohim" or "Ambassador of the Elohim," because you will be our ambassador on Earth and we will come only officially to your Embassy.

The "embassy" they spoke of was no figure of speech; one of the Raëlians' goals is to build a flying saucer landing pad in Israel. (There is a certain Zionist component to Raëlism, in that the ancient Israelites are said to have been hybrids of humans and Elohim; their descendants—Vorilhon among them, since his unknown father is believed to have been a Jewish war refugee—are thus superior to gentiles, whose ancestors were entirely laboratory grown.)

The Raëlians believe that democracy should be replaced with a "Geniocracy," in which only those whose intellectual capacity is 50 percent above average are eligible to hold public office. They also believe in the abolition of private property and the establishment of world government. Nuclear weapons (but not nuclear energy) should be abandoned and population control strictly enforced (the Raëlians have been known to hand out condoms). Also very important to the Raëlians is physical pleasure, which perhaps more than anything else accounts for the movement's popularity (the Raëlians claim up to eighty thousand members in ninety countries).

Raël writes about a memorable banquet that he attended on the home planet of the Elohim (other guests included Jesus, Elijah, Muhammad, Buddha, and many other religious luminaries), where he was told that "all things that bring pleasure are positive, as long as that pleasure is not harmful to anyone in any way. This is why all sensual pleasures are positive." Later that same night, in a sybaritic scenario that could have come out of a soft-porn sci-fi movie like *Barbarella* or *Flesh Gordon*, he was bathed and pleasured by six cloned geishas. Their bed was shaped like a giant seashell; each of his eager partners, he said, was a perfect exemplar of one of the ethnic categories of feminine pulchritude—Nordic, Mediterranean, African, Asian, etc. Writing in *Salon* in 2000, Taras Grescoe noted that Raël's success "seems to derive from providing a structured environment for decadent behavior: He offers a no-guilt playground for hedonism and sexual experimentation." While attending a Raëlian convention in Montreal, Canada (where the Raëlians had their world headquarters at the time—they have since announced plans to decamp to Las Vegas, Nevada), Grescoe observed that a seemingly disproportionate number of them were exotic dancers and bodybuilders.

But most importantly (and most notoriously in recent years), the cornerstone of the Raëlians' scientific religion is the technology of human cloning, which they believe holds the key to eternal life. Clonaid is a corporation headed by a Raëlian bishop named Dr. Brigitte Boisselier (she holds PhDs in physical and analytical chemistry from the University of Dijon in France and the University of Houston in the United States) which purports to have produced as many as thirteen human clones—claims that have been greeted with universal skepticism by the scientific community. Clonaid has thus far refused to make genetic samples of the infants available for independent verification for fear, it claims, that the babies' anonymity will be compromised and their parents will lose custody of them. Those fears are not unfounded. A lawyer named Bernie Siegel has already brought suit in a Florida court to have himself named as the first Clonaid baby's ad litem guardian.

The Raëlians' persecutor is not a religious fundamentalist or an obscurantist—quite the opposite. The Raëlians, Siegel wrote in a publication of the Genetics Policy Institute (a lobby that supports stem cell research, which he founded), are "cartoon mad-scientists." He embarked on his court challenge, he said, to prove that "their claim was a wild fantasy foisted on the world by publicity seekers," thus eliminating a potential stalking horse for the pro-life movement.

Roch "Moses" Thériault

Currently serving a life sentence for murder, Roch Thériault was born in rural Quebec to Catholic parents in 1947. When he was in his early twenties he left his wife and children and took up with a girlfriend in Quebec City. Around the same time, he became involved with the Seventh-Day Adventists. He soon attracted a core of devoted, mostly female followers, with whom he moved to the rural village of Sainte-Marie, in the Beauce region south of Quebec City. Living communally, they opened up an alternative medical practice called the Health Living Clinic.

Disturbed by Thériault's burgeoning cult of personality and concerned about his relations with his female followers, the Adventists disfellowshipped him (eventually he would form ties with a fundamentalist Mormon group in Utah). When a cancer patient they were treating with grape juice and organic foods died, local authorities began to pay them unwelcome attention. They moved deeper into the wilderness and built a large cabin.

Thériault and a number of his followers served short prison sentences after a follower's baby died from complications from a botched circumcision (and possibly a beating); on Thériault's orders, a member of the group was castrated. When they reconvened upon their release, the physical and psychological abuse became even worse. Thériault asserted conjugal rights with all of his female followers. As more and more of them bore his children, he abused their half siblings (the children of other fathers), treating them as "animals" and "slaves" and forcing some of them to have sex with him.

By this time Thériault claimed to be the reincarnation of Moses. Demanding absolute obedience, he committed brutal acts of torture to enforce his authority. As with many abused families, the worse Thériault treated them, the more cravenly dependent on him they became. When one of his wives became seriously ill, Thériault's attempted surgery killed her. Then he attempted to resurrect her by digging up her body, drilling a hole in her skull, and masturbating into it. The straw that broke the camel's back was when he chopped off another wife's arm with a meat cleaver. When the hospital reported her injuries to the police, Thériault and three of his followers were arrested. Thériault would plead guilty to second-degree murder and was sentenced to life in prison in 1993.

Satanism
One of the ironies implicit in any discussion of Satanism is the fact that the vast majority of its supposed adherents

didn't even acknowledge the existence of the Prince of Darkness, never mind worship him. The *Malleus Maleficarum*, the Inquisition's handbook for witch-hunters, was written by Heinrich Kramer and James Sprenger, two Dominican monks, in 1486. As testimony to the superstitious obsessions that characterized medieval Roman Catholicism—its abiding fear of the vestigial animism, nature worship, and practical sorcery that could still be found in Europe's peasant cultures; its terror of female sexuality; its abhorrence of alternative spiritualities and nontraditional conceptions of the divine—it is quite trustworthy. But most of the thousands of herbalists, spell casters, midwives, pagans, shamans, oddballs, epileptics, victims of mental illness, and sexually threatening women who were tortured and killed on its authority wouldn't have recognized themselves in its pages. Satan is a Christian invention. Explicitly Satanic cultists who celebrate Black Masses and desecrate the host, say the Lord's Prayer backward, and invite the devil to join them in their orgies learn their rites from the writings of their Christian persecutors. Wicca was largely invented in the 1950s. The vast majority of the alleged witches and sorcerers that the Church put to death for worshipping Satan did nothing of the sort.

Evangelical Protestants rather than Roman Catholics are the chief inquisitors of suspected Satanists and witches today. Some of the satanic conspiracies they purport to have uncovered are the infiltration of schools and day care centers in order to carry out horrific acts of sexual abuse on innocent children, the mutilation of livestock to use as offerings in their profane rites, and the imposition of One-World government through cutout organizations like the **Bilderberg Group**.

There are religious Christians who aren't the least bit paranoid or delusional or given to extreme political enthusiasms but who nonetheless believe that Satan makes use of pop music, books, TV shows, and movies not only to draw children away from the Christian faith, but to convert them to his own rival religion. Thus an article in the February

2002 edition of *Good News*, a Church of God publication,
warns parents about the dangers of the Harry Potter books.
While it generally acknowledges that they are entertaining,
encourage children to read, and even portray their heroes
(who aren't real witches but only make-believe fantasy characters) as courageously resisting the powers of evil, Harry
and his friends, the article cautions, nonetheless cast spells—
a practice that the Bible explicitly forbids. And they pose a
more insidious danger as well:

> Perhaps some innocent Harry Potter devotees will succumb
> to the notion that witchcraft is noble and later seek to
> become Wiccans or join covens. . . . Or consider children who,
> fed on a steady diet of supernatural fantasy, begin to believe
> that they need to find their own "power within"—and begin
> unwittingly communing with demons.

In the days leading up to the presidential election in
November 2008, a posting made the rounds of the Internet
that noted that Barack Obama (already regarded by some as
the Antichrist) was an admirer of the legendary community
organizer Saul Alinsky (1909–1972). In an instance of six
degrees of separation (actually fewer than that), Alinsky
had also been the topic of Hillary Clinton's senior honors
thesis at Wellesley College. Alinsky was hardly a bomb
thrower like the Weather Underground's Bill Ayers (who was
also a much-talked-about figure in the 2008 campaign); in his
lifetime his books were praised by such respectable figures as
Jacques Maritain (1882–1973) and Whittaker Chambers
(1901–1961). But one of them, *Rules for Radicals* (1971),
bore the following dedication:

> Lest we forget at least an over-the-shoulder acknowledgment
> of the very first radical: from all our legends, mythology, and
> history . . . the first radical known to man who rebelled

against the establishment and did it so effectively that he at least won his own kingdom—Lucifer.

Ipso facto, the Internet rumor concluded, Obama and Clinton were not only dangerous radicals but partisans of the devil. Alinsky would have been dumbfounded. He thought he was echoing the sentiments of the great English poet William Blake (1757–1827), whose *Marriage of Heaven and Hell* declared, "The reason Milton wrote in fetters when he wrote of Angels & God, and at liberty when of Devils & Hell, is because he was a true Poet and of the Devils party without knowing it." But Alinsky's (and Clinton's and Obama's) inquisitors believe in the literal existence of the goat-horned, spike-tailed, pitchfork-wielding Father of All Lies, the ruler of Hell, a terrifying supernatural figure: something that is utterly foreign to the belief systems of the vast majority of people they accuse of being his cohorts.

Even some who loudly and gaudily proclaim themselves to be Satanists don't believe he is real. The shock rocker Marilyn Manson* (his given name is Brian Warner) is reputed to be a member of the Church of Satan, founded in Los Angeles in 1966 by Anton Szandor LaVey (1930–1997). But Marilyn Manson doesn't believe in Satan. "Satan is a word that you can use to describe your animalistic side," Manson told an interviewer. "I guess Satan exists in that sense—that part of everyone's personality. I don't believe in it as a 'being.'" Neither did Anton LaVey.

Like his disciple Marilyn Manson, Anton LaVey was first and foremost a provocateur. His parents (who were not gypsies, as he later claimed) named him Howard Stanton Levey. He was a calliope player and carnival mentalist in his early

---

*Charles Manson, whom Marilyn Manson's stage name honors, himself participated in orgies with avowed Satanists: Family member Susan Atkins, who stabbed Sharon Tate to death, had been a member of the Church of Satan; Bobby Beausoleil, the Family member who killed Gary Hinman, was in the cast of Kenneth Anger's movie *Lucifer Rising*.

days, but it's hard to say anything else about him with any degree of certainty. An unabashed fabulist, he ghostwrote his own biographies and filled them with colorful stories that have subsequently been satisfactorily debunked. For example, he didn't play the role of Satan in the movie *Rosemary's Baby*; he didn't have love affairs with Jayne Mansfield and Marilyn Monroe, and he never worked as a lion tamer.

LaVey borrowed most of his ideas from better-known writers, such as the occultists John Dee and Aleister Crowley and the philosophers Friedrich Nietzsche (1844–1900) and Ayn Rand (1905–1982). He also plagiarized much of his bestselling book *The Satanic Bible* (1969) from Ragnar Redbeard, the pseudonymous author of the social Darwinist screed *Might Is Right* (1896). Though LaVey mined occult texts for rituals and created and recorded Black Masses, his church was based on the principled rejection of supernaturalism and the embrace of sheer will to power; mostly, it was about performance, self-promotion, and especially self-indulgence. The nine tenets of The Church of Satan, as LaVey laid them out, were:

1. Indulgence, instead of abstinence;
2. Vital existence, instead of spiritual pipe dreams;
3. Undefiled wisdom, instead of hypocritical self-deceit;
4. Kindness to those who deserve it, instead of love wasted on ingrates;
5. Vengeance, instead of turning the other cheek;
6. Responsibility to the responsible, instead of concern for psychic vampires;
7. Man as just another animal . . . who because of his divine spiritual and intellectual development, has become the most vicious animal of all;
8. Satan represents all of the so-called sins, as they lead to physical, mental, or emotional gratification;
9. Satan is the best friend the Church has ever had, as he has kept it in business all these years.

Scientology

Scientology came into the world in 1950 as *Dianetics*, a best-selling self-help book by L. Ron Hubbard (1911–1986), who at the time was a marginally successful writer of science fiction and Westerns. Interestingly, *Dianetics* was published in the same season as *Worlds in Collision* by Immanuel Velikovsky (1895–1979), a much-touted book which purported to explain some of the miraculous incidents recounted in the Old Testament—specifically the plagues of Egypt, the parting of the Red Sea, and Joshua's ability to stop the sun in its tracks, as recounted in Joshua 10:12 and 13—as actual, historical events with a natural cause: a comet that suddenly erupted out of Jupiter and went careening through the solar system, brushing past earth several times before settling into a stable orbit of its own as the planet Venus. Velikovsky was trained as a psychiatrist and had scant knowledge of or interest in astronomy. Though his books sold by the truckload, his theories are universally derided by the scientific establishment. L. Ron Hubbard, though he later falsely claimed to be a nuclear physicist, never trained as a psychiatrist. Even so, he claimed, with characteristic modesty, that his discovery of the principles of Dianetics marked "a milestone for man comparable to his discovery of fire and superior to his invention of the wheel and arch." Hubbard coined the word "Dianetics" by combining the Greek *dia*, or "through," with *nous*, or "soul"; it means, he said, "what the soul is doing to the body through the mind."

Dianetics operates on the theory that everything that ever happens to us—from the moment of conception on—leaves "engrams," or memory traces that are literally hardwired into our brains. When these engrams are stimulated, our "reactive mind" hijacks our "analytic mind," short-circuiting our mental and emotional functioning. Dianetics offers a cure through a process called "dianetic reverie," in which the patient reveals his engrams to a trained "auditor," who then erases them. When the process is complete, the patient is "clear."

Scientology didn't officially become a religion until 1953, when Hubbard elaborated his theory of "thetans," or immortal souls, which carry their engrams from one incarnation to another. He also devised a creation story that featured an evil galactic warlord and tax collector named Xenu, a character who might have stepped out of one of Hubbard's space operas. Scientology's religious status brought it certain tax benefits while exempting it from the sort of scrutiny that the FDA applies to medical products.

But to argue about whether Scientology is a mental health regimen or a religion is to miss the point. It's a *business*. By the end of 1950, when *Dianetics* had sold more than half a million copies, *Look* magazine noted that Hubbard was charging $500 for the one-month course that auditors were required to take before they received his certification (that's more than $4,000 in today's dollars, according to the consumer price index—chicken feed compared to the cost of a medical degree, but serious money nonetheless). It cost $200 to attend a series of fifteen lectures ($1,500-plus today), and $25 an hour ($200-plus) to be audited. Since auditing took approximately 220 hours, the cost of a cure was $5,500 (more than $50,000 in today's dollars). Back then, the worst that anyone had to say about Scientology was that it was pseudoscientific snake oil; no one was yet calling it a cult. Actually that's not quite true—"cult" is precisely the word that *Consumer Reports* used when it wrote about Dianetics in 1950, decrying the even higher costs and no-less-questionable methods of mainstream psychiatry:

> It is little wonder that irrational cults have flourished. The popularity and commercial success of some of these cults are eloquent testimony to the enormous need of the people for help for chronic anxiety states and mental sicknesses and the failure of society to meet these needs.

Scientology was a cash cow, and it was also a cult of personality—an institutional extension of the greed and narcissism of the man who told the first of his three wives in 1938 that "I have high hopes of smashing my name into history so violently that it will take a legendary form." Its tentacular organization, with its nested shell companies and interlocking directorates, was designed to protect Scientology's (and L. Ron Hubbard's) assets from tax collectors; it was also a totalitarian apparatus that allowed its creator to assume Godlike powers over his followers and, not incidentally, extract tens of millions of dollars from them.

According to a six-part investigative piece by Joel Sappell and Robert W. Welkos that ran in the *Los Angeles Times* in 1990, Scientology's governing financial policy, in Hubbard's own words, was "MAKE MONEY, MAKE MORE MONEY, MAKE OTHERS PRODUCE SO AS TO MAKE MONEY." Once a "body was in the shop," to borrow one of the movement's colorful names for its patients/students/followers, the goal was to keep them perpetually hungry for more. "One can keep doing this to a person—shuttle them along using mystery," Hubbard declared.

Hubbard confabulated obsessively over his past, whether he was embellishing his checkered naval career or concocting false documentation for his oft-told story about Blackfeet Indians initiating him as a blood brother when he was a child. Here he is in 1967, sounding uncommonly like Lyndon LaRouche at his bombastic worst: "Our enemies on this planet are less than twelve men. They are members of the Bank of England and other higher financial circles. They own and control newspaper chains and they are oddly enough directors in all the mental health groups in the world which have sprung up." Not only was Hubbard grandiose and paranoid; he was ruthless and vindictive. Heretics within his church were reeducated with shunning and humiliating manual labor. Apostates, Hubbard said, may "be deprived of property or injured by any means by any Scientologist. . . .

[They] may be tricked, sued or lied to or destroyed." In the last years of Hubbard's life, his wife and ten top Scientology officials were jailed for bugging and burglarizing government offices. Hubbard himself became a fugitive, hiding from federal authorities under assumed names.

Since Hubbard's death in 1986, the organization has been overseen by David Miscavige, a second-generation Scientologist who became Hubbard's closest associate when he was still a teenager. Though Scientology claims a worldwide membership of between five and ten million—including such high-wattage celebrities as the movie stars John Travolta and Tom Cruise*—critics believe it is probably closer to one hundred thousand.

The Unarius Society (see **Area 51** in Conspiracies)

Unification Church
Religious movement founded in Seoul, South Korea, in 1954 by the Reverend Sun Myung Moon as the Holy Spirit(ual) Association for the Unification of World Christianity. The basic teachings of the church are summarized in the *Divine Principle* (which Moon introduced in book form in 1946). In a nutshell, it teaches that the fall of man occurred because of the Archangel Lucifer's jealousy. Lucifer seduced Eve, who seduced Adam in turn.

Sex—not implicitly wicked in itself, but a dangerous and destructive force when unregulated—was the conduit through which evil came into the world.

> By engaging in a sexual relationship prematurely, Adam and
> Eve let selfish love, centered on their physical bodies, take
> the place of selfless love, centered on their spirits and God's
> Word. Thus, they fell. As a result, Adam and Eve could not

*Since 1955, Scientology's Celebrity Centre International has provided special services to "artists, politicians, leaders of industry, sports figures and anyone with the power and vision to create a better world."

give birth to and raise good, sinless children. Instead they gave birth to children who inherited from them the selfish nature they acquired through their relationship with the angel, Lucifer.

Marriage is a key method of sexual regulation. Thus the Unification Church's signature mass weddings—twenty thousand couples exchanged vows in Seoul Stadium on February 13, 2000, for example.

Jesus (who was not divine) tried but failed to redeem mankind. "The way of salvation is a path of self-denial and self-sacrifice," Moon wrote. Only when mankind has sufficiently denied its selfish, satanic nature, will the Messiah come "to end Satan's dominion, to liberate us from false, selfish love and to establish God's kingdom." And who is this Messiah? A Unification Church document entitled "A Cloud of Witnesses" (which can be found on the church's official Web site) provides the answer. At precisely twelve noon on Christmas Day of the year 2001, a seminar was convened in heaven. Attendees included Jesus, Confucius, Muhammad, and Buddha, as well as a host of lesser religious luminaries, such as Karl Barth, Martin Luther, Saint Peter, Saint Augustine, Jonathan Edwards, and John Calvin. Many holy men from the Islamic, Hindu, Buddhist, and Confucian faiths, whose names would be less familiar to Americans, also attended—such as Abu Bakr, the first Caliph; Al-Ashari, founder of Sunnism; Buddha's cousin the Venerable Ananda; and Gautama Maharishi, an originator of the practice of yoga. Marx, Lenin, Stalin, and Deng Xiaoping were also there, as was God, the Creator of the Universe. All of them signed a resolution affirming, among other things, that "Reverend Sun Myung Moon is the Savior, Messiah, Second Coming and True Parent of all humanity."

Moon, who served time in prison for tax evasion in the 1980s, was once widely feared as a sinister cult leader who used mind control methods on his millions of young recruits.

By most accounts the membership of the Unification Church (its official name is now Family Federation for World Peace and Unification) currently numbers in the low hundreds of thousands worldwide, with three to six thousand in the United States. Nonetheless, the organization remains formidable. Moon has invested billions of dollars in a host of businesses (everything from munitions to seafood, real estate to motels), and has generously subsidized conservative causes, to which he also supports through the editorial page of his newspaper, *The Washington Times*. In 2004, he was honored at a gala reception in Washington, D.C. "Rep. Danny K. Davis (D-Ill.) wore white gloves and carried a pillow holding an ornate crown that was placed on Moon's head," wrote the *Washington Post*.

> The Korean-born businessman and religious leader then delivered a long speech saying he was "sent to Earth . . . to save the world's six billion people. . . . Emperors, kings and presidents . . . have declared to all Heaven and Earth that Reverend Sun Myung Moon is none other than humanity's Savior, Messiah, Returning Lord and True Parent."

According to John Gorenfeld, who reported the story for *Salon*, "Members of Congress assisting at the event included Sen. Mark Dayton, Minnesota Democrat, Reps. Roscoe G. Bartlett of Maryland, Christopher B. Cannon of Utah and Curt Weldon of Pennsylvania, all Republicans, and Democratic Reps. Danny K. Davis of Illinois, Harold E. Ford Jr. of Tennessee and Sanford D. Bishop Jr. of Georgia."

In April 2008, the eighty-eight-year-old Moon named his twenty-nine-year-old son Hyung Jin Moon his successor as president of the church.

CONSPIRACIES

The Conspiratorial Frame of Mind

• A career criminal bumps into an old cellmate in a bar, who introduces him to two of his friends. In the course of a long night of drinking, the four felons conceive a plan to rob the armored car that collects the cash from the grocery store where one of them stocks shelves.

• Nine of New England's biggest cranberry growers surreptitiously convene in a suite at a Days Inn outside of Pawtucket, Rhode Island, where they agree to fix the price for this year's bumper crop at last year's drought-inflated level.

• The CEOs of Amoco, Exxon, Dutch Shell, BP, and Chevron teleconference on a scrambled line after they learn that an obscure inventor is on the brink of bringing a cheap, easily manufactured device to market that will enable any automobile to run on tap water. They resolve to deal with the matter as expeditiously as possible—by hiring a contract killer.

Each of these invented scenarios is instantly recognizable as a criminal conspiracy. When a police officer or a prosecutor talks about a conspiracy, he or she is referring to a secret scheme, planned by more than one person, to accomplish a specific illegal end—to commit larceny, to fix prices, to murder a potential competitor. The planning itself is a serious crime, even if the plot fails—indeed, even if it never gets off the ground.

There are political conspiracies too, and history is replete with them. On the Ides of March in 44 BCE, Marcus Junius Brutus, Gaius Cassius Longinus, Publius Servilius Casca, and many other Roman senators took turns stabbing Julius Caesar to death. In 63 BCE, Cicero exposed Lucius Sergius Catilina's plot to overthrow the Roman government. The Gunpowder Plot, a foiled attempt to blow up the English houses of parliament while James I was presiding over the commencement of its 1605 session—what might have been the most devastating act of terrorism in history—was orchestrated by a cabal of Catholics; the plotters who killed Archduke Franz Ferdinand in 1914 were affiliated with a Serbian secret society called the Black Hand. Csar Alexander II was killed by bomb throwers belonging to a Nihilistic revolutionary group called Narodnaya Volya (People's Will) in 1881; John Brown's 1859 raid on Harpers Ferry was secretly sponsored by six prominent Northern abolitionists; the coordinated attacks on the World Trade Center and the Pentagon on September 11, 2001, were planned and executed by members of the Islamist terrorist syndicate **Al Qaeda**. Even Hillary Clinton's hyperbolic complaint in 1998 that her husband was the victim of a "vast right-wing conspiracy" was not entirely unfounded. Though the Clintons were the authors of most of their troubles, some of their persecutors did indeed "pop up in other settings," as Hillary claimed—and much of their funding came from the same sources.

Most of the conspiracies covered in this book are different. For one thing, they have a much wider scope. They may involve thousands or even millions of plotters (**Freemasons**, international Communists, **Jesuits**, the **Illuminati**, wealthy financiers, the Jews) working over the course of generations, and their goals may be as vague and as all-encompassing—as satanic, let us say—as "the destruction of freedom" or "world domination." The plots themselves run the gamut from planting a Manchurian candidate in the White House to aiding and abetting alien space invaders. As bizarre and fantastical as these schemes may sound, the schemers seem even stranger still. For one thing, they often behave irrationally. For instance, as a number of writers on the **Kennedy assassination** have claimed, they might kill dozens of witnesses, years after the event, lest they tell a new set of investigators what they'd already told the old—all the while allowing those same new investigators to go about their business of lecturing, writing books, and making movies unmolested. Some of their schemes may seem oddly redundant. For example, researchers belonging to the so-called **9/11 Truth** community claim that the World Trade Center complex was brought down by explosives planted inside the buildings—that those plane crashes (if they even occurred) were merely decoys. And these other kinds of conspirators are less secretive than their criminal counterparts—in fact they compulsively call attention to their activities, scattering a plethora of symbolic and numerological clues in their wake that are easily decipherable by anyone possessing sufficient patience, imagination, and a high-speed modem.

In cases like these, the word "conspiracy" is more of a metaphysical than a legal concept. Forensic evidence or even a logically consistent chain of reasoning isn't required to compel belief as it would be in a courtroom, just a specific view of the world and a congenial frame of mind. When used in conjunction with "theory," the word "conspiracy" is practically synonymous with "determinism," and a malign determinism at that: it is the paranoid certainty that nothing happens by accident, that somebody bad is pulling all the strings. Once such a belief is planted in a certain type of mind, it's virtually impossible to uproot it. As Carl Sagan wrote, "You can't convince a believer of anything; for their belief is not based on evidence; it's based on a deep-seated need to believe."

Those who believe that the Jews are responsible for most of the world's ills, or that those guys with funny red fezzes on their heads, driving tiny cars in local parades (members of the Ancient Arabic Order, Nobles of the Mystic Shrine, or Shriners, a rite of Freemasonry), are really Satan's authorized representatives, or that multiple generations of the Bush family have fostered the nefarious schemes of socialist, drug-dealing billionaires, believe what they believe about the world because of what's already inside of their heads—not because of any truths that are objectively and verifiably "out there" (to borrow a phrase from television's hyperconspiratorial *The X-Files*). There are individuals and organizations (real and imagined) whose very being irritates the gray matter of the conspiratorially inclined. Take David Rockefeller. For those who blame Godless internationalism, paper money, or some other such monism for all the ills of the world, his family name alone, never mind his long-standing connections to such think tanks and public policy conferences as the **Council on Foreign Relations**, the **Bilderberg Group**, and the **Trilateral Commission**, suffices to set their mental gears spinning into overdrive. Semimythical associations like the **Knights Templar**, the Freemasons, and the Bavarian Illuminati continue to vex, fascinate, outrage, and otherwise obsess and dismay conspiracy theorists.

The Knights Templar was disbanded in the fourteenth century, but it remains a perennial subject of speculation. A number of recent popular novels—such as *The Da Vinci Code* (2003), which, according to its author, was based entirely on documented facts—depict the Templars as surviving into the present. Hundreds of years ago, when Freemasonry counted George Washington (1732–1799), Mozart (1756–1791), Voltaire (1694–1778), and Benjamin Franklin (1706–1790) among its members, its claims of ancient provenance and its esoteric scriptures might have seemed more significant than they do today, now that its membership is rapidly dwindling and the celebrities that it claims are so few and of such a decidedly dimmer wattage.* Yet to conspiracists of a certain stripe, Freemasonry presents as clear and present a danger today as it did in 1828, when the Anti-Masonic political party was founded in upstate New York. As for the Bavarian Illuminati—which was indeed created by the Jesuit-trained Adam Weishaupt (1748–1830) in Ingolstadt in 1776 but fell apart before the nineteenth century began—it still provides fodder for theorists on both sides of the political spectrum, from the John Birch Society to antiglobalist, postmodern anarchists.

And then there are the Jewish moneylenders—a perennial bane of conspiracy theorists. Most notorious of all were the Rothschilds, whose patriarch Mayer Amschel (1744–1812) emerged from the *Judengasse* (Jew Alley) of Frankfurt, groomed his eldest son, Amschel (1773–1855), as his successor, and installed his four younger sons in the capitals of Europe—Solomon (1774–1855) in Vienna, Nathan (1777–1836) in London, Calmann (1788–1855) in Naples, and James (1792–1868) in Paris—where they were ideally situated to profit from the industrial revolution and the Napoleonic wars that roiled the continent throughout the first half of the nineteenth century. Moses and Gerson Warburg founded M. M. Warburg & Co. in Hamburg in 1798; Paul Moritz Warburg (1866–1932) was one of the creators of the U.S. Federal Reserve; Siegmund George Warburg (1902–1982) would found S. G. Warburg in London. Jacob Henry Schiff (1847–1920) married into the Kuhn family and became the head of the bank Kuhn, Loeb & Co., where Otto Herman Kahn (1867–1934) would also make his fortune. But it wasn't just the supposed Jewish penchant for moneymaking that

---

*Shriner member Michael Richards, for example (who played Cosmo Kramer on *Seinfeld*). Some Internet postings connected the dots, as it were, between his career-ruining racist rant, which was widely viewed on YouTube a few years ago, and the white supremacist views of the Confederate general Albert Pike (1809–1891), the longtime Sovereign Grand Commander of the Scottish Rite's Southern Jurisdiction.

infuriated anti-Semitic conspiracists. Decadent Jewish artists were accused of attacking moral and aesthetic standards; Sigmund Freud (1856–1939) and his psychoanalytic successors were castigated for sexualizing family dynamics; Jewish revolutionary theorists like Karl Marx (1818–1883) were seen as undermining the very foundations of society. And they were just the tip of the iceberg, the most visible representatives of their secretive, greedy, deicidal race, whose dreams of messianic vindication and world domination are inscribed in their DNA.

The English novelist and historian Nesta Webster (1876–1960)—the mother of modern conspiracy theory—had much to say about the Jews in her monumental *Secret Societies and Subversive Movements* (1921):

> I do not think that the Jews can be proved to provide the sole cause of world-unrest. . . . But this is not to underrate the importance of the Jewish peril. . . . Jewry in itself constitutes the most effectual Freemasonry in the world. What need of initiations, or oaths, or signs, or passwords amongst people who perfectly understand each other and are everywhere working for the same end? Far more potent than the sign of distress that summons Freemasons to each other's aid at moments of peril is the call of the blood that rallies the most divergent elements in Jewry to the defense of the Jewish cause.

Robert Cooper Lee Bevan, Webster's father, was a director of Barclays Bank; her mother was the daughter of an Anglican bishop. Both were deeply religious and Webster was something of a spiritual quester herself. Educated at the University of London, she traveled widely in the East before she married Captain Arthur Webster, a district police superintendent in India. Around 1910, while researching a novel set during the French Revolution, Webster had a mystical experience that left her convinced that she was the reincarnation of the Comtesse de Sabran. In *The French Revolution: A Study in Democracy* (1919), she revived the theory (first popularized in 1798 by Abbé Augustin Barruel and John Robison) that her beloved *ancien régime* had been brought down not by a spontaneous revolutionary uprising but by the subversive efforts of the secularists in the Bavarian Illuminati, working hand in hand with French Freemasonry.

With the publication of *Secret Societies and Subversive Movements*, she cast a much wider net, arguing that occultist secret societies—especially Jewish **Kabbalists**—had been conspiring to overthrow legitimate religions and polities since the beginnings of time; that they not only caused the French Revolution, but were the secret impetus behind Russia's Bolsheviks, an idea she explicated further in *World Revolution: The Plot Against Civilization* (1921). Webster's involvement with Oswald Mosley's (1896–1980) British Union of Fascists left her stranded on the margins of British political and intellectual life by the time of World War II. Nevertheless, her writings would have a profound influence on America's John Birch Society (which did not share her anti-Semitism) and the racialist, neo-Nazi Liberty Lobby, which reprinted some of her books through its Noontide Press.

Lined up with the Jews, Freemasons, billionaires, and communists as an archetypical force for evil and subversion is the Roman Catholic Church—a long-standing bugaboo to many Americans since the country's beginnings. We all learn about the Pilgrims in elementary school, but how many of us were taught about the annual November 5 Pope's Day celebrations that were held in colonial Boston, when the colonists burned images of the Pope in effigy to commemorate the defeat of the Gunpowder Plot?* Until 1821, Catholic immigrants were denied U.S. citizenship unless they publicly abjured their allegiance to the Pope. The American political movement called Know-Nothingism (because its members

---

*The English call it Bonfire Day or Guy Fawkes Day after the plot's hapless chief conspirator, who was executed in 1606.

were enjoined to say that they "knew nothing" when asked about its secrets) kept anti-Catholic feelings burning at a fever pitch until the outbreak of the Civil War; its traces lingered long afterward. As late as 1960, presidential candidate John F. Kennedy (1917–1963) was obliged to give a speech to reassure voters that he believed in "an America where the separation of church and state is absolute—where no Catholic prelate would tell the president (should he be Catholic) how to act."

A 1,836-page-long publication called *Vatican Assassins* can be purchased on CD via the Internet. Its quaintly prolix subtitle, more characteristic of a polemic from the eighteenth century than the twenty-first, is worth quoting in full, since it touches so many bases. Its author, Eric Jon Phelps, self-identifies as a "White American Freeman Dispensational, Fifth Monarchy, Seventh-Day Baptist-Calvinist." Take a deep breath:

> *After Thirty-Eight Years of Suppression (1963–2001) Exposing the Murder of Knight of Columbus President John F. Kennedy, by the bloody hand of the Society of Jesus, by Order of its Jesuit General being "the Black Pope," in Command of His Most Obedient Servant, the "infallible" Pope Paul VI being "the White Pope," He Controlling the Soviet KGB and Jesuit-trained Fidel Castro's Communist Cuba through the British, Russian and American Branches of the Knights of Malta, While in Command of His Jesuit-trained Most Obedient Servant: The Archbishop of New York and Knight of Columbus Francis Cardinal Spellman, Directing the Cast of Organized American Traitors, They Being the High Command of The Knights of Malta, Shriner Freemasonry The Knights of Columbus, The Mafia and therefore, The New York Council on Foreign Relations, Controlling the "Holy Roman" Fourteenth Amendment American Empire Including Its: Commander-in-Chief, President Lyndon Johnson, Federal Government and War Machine, Federal Reserve Banking System, Military Industrial*

Complex, National "Lucepress" Media, Federal Bureau of Investigation, Central Intelligence Agency, National Security Agency, Secret Service, Chief Justice of the Supreme Court with his Warren Commission, Speaker of the House of Representatives with His Assassinations Committee, and Vietnam War

Of course America is nowhere near as overtly anti-Catholic as it once was, even on the militant fringes of Protestantism. Starting in the 1970s, the Christian broadcaster, minister, author, onetime U.S. presidential candidate, and conspiratorial thinker par excellence Pat Robertson began to build bridges between his evangelical flock and their Roman Catholic "brothers in Christ," the better to fight their common enemies. Jerry Falwell (1933–2007), the leader of the Moral Majority, and James Dobson, of Focus on the Family, followed his lead. In his book *The New World Order* (1991), Robertson reserved his greatest ire for the Rothschilds, the Masons, the Illuminati, the United Nations, and the forces of secular humanism. But not all evangelical Protestants are so open-minded. Robertson's ecumenicism makes the Presents of God Ministries (a breakaway Seventh-Day Adventist sect founded by an ex-Catholic) downright apoplectic. Their Web site is replete with scorching references to him:

This man named Pat Robertson is a Roman Catholic short robed Jesuit who will do for the church what prophecy calls the last straw. He has stretched out his hands to Rome and has embraced all it has to offer.

To be sure, the Presents of God Ministries is not exactly in the mainstream of American Christianity. But the phenomenal success of the novel *The Da Vinci Code* (2003), with its terrifying albino **Opus Dei** hit man and its portrayal of a cynical Vatican that will stop at nothing to preserve its power and prerogatives, suggests that anti-Papist prejudice is not entirely a thing of the past.

John Hagee, the pastor of the seventeen-thousand-member Cornerstone Church of San Antonio, Texas, and the founder of the pro-Zionist political lobby Christians United for Israel, is as outspokenly anti-Catholic as he is fulsomely philo-Semitic. Presidential candidate John McCain was forced to reject Hagee's endorsement in the spring of 2008 after some of his more inflammatory statements on the subject of Catholicism were publicized. ("The Roman Catholic Church, which was supposed to carry the light of the gospel, plunged the world into the dark ages," is one example. In a widely distributed YouTube video, Hagee could be seen and heard equating "the Great Whore of Babylon" with "the Roman Church.")

When seeking to understand the conspiratorial mind, the focus of its obsession is less important than the presence of the obsession itself. Jim Marrs has published a string of bestsellers on everything from the Kennedy assassination and the role played by space aliens in Biblical history to the complicity of U.S. intelligence agencies in the events of 9/11. David Icke, a retired British soccer player and sports announcer turned writer and lecturer, has discerned a conspiracy of shape-shifting reptiles of extraterrestrial origin—among them the British royal family, the Bushes, Gorbachev, and Henry Kissinger—who are striving to subjugate the human race.* Adolf Hitler's (1889–1945) *Mein Kampf*, with its fixation on a fanciful, romanticized Aryan culture locked in a death struggle with decadent international Judaism, and the poet Ezra Pound's (1885–1972) screeds about the evils of paper money and the Jews who loan it out for interest ("USURY is the cancer of the world, which only the surgeon's knife of Fascism can cut out of the life of the nations,"

---

*Icke might have been influenced by the early 1980s camp classic TV show *V*, in which reptilian alien invaders were disguised as soap opera–handsome villains and icily beautiful, impeccably lipsticked vixens. The John Carpenter movie *They Live* (1988) also comes to mind, in which the hero dons a pair of sunglasses that enables him to see the world as it really is—a dictatorship ruled by monstrous aliens who control their human subjects with subliminal advertising.

he wrote) are no different in kind than the poisonous rantings that pollute so much of cyberspace today.

As an experiment, type the words "Princess Di" and "Illuminati" into Google. Within three-tenths of a second, links to thousands of pages will be delivered to your desktop. If you click on almost any of them, you will hit pay dirt. Here is an extract from an article by T. Stokes, a palmist, astrologer, and lecturer on the paranormal:

> There has long been a Jewish connection to the royal family. . . .
> Prince Charles, who is head of the Church of England, yet
> strangely was circumcised by the London Jewish communities'
> mohel, Dr. Jacob Snowman. Princess Diana refused to have
> her sons similarly sexually mutilated, bringing her onto a col-
> lision course with vested control interests. The queen at one
> point said, *"There are powers at work in this country of which
> we know nothing."*

"The Jews," "the royal family," "powers of which we know nothing." They are words that could have just as easily been generated by a computerized "conspiracy generator" as by a flesh-and-blood parapsychologist.

Some conspiracy theorists are content merely to declaim and defame. Others not only see the world through a conspiratorial lens, but are active conspirators themselves. Adolf Hitler and Joseph Stalin (1879–1953) mixed theory and praxis; so does Lyndon LaRouche today, though with less spectacular results. Mark Lane, the bestselling author of *Rush to Judgment* (1966), one of the first books to question the Warren Commission's report on the Kennedy assassination, and *Plausible Denial* (1992), which laid the blame for it on the CIA, was one of Jim Jones's lawyers; he was present at Jonestown on the night that Jones and more than nine hundred members of his **Peoples Temple** took their lives.

In the course of his short but eventful life, Lee Harvey Oswald (1939–1963) associated with any number of individuals whose life paths were as twisted and unconventional as his own. Long before his abortive attempt to defect to the Soviet Union, when he was a teenage cadet in the Civil Air Patrol in Louisiana, Oswald came into contact with David Ferrie (1918–1967), who was one of his squadron's instructors. A gay, hairless (he suffered from alopecia) hypnotist who had been active in the heretical Old Roman Catholic Church in North America, the ardently anticommunist ex–Eastern AirLines pilot hovers on the margins of many accounts of the Kennedy assassination. In Dallas, Oswald would become friendly with George de Mohrenschildt (1911–1977), a shadowy, Russian-born petroleum geologist who in earlier years had been an intimate of Jacqueline Kennedy's eccentric relative Edith Ewing Bouvier Beale (1895–1977) of *Grey Gardens* fame, and whose brother Dmitri was a senior figure in the CIA. Bruce Campbell Adamson's epic *Oswald's Closest Friend* extends backward in time to the assassination of Leon Trotsky (1879–1940) and forward to the death of Princess Di over the course of fourteen self-published volumes, charting the intricate web of the de Mohrenschildt brothers' associations.

Before Oswald ever dreamed of assassinating the ultra-right-wing General Edwin Walker (1909–1993) or President John F. Kennedy, he believed that he had an important role to play in history. But when at last he had captured the world's undivided attention, he protested desperately that he was only a "patsy"; that somebody else was pulling all the strings. Perhaps they were. Fifty years later, most people seem to think so.

It makes a rough sort of sense that conspiracy theorists would be tempted to join conspiracies and that potential conspirators would be drawn to each other, in the same way that a practicing Catholic is more likely than a Muslim to enlist in the Jesuits, or that a communist is more likely than a **Rotarian** to join a revolutionary cell. Still, it is interesting to note the underlying similarities between the conspiratorial views of a number of demagogues and cult leaders whose ideologies appear to be starkly opposed. Hitler and Stalin, for example, occupied opposite ends of the ideological spectrum, yet they both feared Jews; the erstwhile science fiction writer L. Ron Hubbard (1911–1986) and the ex-Marxist Lyndon LaRouche each claimed to have been the victims of a cabal of international bankers. Both the House of Windsor and the Bush family have been the objects of intense suspicion in conspiracist thinking. 9/11 Truthers are as likely to be right-wing racists as left-wing anarchists, but they all loathe their government with equal intensity. Some of these people are mentally ill: their personalities and ideations are shaped (or distorted) by the same pathologies; they don't so much agree with each other as exhibit the same symptoms. Because they are narcissistic, they think of themselves as gods; because they are paranoid, they are secretive and defensive; because they are grandiose, they fancy themselves the victims of vast conspiracies—or they organize and even execute vast conspiracies themselves.

What else do the conspiratorially minded have in common? Richard Hofstadter's indispensable essay "The Paranoid Style in American Politics," written in 1964, provides invaluable historical context. Just as the midtwenieth century was marked by anticommunist hysteria, Americans in the nineteenth century did their own share of witch-hunting. Rumors about Illuminism sparked a transient panic in America in 1798; a few decades later, Illuminism's cousin Freemasonry came into disrepute. Specifically, the Masons were accused of murdering William Morgan, a bricklayer from Batavia, New York, who'd threatened to expose their secrets; in general, the Masons were feared and resented as an aristocratic, conspiratorial, irreligious elite who owed their loyalty to each other rather than to their country. The Anti-Masonic political party absorbed many of the forces opposed to Andrew Jackson (1767–1845), who was a high-ranking Mason, and returned John Quincy Adams (1767–1848), whom Jackson had driven from the White House in 1828, to Washington as a congressman. As anti-Mason feelings subsided, the mounting pace of immigration from non-Protestant countries raised new anxieties. None other than the distinguished portrait painter Samuel F. B. Morse (1791–1872)—who also invented the telegraph—warned of a Vatican-sponsored plot to install one of the Hapsburgs as emperor of the United States. Decades later, during the depression of 1893, a similar hoax to the ***Protocols of the Learned Elders of Zion*** was perpetrated against Catholicism, when a forged encyclical attributed to Pope Leo XIII was widely circulated, in which its putative author exhorted his American flock to slaughter their heretical countrymen. Anti-Masonry and anti-Catholic nativism were highly emotional, irrational responses to social, economic, and demographic changes that pulled the rug out from under groups that had formerly considered themselves secure. At their extremes, they manifested as clinical hysteria, with hallucinations and delusions of persecution.

The tectonic upheavals of the twentieth century (World War I, the Depression, World War II, the Cold War, the civil rights movement, the advent of legal abortion, feminism, gay liberation, rising divorce rates, the rapid transition from a rural to an urban economy) left countless more Americans reeling. Some, writes Hofstadter, took refuge in a conspiratorial worldview that allowed them to indulge their feelings of victimization. To them, there was no such thing as accidents, tragic misunderstandings, unforeseen consequences, or good intentions gone awry, only the calculated maliciousness of implacably evil adversaries. In Senator Joseph McCarthy's (1908–1957) words, it was a conspiracy "on a scale so immense as to dwarf any previous such venture in the history of man."

America, right-wing conspiracists who flocked to the John Birch Society and other ultra-right-wing groups came to believe, was an occupied nation. Its puppet government was the tool of evil powers who pulled the strings of its financial system through the manipulation of debt and the monetary supply and waged foreign wars and created internationalist organizations like the UN and the World Bank to prepare the way for the eventual dominion of a One-World government. Woodrow Wilson was a socialist; FDR had prior knowledge of the attack on Pearl Harbor; Eisenhower was a "dedicated, conscious agent" of international Communism.

Disoriented, dispossessed, and overwhelmed by feelings of their own powerlessness, the paranoid perceive their enemy, Hofstadter writes, as "a perfect model of malice, a kind of amoral superman—sinister, ubiquitous, powerful, cruel, sensual, luxury-loving . . . [who] manufactures disasters, and then enjoys and profits from the misery he has produced." Perhaps, Hofstadter concludes, a certain number of individuals have always been predisposed toward this sort of thinking. Add enough significant social, economic, or cultural stressors and a mass movement can coalesce around them—the Know-Nothings, Hitler's Brown Shirts, the burgeoning readership for Tim LaHaye and Jerry Jenkins's *Left Behind* series, with its UN-affiliated Antichrist and its Rapture-destined Elect.*

The philosopher of science Karl Popper (1902–1994) wrote about the "conspiracy theory of society" in the second volume of his landmark *The Open Society and Its Enemies* (1952), defining it as "the view that an explanation of a social phenomenon consists in the discovery of the men or groups who are interested in the occurrence of this phenomenon . . . and who have planned and conspired to bring it about." Popper attributed this way of thinking to the "secularization of . . . religious superstition":

> The gods are abandoned. But their place is filled by powerful men or groups—sinister pressure groups whose wickedness is

---

*H. L. Mencken put it less politely. "The central belief of every moron," he wrote in 1936, "is that he is the victim of a mysterious conspiracy against his common rights and true deserts. He ascribes all his failure to get on in the world, all of his congenital incapacity and damfoolishness, to the machinations of werewolves assembled in Wall Street, or some other such den of infamy. If these villains could be put down, he holds, he would at once become rich, powerful and eminent."

responsible for all the evils we suffer from—such as the Learned Elders of Zion, or the monopolists, or the capitalists, or the imperialists.

Popper didn't deny that secret societies and conspiracies do in fact exist, or that when people who believe in conspiracies gain political power and launch counterconspiracies of their own much mischief can follow; he merely noted that social, political, and historical events don't take place within a vacuum. Even when an action is deliberately intended, its consequences rarely are: effects provide unreliable evidence for causes and vice versa. The plotters who killed Abraham Lincoln (1809–1865), for example—and America's sixteenth president was indeed the victim of a conspiracy—accomplished their immediate aim, but they could never have anticipated even a small fraction of its sequelae.

Popper's categories of "falsifiable" and "unfalsifiable" statements have given us one of the most potent tools we have for distinguishing pseudoscientific assertions from the real thing. His reminder of "the unwieldiness, the resilence or the brittleness of the social stuff, or its resistance to our attempts to mould it and to work with it" could have an equally clarifying influence on the social sciences.

Though conspiracists invariably describe themselves as hard-boiled types, skeptical, unillusioned, and cynical to the core, there is much that is reassuring and optimistic in their worldview. Conspiracists believe in prophecy; they have a congenital distaste for shadings, nuances, and uncertainties. However Manichaean their world might be, however Gnostic in its manifold deceptions and depravities, ultimately it is a profoundly meaningful place. Not only do its events admit of neat explanations; salvation remains a distinct possibility. The day of reckoning will come, they believe, when they can convince enough "sheeple" to see through the enemy's "big lies." Truth and justice will have their day.

The illusion of understanding restores the conspiracists'

sense of control—it places them back at the center of things, masters of their own destinies. Hence the crude rumors pervading communities that feel as though they're under siege. The twin scourges of **AIDS** and crack were created by the white man and deliberately introduced into the communities of people of color to destroy them. O. J. Simpson was framed; the pop singer Michael Jackson was prosecuted for pederasty because the white power structure could not tolerate a black man becoming so successful. Huge segments of the Arab world are firmly convinced that 9/11 was jointly planned by Israel and the United States to provide a casus belli for invading Iraq—for example, this Cairo electrician, quoted in the *New York Times* on September 9, 2008:

> "Why is it that they never caught him, bin Laden? How can they not know where he is when they know everything? . . . What happened in Iraq confirms that it has nothing to do with bin Laden or Qaeda. They went against Arabs and against Islam to serve Israel, that's why."

But you don't have to travel to the Middle East to hear such theories—any number of Americans (including a handful of celebrities, such as the actor Charlie Sheen and the ex-wrestler and former governor of Minnesota, Jesse Ventura) will tell you that 9/11 was an "inside job."

Our susceptibility to conspiratorial thinking is literally hardwired in our brains. The October 2, 2008, issue of *Science* documented a series of experiments conducted by Jennifer Whitson of the McCombs School of Business at the University of Texas, Austin, and Adam Galinsky of the Kellogg School of Management at Northwestern University. Subjects were asked to examine a number of abstract patterns, some of which had recognizable images embedded in them. Immediately before they were tested, half of the participants had been placed in a situation that was designed to induce a feeling of powerlessness (specifically, they were given a battery of questions to answer, only to be told that an arbitrarily selected portion of their answers were incorrect). Ninety-five percent of both groups spotted the embedded images—but 43 percent of the group that had been deliberately frustrated (a much higher percentage than the other) also found patterns where none actually existed. "Lacking control leads to a visceral need for order, even imaginary order," Whitson observed. "The less control people have over their lives, the more likely they are to try and regain control through mental gymnastics," added Galinsky.

While psychologists may be able to identify specific clinical pathologies in the thought patterns and behavior of the conspiracy-minded,* for me the hallmark of the conspiracist personality is its naive religiosity, which is surprisingly akin to the all-encompassing, steadfast piety of very young children. Children and conspiracy theorists are philosophical occasionalists, in that they believe that everything that ever happens is an occasion for a transcendent power (God, proponents of One-World government) to impose its will. They are magical thinkers (if I step on this crack, I'll break my mother's back) and obsessive pattern seekers (if a Rothschild handled Cecil Rhodes's money, then Rhodes scholars must all be Zionists). They accept that appearances can be deceiving (a frog may turn out to be a prince; Hillary Clinton is really a Jewish lesbian named Rodenhurst) and never doubt for a moment that someone, somewhere, can provide the answer to any question, no matter how vexing (a parent, a pastor, a third-party political candidate). Not that there aren't significant differences between children and conspiracists. Children forgive and forget; conspiracists store up their grudges and grievances and keep them fresh for centuries.

Quoting the Roman poet Archilocus's aphorism that "the

---

*Anyone who has read more than a page or two of the writings of Lyndon LaRouche is likely to recognize their author in the *DSM-IV*'s description of Narcissistic Personality Disorder— "Pervasive pattern of grandiosity . . . need for admiration, and lack of empathy." David Icke's Draco-Reptilian **New World Order** is highly suggestive of the *DSM-IV*'s Grandiose Delusional Disorder, in which the patient "might believe . . . he or she has made an important discovery."

fox knows many things, but the hedgehog knows one big thing," the philosopher Isaiah Berlin famously contrasted the intellectual styles of pluralists and monists. If conspiracists were intellectuals, they would be hedgehogs, but they're not usually thinkers—they're people of faith, more often than not, and usually of a fundamentalist bent. The object of their faith is not necessarily religious (though it frequently is)—I am referring to the manner of their believing rather than its contents. Uncritical and credulous in regard to their own authoritative texts, dogmatic and literal-minded in the ways they interpret them, conspiracists attribute those same qualities to their adversaries. Not only do they grant credence to outrageous libels—for example that the Talmud instructs Jews to defraud gentiles, or that Jesuits pledge to murder as many Protestants as they possibly can; they take it for granted that all Jews and Jesuits would honor such unholy covenants. Instead of dismissing the blasphemous writings of occultists out of hand, the conspiracist fears them; stranger still, he believes them. Because the conspiracist is God-fearing, he sees the hoofprints of Satan everywhere.

The poet John Keats (1795–1821) attributed Shakespeare's greatness to his capacity for "negative capability," which he defined as "when a man is capable of being in uncertainties, Mysteries, doubts without any irritable reaching after fact & reason." The authorial impulse to overexplain, Keats recognized, can be fatal to storytelling—but his insight was not merely a literary one. As illustrated by innumerable Zen parables, the ability not just to tolerate but to revel in mystery and ambiguity is a signature of enlightenment—an attribute no conspiracist, for all the privileged knowledge he or she claims to possess, can lay claim to.

"The only true wisdom is knowing that you know nothing," said Socrates. Conspiracism is the delusion that one knows everything.

AIDS and the Black Death

Inchoate in the collective consciousness of almost every community that's ever been touched by HIV/AIDS is a myth that explains how the affliction came to be—and that offers up a cast of human villains to blame for either its existence or its persistence (or both). The gay American writer and activist Larry Kramer called Ronald Reagan "Adolf Reagan" and held him "responsible for the death of more gay people than . . . Hitler." The Reverend Jeremiah Wright, who gained notoriety as Barack Obama's pastor and ex-pastor during the 2008 U.S. presidential campaign, said that "the government lied about inventing the HIV virus as a means of genocide against people of color." The Kenyan political activist and Nobel laureate Dr. Wangari Muta Maathai has been widely quoted as saying of AIDS that "in fact it is created by a scientist for biological warfare" (a view, it should be pointed out, that she later emphatically and explicitly disavowed).

According to "AIDS: USA Homemade Evil" (1986), a pamphlet written by Jakob Segal, an East German biologist whom a KGB defector would later identify as a Soviet disinformation agent, the HIV virus was created at the U.S. military's Fort Detrick, Maryland, bioweapons laboratory in 1978 when scientists combined the retrovirus HTLV-1 (which causes T cell leukemia) with the sheep virus VISNA, then infected prisoners with the lethal synthesis.

Boyd E. Graves has argued that AIDS's origins date all the way back to the establishment of the Federal Quarantine Act in 1878, when eugenicists first got a toehold in the government. Since 1889, when mycoplasmas (tiny protean "stealth pathogens" whose lack of a cellular wall makes them notoriously difficult to culture or identify, and which can invade cells without killing them) were first discovered, America has had the ability to manufacture epidemics and target them at undesirable classes of people. Graves claims that the English mathematician, philosopher, and peace activist Bertrand Russell "supported the necessity for organized plagues against the Black population" in 1921. And so his account continues down the years:

> In 1972, the United States and the Soviet Union entered into a biological agreement that would signal the death knell for the Black Population. . . . In 1974, Führer Henry Kissinger releases his NSSM-200 (U.S. Plan to Address Overpopulation). . . .

Still another theory has it that the HIV virus was engineered at Cold Spring Harbor Laboratory on New York's Long Island and disseminated throughout the third world by the World Health Organization in the guise of smallpox vaccinations. Other conspiracy theorists implicate giant drug companies, who deliberately spread the disease, arbitrarily withhold cures, or unfairly profit from their overpriced medications.

On the opposite extreme are the so-called AIDS denialists, most prominently the German-born cell biologist Peter H. Duesberg, who insists that AIDS is not caused by HIV at all, but by drug use and promiscuity in the West and by malnutrition in Africa. Though not a conspiracy theory per se, Duesberg's and others' influence on decision makers like South Africa's president Thabo Mbeki delayed an effective response to the epidemic. Their theories appealed to the political right, as well, because it put most of the onus for the disease on its victims.

A study released by Oregon State University and the Rand Corporation and reported in the *Washington Post* in January 2005 found that almost half of African Americans believed that AIDS was man-made; 25 percent that it was manufactured by the government; and 12 percent that it was spread by the CIA. Fifteen percent believed that AIDS was a form of genocide; more than 50 percent that a cure existed but was being deliberately withheld from the poor.

Denial, anger, and scapegoating are common reactions to

a catastrophe of this magnitude. Six and a half centuries ago, when the Black Death swept across Europe, killing tens of millions in just two years—as much as a third of the continent's population—some, convinced that humanity was being punished for its sins, tried to do something about it. Flagellants sought to appease God with their own extravagant acts of penance, and also by carrying out acts of vengeance against Christ's enemies, earning a rebuke from Pope Clement VI, who, unusually for a Catholic pontiff of his era, complained that the flagellants, "beneath an appearance of piety, set their hands to cruel and impious works, shedding the blood of Jews, whom Christian piety accepts and sustains." Others followed the flagellants' lead. In October 1348, in Geneva, Switzerland, authorities responded to rumors of poisoned wells by arresting a number of Jews. One of them, a man named Agimet, "was put to the torture a little," as a chronicle delicately phrased it, and quickly confessed. As he was preparing to leave on a journey, he told his questioners, he had received a summons from Rabbi Peyret of Chambéry.

"We have been informed that you are going to Venice to buy silk and other wares," the rabbi said to him. "Here I am giving you a little package of half a span in size which contains some prepared poison and venom in a thin, sewed leather-bag. Distribute it among the wells, cisterns, and springs about Venice and the other places to which you go, in order to poison the people who use the water." Agimet admitted that he had done as he was told, poisoning wells not just in Venice but in Calabria, Puglia, Ballet, and Toulouse. Jews in Basel, Strasbourg, Freiburg, and many other towns were burned at the stake as news of his confession spread.

In medieval Europe, the terrified majority population blamed a hated minority for its afflictions. With AIDS, minorities not only have had to bear a disproportionate share of the suffering; they've carried its stigma too. "AIDS is not just God's punishment for homosexuals," thundered the Moral Majority's Jerry Falwell. "It is God's punishment for the society that tolerates homosexuals."

When AIDS first began to spread into the African American community, memories of the 1932–1972 Tuskegee Experiment—in which some four hundred mostly illiterate black sharecroppers who had been promised free syphilis treatments were given placebos instead, so scientists could observe them as the disease progressed into its advanced stages—were still fresh. When the experiment was belatedly called off, decades after penicillin had been discovered to cure syphilis, 128 of the subjects had already died, forty of their wives had been infected, and nineteen of their children had been born with congenital syphilis. "Nothing learned," an appalled Public Health Service analyst concluded of the study, "will prevent, find, or cure a single case of infectious syphilis or bring us closer to our basic mission of controlling venereal disease in the United States." To say that Africans and people of African descent have been cruelly exploited historically is a grotesque understatement. As pseudoscientific—and as dangerous—as most AIDS conspiracy theories may be, it's not difficult to understand their emotional appeal.

Al Qaeda

Though its members are secretive and cultish by definition (dedicated as they are to perpetrating deadly terrorist acts in the name of the reactionary Salafist interpretation of Islam that they adhere to), Al Qaeda is more of a criminal and political conspiracy than a social or religious movement.

The organization came into being as a formal entity around 1988 when Ayman al-Zawahiri's Egyptian Islamic Jihad merged with the Maktab al-Khidamat (MAK), the Afghan Services Bureau. Osama bin Laden, one of the Saudi Arabian billionaire Muhammad bin Awad bin Laden's fifty-four children, had founded the MAK with his mentor, the

Palestinian intellectual Abdullah Yusuf Azzam (who was killed in 1989), to recruit and train guerillas to fight the Soviet troops that had been occupying Afghanistan since 1979. *Al Qaeda* means "the base," which refers to the guest-house in Peshawar where recruits reported for duty, as well as to the database in which their names—tens of thousands of them, from more than fifty countries—were entered. Under Osama bin Laden's leadership Al Qaeda would grow into the largest and deadliest terrorist movement in the world. In addition to the MAK and the Egyptian Islamic Jihad, some of the other international jihadist movements gathered under Al Qaeda's umbrella are: the Libyan Islamic Fighting Group; the Islamic Army of Aden; Jama'at al-Tawhid wal Jihad (now known as Al Qaeda in Iraq); the Pakistan-based Lashkar-e-Taiba (which carried out a hor-rific series of attacks on hotels, a train station, and a Chabad guesthouse in Mumbai, India, in November 2008); Jaish-e-Muhammad (Kashmir); the Islamic Movement of Uzbek-istan; Al Qaeda in the Islamic Maghreb and the Armed Islamic Group (Algeria); Abu Sayyaf Group (Malaysia and the Philippines); and Jemaah Islamiya (Southeast Asia).

Al Qaeda's stated goal was to purify the Islamic world, to rid Islamic countries of decadent, secular, Western influences and institutions and restore sharia (Koranic law) as the law of the land. After the first Gulf War, the presence of infidel American troops in Saudi Arabia, "the land of two Holy Places," was added to Al Qaeda's list of grievances. In 1996 bin Laden issued a fatwa calling for an all-out war against the Crusader Zionist alliance; another fatwa in 1998 specifi-cally called for American blood:

> The ruling to kill the Americans and their allies—civilians and military—is an individual duty for every Muslim who can do it in any country in which it is possible to do it, in order to liberate the Al-Aqsa Mosque and the holy mosque [Mecca]

from their grip, and in order for their armies to move out of all the lands of Islam, defeated and unable to threaten any Muslim. This is in accordance with the words of Almighty God, "and fight the pagans all together as they fight you all together" and "fight them until there is no more tumult or oppression, and there prevail justice and faith in God."

After the fundamentalist Islamic Taliban regime (*taliban* is the Pashto word for "students") rose to power in Afghanistan in 1996, Al Qaeda operated openly there, running training camps for aspiring jihadists; planning, financing, and coordinating international operations; orchestrating a worldwide propaganda campaign; reaching out to militant Shiites in Hezbollah; and, most alarming, actively seeking to acquire nuclear and chemical weapons. In 1998, Al Qaeda was responsible for deadly embassy bombings in Nairobi, Kenya, and Dar es Salaam, Tanzania. In 2000 the USS *Cole*, a guided-missile destroyer, was attacked in port in Aden, Yemen, by waterborne suicide bombers. In 2001, Al Qaeda launched its most spectacular operation yet, the coordinated attacks on the Pentagon and the World Trade Center.

America's response was massive and sustained. Forced underground by the U.S. invasion of Afghanistan and the worldwide "War on Terror," and with many of its leaders dead or captured, by mid-2002 Al Qaeda had been reduced to a decentralized confederacy; its embattled leadership was forced to shift its focus from implementation to ideology. But the forces Al Qaeda unleashed continued to present a formidable threat to the West—as witness the bombings on the Madrid railroad on March 11, 2004, which killed 191 commuters and influenced a national election (three days after the attacks, the Bush-friendly administration of José María Aznar was voted out of office; his successor José Luis Rodríguez Zapatero made good on his campaign promise to withdraw Spanish troops from Iraq), and on the London

Underground on July 7, 2005, in which fifty-six people died, including the bombers.

Ironically, the U.S. invasion of Iraq provided Al Qaeda with a renewed lease on life. Testifying before the House Select Intelligence Committee in April 2008, the journalist and terrorism expert Peter Bergen noted that the pool of available jihadists had grown much larger since the invasion and that the pace of their attacks had accelerated. "To test that thesis empirically," he continued,

> Paul Cruickshank of New York University and I compared the period after September 11 through the invasion of Iraq in March 2003 with the period from March 2003 through September 2006. Using numbers from the authoritative RAND terrorism database and a conservative methodology, we found that the rate of deadly attacks by jihadists had increased sevenfold since the invasion. And, even excluding terrorism in Iraq and Afghanistan, fatal attacks by jihadists in the rest of the world have increased by more than one-third since March 2003. Iraq, of course, did not cause all of this terrorism, but it certainly increased the tempo of jihadist attacks from London to Kabul to Amman.

Bergen held out hope that Al Qaeda might eventually wear out its welcome in the Islamic world. Although its attacks on Western targets receive the bulk of publicity, the overwhelming majority of Al Qaeda's and its affiliates' victims have been Muslims. The Tamil Tigers, who virtually invented the suicide bomb, carried out seventy-six attacks between 1987 and 2001. Al Qaeda in Iraq conducted ten times that many in a third of the time. Al Qaeda has been spectacularly effective at channeling the Arab world's long-standing grievances and rage, much less so at promoting a positive vision. "We know what bin Laden is against, but what's he really for?" Bergen asks.

If you asked him he would say the restoration of the caliphate. In practice that means Taliban-style theocracies stretching from Indonesia to Morocco. A silent majority of Muslims don't want that. An interesting poll in Saudi Arabia in 2003 gets to this. In that poll 49 percent of Saudis admired bin Laden, while only 5 percent wanted to live in a bin Laden–run state. Many Muslims admire bin Laden because he "stood up" to the West. That doesn't mean they want to live in bin Laden's Islamist utopia. Sudan under Turabi, Afghanistan under the Taliban, and Iran under the ayatollahs don't look very attractive to most Muslims.

Area 51, Stealth Blimps, Majestic-12, Alien Abductions, and Divine Revelations

Also known as Groom Lake, Dreamland, Homey Airport, the Nellis Range Complex, Paradise Ranch, The Farm, Watertown Strip, Red Square, "The Box," and, most prosaically, Air Force Flight Test Center, Detachment 3, Area 51 is a highly restricted military base located about ninety miles north of Las Vegas, Nevada. The closest town to Area 51 is Rachel, Nevada (population 98), about twenty-five miles away.

The first mystery about Area 51 is the origin of its name. The red square on the map that designates its precincts (the restricted airspace above it is labeled R-4808N on aviation charts) is bordered by the Air Force's Nevada Test and Training Range and the Department of Energy's Nevada Test Site (formerly known as the Nevada Proving Grounds), where more than a thousand nuclear devices were detonated between 1951 and 1992. The Nevada Test Site is divided into grids numbered one through thirty and much of Area 51 is contiguous with the NTS's "Grid 15." Perhaps the NTS number was deliberately transposed, the better to distinguish the two sites. Assigning so much higher a number to the Air Force Flight Test Center's domain also guaranteed that a grid with an identical number wouldn't eventually turn up on the NTS site, since even if the NTS were to expand, it is unlikely to ever add as many as twenty-one grids to its vast extent (the NTS is already as large as the state of Rhode Island).

Groom Lake is not a lake at all—or rather it hasn't been for a long time; its water has long since evaporated. Its flat, firm clay surface and remote location made it an ideal site to test the U-2 spy plane in 1955, although the five-thousand-foot runway at the existing airbase was much too short and had to be extended by another thirty-five hundred feet. The facility has been considerably expanded in the intervening half century; hundreds of workers commute to it daily from Las Vegas on unmarked 737s and other planes that fly in and out of McCarran International Airport. A terse official statement conceded the base's existence a few years ago, but not much else:

> The Air Force has acknowledged the existence of the Nellis Range Complex near the Groom Dry Lake for many years now. There are a variety of activities, some of which are classified, throughout the complex. The range is used for the testing of technologies and systems training for operations critical to the effectiveness of U.S. military forces and the security of the United States.

Such activities have almost certainly included putting the SR-71 Blackbird, the F-117A Nighthawk stealth fighter, and other "black" experimental aircraft (not to mention a host of drones and smart bombs and cruise missiles) through their paces as they were being developed, but we can't be sure, because that same Air Force release included the caveat that "some specific activities and operations conducted on the Nellis Range, both past and present, remain classified and cannot be discussed." One hypothetical experimental aircraft that has been much speculated about on the Internet of late is an enormous "stealth blimp" powered by an "electrokinetic propulsion" device. Prototypes of this vehicle, if they indeed exist, might account for recent sightings of vast V-shaped formations of lights in the night skies over Arizona, Texas, Illinois, California, and New Jersey.

But many military facilities are kept off-limits to civilians, even ones where top secret technology isn't likely to be on display. Why all the fuss about Area 51? Earnest, unfanciful, workaday souls like former Indiana congressman Lee Hamilton have suggested that "the Air Force is classifying all information about Area 51 in order to protect themselves from a lawsuit." The lawsuit that Hamilton referred to (during an interview with Leslie Stahl on CBS's *60 Minutes*, which aired in March 1996) was filed against the Air Force and the EPA on behalf of five unnamed civilian contractors and two contractors' widows, who were said to have been poisoned by the dioxin, dibenzofuran, and trichloroethylene that they were exposed to in the course of their work. Citing national security concerns, the government successfully held back evidence and the suits were dismissed.

But that's not why Area 51 is included in this book. As anyone who has ever watched *The X-Files* on television or caught *Independence Day* in a theater, glanced at the covers of tabloids like the *National Enquirer*, or flipped through a handful of the ever-burgeoning library of books about UFOs well knows, the barracks and hangars and airfields that show up in satellite photographs of Area 51 (and the government has gone to considerable trouble to restrict or redact those too) are only the tip of the iceberg. Beneath the ground (as many as forty levels underground, according to some breathless accounts) are sleek, high-tech facilities where hardware from crashed UFOs is studied and adapted for earthly purposes. Without any apparent sense of irony or inconsistency, some of the same people who claim that the U.S. government has long possessed alien technologies like electromagnetic pulse engines and "gravity amplifiers" that can compress space-time, making faster-than-light travel feasible, also insist that the moon landing was faked. Area 51, in their telling, is where Neil Armstrong's and his fellow Apollo astronauts' moon walks were staged and filmed. But that's not all: there are medical facilities in Area 51 where alien corpses are autopsied and interrogation rooms where living aliens are questioned. An extreme fringe of ufologists goes so far as to suggest that the facility is actually *run* by aliens; our government stands by helplessly, they say, as these Grays, Nordics, and Insectoid entities harvest human DNA and otherwise exploit our captive planet.

UFOs, the **Council on Foreign Relations**, the ***Protocols of the Learned Elders of Zion***, and Area 51 are all of a piece, according to the writings of arch–conspiracy theorist Milton William Cooper (1943–2001), author of *Behold a Pale Horse* (1991). Cooper relates how Defense secretary James Forrestal (1892–1949) "fell" to his death from a window on the sixteenth floor of Bethesda Naval Hospital, where he had been confined with "involuntary melancholia" after he objected to the unholy deal that his fellow members of Majestic-12 had struck with alien invaders. (Cooper himself would die at the hands of Apache County, Arizona, law enforcement officers, under murky circumstances that many believe have yet to be satisfactorily explained.)

Majestic-12 is alleged to be a supersecret cabal of wise men appointed by Harry Truman (1884–1972) in 1947 to handle UFO-related issues. Top secret government documents that "proved" Majestic-12's existence mysteriously came into the possession of UFO researcher Jamie Shandera in 1984; needless to say, their authenticity remains a matter of great dispute. Along with Majestic-12, **New World Order** theorists also refer to the **Jasons**, a secret cabal of top independent scientists who, starting in 1958, met as paid consultants to evaluate military technology. The Jasons are real—Mildred Goldberger, the wife of scientist Marvin Leonard Goldberger, named them after Greek mythology's Jason, the captain of the *Argo* and the seeker of the golden fleece, because her husband and his colleagues were questers after truth. The Jasons included veterans of the Manhattan Project like Edward Teller, Luis Alvarez, and Hans Bethe, and up-and-coming luminaries like Murray Gell-Mann, John Archibald Wheeler, and Steven Weinberg. Daniel Ellsberg's "Pentagon Papers" exposed many of their names to public view in 1971—causing some of them great embarrassment when their students accused them of abetting the war machine.

But let's get back to Cooper. In his telling, John F. Kennedy was assassinated not by Lee Harvey Oswald, but by his limousine driver (!)—because he had threatened to go public about our visitors from the star system Zeta Reticula. The space race was a fraud because there were already bases on the moon (that's why we haven't returned there since the 1970s—because televised moon walks would inevitably reveal their presence). That's also why so many Mars probes have malfunctioned—because Mars is already as overdeveloped as south Florida and its inhabitants prefer to keep their presence secret. The **Trilateral Commission** was set up to liaison with space aliens, not to improve relations between Asia and Europe and North America.

And exactly who are the planetary traitors who sold out to the Zeta Reticulans? If you've had even a modicum of exposure to conspiracist tracts, the answer will not surprise you: they are the **Illuminati**, the **Masons**, the ultrarich enemies of Christianity (secularists and Jews), the proponents of One-World government who secretly sponsored the Bolsheviks in Russia and perpetrated the odious federal income tax in the United States, and who brought down the Twin Towers and attacked the Pentagon in September of 2001. Near the end of his life, Cooper came to believe that the alien invasion he had spilled so many words about in print wasn't real, but was in fact a fiendishly clever specimen of disinformation. The Illuminati had been using conspiracy theorists, of all people, to disseminate fictitious rumors about extraterrestrials, hoping to distract the public's attention from the awful truth about their own even more horrifying existence.

But I digress. It's not surprising that a supersecret military test facility like Area 51 would become a mecca for UFO sightings. Not only would the local skies be filled with strange-looking aircraft; high-intensity flares and chaff might be deployed in the course of testing them, causing spectacular visual effects.*

Flying saucer enthusiasts really began flocking to Area 51—specifically to a storied black mailbox between mile markers 29 and 30 on the southwest side of Highway 375, where a dirt road branches off toward Groom Lake—when a man named Bob Lazar started telling everyone within earshot about the incredible things that could be seen there. In November 1989, Lazar appeared on a Las Vegas television talk show to talk about his former work at S-4, another ultrasecret government facility, about ten miles south of Area 51, near Papoose Dry Lake, where he had seen nine flying saucers stored in a hillside hangar. Not only that; he had helped reverse-engineer the propulsion system of one of them (a vehicle he called "the sports model"; its antigravity engines, he discovered, were fueled by the highly unstable Element 115. Lazar later marketed a scale model of this spacecraft).

Although he claimed to have studied at MIT and Caltech, Lazar's name doesn't appear in either university's records. He did work at Los Alamos before he came to Las Vegas, but as a technician rather than a senior scientist; there are no

---

*When I was a little boy, back in the Vietnam era, one afternoon I looked up and spotted a pair of hovering military helicopters. Below them was a glittering, shimmering cloud of light. My father was an engineer at nearby Fort Monmouth, the home of the Army Signal Corps. He told me that they were dropping chaff—strips of aluminum or glass or plastic fibers that distort radar images as they float through the air, frustrating guided missiles. Almost certainly, they were either training their crews or testing new equipment on the ground. Had my father not explained this to me, I might well have believed I'd witnessed something truly extraordinary—perhaps a creature made out of pure energy plasma, like the ones that were always turning up on television's *Star Trek*.

records to confirm that he was ever employed at S-4 or Area 51. Lazar countered that the government had erased his traces to discredit him. Lazar would plead guilty to pandering in 1990 (he had a business interest in a brothel, in which he installed electronic surveillance devices); in 1993 he sold his life story to the movies—a story that seems increasingly unlikely ever to be filmed. He lives in relative seclusion in New Mexico today, where he runs a scientific supply company and is purportedly developing a kit that will enable anyone to convert their car to run on hydrogen fuel.

Another person who did much to spread the word about Area 51 was Bob Lazar's friend John Lear. The son of Bill Lear, the inventor of the Learjet, John Lear is himself a storied figure in aviation. He holds numerous world records for speed and has worked as a civilian airline pilot, a soldier of fortune, and for the CIA. Here is his own characteristically understated account of himself, excerpted from a career summary he provided to the Las Vegas chapter of the Quiet Birdmen Association, a fellowship of professional pilots:

> What I did get . . . that no other airman got was most FAA certificates: these are the ATP, Flight Instructor with airplane single and multi engine, instrument, rotorcraft helicopter and gyroplane and glider. . . . I have 19,488 hours of total time of which 15,325 hours is in 1, 2, 3, or 4 engine jets. . . . I have flown 119 types of airplanes, helicopters, gyroplanes, and gliders.

Lear was one of the first people whom Lazar took out to Highway 375, where they witnessed saucers in flight. After they were intercepted by Area 51 guards, Lear says, his security clearance was revoked and he lost his job. He has since lectured extensively, not just on Area 51, but on the alien invasion that commenced twenty-five thousand years ago; 9/11 (which was planned and executed not by Osama bin Laden, but by his drug dealer enemies, who framed him so that Washington would remove him from power, allowing the illegal drug trade to flourish in Afghanistan again); AIDS (which was developed by the U.S. Navy in 1972); the *Challenger* space shuttle disaster (the Russians did it); the so-called Strategic Defense Initiative (Majestic-12 member Edward Teller, who personally recruited Bob Lazar to work at S-4, spearheaded the SDI program as a weapon to be used against the EBEs—Extraterrestrial Biological Entities— that Teller had belatedly come to realize were our enemies); and much, much more. Lear's Gnostic conviction that so many of the things that the rest of us take for granted are really blatant lies fomented by hidden powers, his arrogant certainty that he alone has the perspicacity to see through them, not to mention the patent (and frequently offensive) weirdness of so many of his claims—for example, that the hijacked airliners that are widely believed to have been flown into the World Trade Center were really harmless holo-grams—test the forbearance of even the fringe conspiracy community, where many regard him as a huckster at best, a sinister purveyor of Illuminati disinformation at worst.

In 1993, Glenn Campbell (not the singer), a resident of Rachel, Nevada, wrote and self-published a book called *The Area 51 Viewer's Guide*, which directs its readers to White Sides, a mountaintop that provided a legal vantage into Area 51. He also blazed a road onto Freedom Ridge, another, more accessible viewing site. When the Air Force tried to close both platforms down, Campbell sent out press releases. Rachel, Nevada's home page tells the rest of the story.

That's when the biggest wave of publicity began, with many major media outlets visiting Freedom Ridge to report on the "nonexistent" base. *The Wall Street Journal, Popular Science, The New York Times,* and many other publications ran sto-ries on the base and on Rachel, as did dozens of TV outlets, including ABC News, CNN, *Encounters,* and *Sightings.* On October 1, 1994, Larry King brought a crew of fifty to

Rachel for a live, two-hour special on TNT. . . . Millions around the country saw it.

Rachel's entrepreneurs are still reaping the benefits of the Air Force's heavy-handedness. The Rachel Bar & Grill changed its name to The Little A'Le'Inn and does an active trade in T-shirts and souvenirs; Highway 375 was officially renamed Extraterrestrial Highway in 1996. Tour outfits in Las Vegas have cashed in as well. "After a great Alien Burger at the Little A'Le'Inn," reads one ad, "we will travel . . . to the absolute perimeter of Area 51." It goes on:

> You can wave at the heavily armed guards in the 4 × 4 parked on the desert hillside but they don't wave back, they just watch from behind their darkened windows. As much as the United States Air Force has denied the existence of this base, we know it is there but no one knows what it is they do there. . . . This is an Extreme tour to the world's most top secret military facility, the real home of *The X-Files.*

Almost seven hundred miles separate Roswell, New Mexico, from Rachel, but it too occupies a special place in UFO lore. Consider this: if you divide Roswell's longitude by its latitude you get a number that's fairly close to pi. Coincidence? Hardly. There are true believers who will tell you that the doomed alien pilots of a disabled UFO guided it to its landing place near Roswell to send us a message. If you log on to the Internet you can read gematrical interpretations of Roswell's coordinates that would dazzle even the most jaded of **Kabbalists**. But we're getting ahead of ourselves.

On July 8, 1947—just two weeks after a businessman and amateur pilot named Kenneth Arnold (1915–1984) told newspaper reporters that he had seen nine "saucer-like" objects whiz across the sky near Mount Rainier, coining the word "flying saucer," inspiring countless copycat reports all over the world and igniting a media firestorm that is still

burning today—the Roswell Army Air Field public information office reported the crash and recovery of a "flying disc."
It was a potentially huge story, but less than twenty-four
hours later, the military tried to unring the bell. In the words
of the July 9, 1947, *Las Vegas Review Journal*:

> Brig. Gen. Roger B. Ramey, commander of the 8th Air Force
> said at Fort Worth that he believed the object was the "rem-
> nant of a weather balloon and a radar reflector," and was
> "nothing to be excited about."

The fact that the wreckage weighed only five pounds and
that W. W. Brazel, the rancher who found it, described it to a
reporter from the *Roswell Daily Record* at the time "as rubber
strips, tinfoil, a rather tough paper and sticks," lends credence to the military brass's decidedly blasé reaction. Nevertheless, in a 1978 interview with ufologist Stan Friedman,
Jesse Marcel, the intelligence major who authorized the original Army press release and who thirty-one years later was
still seething about the way his superiors had left him to
twist in the wind, adamantly insisted that the objects whose
recovery he'd supervised had had their origin in another
world. Jesse Marcel, Jr., defended his father in a book he
published in 2008, called *The Roswell Legacy: The Untold
Story of the First Military Officer at the 1947 Crash Site*.

Building on the renewed interest in the Roswell story,
Charles Berlitz and William L. Moore published *The Roswell
Incident* in 1980. Other notable titles in the stream of books
that followed—in which the five-pound bundle of rubber strips
and sticks and strips of paper metastasized into alien cadavers
and truckloads of artifacts—were Kevin D. Randle and Donald R. Schmitt's *UFO Crash at Roswell* (1991) and Philip
Corso's curious *The Day After Roswell* (1997). TV shows,
movies, and countless magazine articles and Internet postings
have since made "Roswell" a byword both for extraterrestrial
contact and outrageously blatant government cover-ups.

Philip Corso (1915–1998) was a highly decorated Army colonel who, near the end of his life, began to retail astonishing tales about his Roswell-related experiences. In his telling, he was on duty at Fort Riley, Kansas, in 1947 when he had the opportunity to examine a shipment en route from Roswell to Wright-Patterson Air Force Base in Ohio. Among its contents was a dead alien, embalmed in a gelatinous fluid. "It was a four-foot, human-shaped creature with . . . bizarre-looking, four-fingered hands . . . and a lightbulb-shaped head," he recalled. Later, when he was assigned to the Foreign Technology desk at the Pentagon, he was asked to evaluate the artifacts that were recovered at Roswell. Realizing their incredible implications, he wrote, he "seeded" them to the R&D divisions of defense contractors so they could be reverse-engineered. Fiber optics, integrated circuits, lasers, night vision goggles, and Kevlar are only a few of the "discoveries" that we know about—particle beam transmitters and psychotronic devices (which transmit thoughts to machines) are still classified.

In response to a 1994 General Accounting Office inquiry into the Roswell incident, instigated at the request of Congressman Steven Schiff (R-NM), the Air Force produced an extensive report in which it admitted that the wreckage recovered at the original Roswell site was a balloon involved in the top secret Project MOGUL, which had lofted microphones and radio transmitters into the upper atmosphere to capture sonic traces of Soviet nuclear tests. Not everyone involved in the recovery was in on the secret, which accounted for some of the initial confusion. The report further opined that glimpses of anthropomorphic crash dummies dropped from balloons at different times in the 1950s (projects that were also conducted under conditions of strictest secrecy), as well as recollections of actual bodies that were recovered from a fatal 1956 airplane crash near Roswell, might have been conflated with the original incident in later eyewitness accounts. But by then the Roswell meme—that the military had orchestrated a massive cover-up following the discovery of an authentic flying saucer—was set in stone. Few minds were changed.*

The Roswell incident has become so encrusted with hype, fantasy, delusional grandiosity, and rank commercialization that at this point it's more of a pop culture phenomenon than a recoverable historical event. This is ironic, because it provides a classic illustration of how blowback from excessive secrecy can be more harmful than a timely and judicious dose of the truth. Carl Sagan wrote about this phenomenon in *The Demon-Haunted World* (1996). Some UFO sightings that the government instantly denied, he suggested, might well have been based on something earthly and real. Unexplained blips on civilian radar, for example, could have been Soviet aircraft, deliberately intruding into U.S. airspace to test the defensive response; mysterious glowing objects in the night sky that were reflexively dismissed as weather balloons or weather or nothing at all could in some cases have been experimental aircraft or rockets or aerial explosions. Crash sites were sealed off by armed soldiers—even when the objects being recovered were as seemingly innocuous as plastic crash dummies. Innocent civilians were harassed when they asked the wrong questions or saw what they weren't supposed to; military careers were damaged or destroyed by a reluctance to hew to the official line. After Vietnam and Watergate, the public intuited that it was being lied to about a host of national security issues that went far beyond flying discs. Paradoxically, that skepticism fostered an unhealthy gullibility in some, a compensatory proclivity to believe even the most outrageous claims.

Which brings us to alien abductions. In September 1961, Barney and Betty Hill, a New Hampshire couple, contacted the Air Force to report a flying saucer sighting. A few years

---

*The word "meme" was coined by the evolutionary biologist Richard Dawkins to describe a unit of cultural information—or just as often, misinformation—that propagates itself and spreads from mind to mind, much as a virus infects bodies.

later, still obsessed by their experience and tormented by nightmares, they sought help from Dr. Benjamin Simon, a Boston psychiatrist. Under hypnosis, they recalled a much more harrowing ordeal than anything that they'd previously talked about, in which they were taken on board a flying saucer and subjected to intrusive medical procedures. Some time after that, their story found its way into the newspapers and then it became the subject of John Fuller's bestselling book, *The Interrupted Journey* (1966). A highly memorable television movie was aired in 1975, starring James Earl Jones and Estelle Parsons as the Hills and Barnard Hughes as their psychiatrist. It would be ironic if the movie provided a template for future abduction scenarios, because there is reason to suspect that the Hills might have confabulated their own recollections with an episode of *The Outer Limits* that they'd seen on TV, shortly before they began their sessions with Dr. Simon. It's worth mentioning that Dr. Simon never believed that the stories the Hills told him under hypnosis recounted real events, although he was satisfied that their therapy had helped them. Another well-known abductee is Betty Andreasson, who was taken with her daughter in 1967 while her six other children and her parents were immobilized in a trance. Under hypnosis, Andreasson revealed that she had received visitations from aliens on many other occasions; also that the aliens, who seemed to share her Christian beliefs, told her that she had been specially "chosen." Raymond E. Fowler has written several volumes about her experiences—which devote especial attention to their theological implications.

A number of books about alien abductions found their way onto the bestseller lists in the 1980s. Whitley Strieber was already a successful author of horror fiction in the mold of Stephen King when he wrote *Communion: A True Story* (1988), a memoir about the terrifying encounters he claimed to have been having with otherworldly entities for most of his life. Interestingly, Strieber had cowritten a novel a few years earlier, *Warday*, in which he cast himself and his family as characters who were struggling to survive the aftermath of a limited nuclear war. As he wrote the book, he told *People* magazine, the boundaries between himself and his fictional avatar began to dissolve. He lost weight and got migraine headaches—symptoms of the radiation sickness that his fictional counterpart was suffering from. "Sometimes," he confessed,

> I'd get to the point where I couldn't believe the war wouldn't start the next second. . . . I cried after every interview I wrote. To me these were real people, talking to me, telling me about that dark wind blowing from the future.

It almost makes one wonder if *Communion* didn't begin its life as a novel as well.

Though Strieber has reaped a fortune from *Communion* (which was made into a movie starring Christopher Walken) and its sequels, he seems disarmingly sincere. He is not a political extremist or a patent charlatan; nor, for all his seemingly paranoid obsessions about mysterious "others" meddling with his mind and body, is he obviously mentally ill. There has been speculation that he suffers from temporal lobe epilepsy (which could account for his lifelong hallucinatory experiences, if that is in fact what they are); the *People* magazine interview above suggests that he sometimes has difficulty distinguishing between products of his imagination and the real world—indeed, that his creative method depends in part upon his ability to sustain that confusion. Plus, he was treated under hypnosis by the artist and UFO abduction therapist Budd Hopkins, who became a celebrity himself by sharing the stories his patients told him about their abductions in his own bestselling books, which include *Intruders* (1987) and *Missing Time* (1988).

Psychiatrists warn that witness testimony elicited under hypnosis is highly suspect, because the patients are so suggestible; worse, unless they are given specific posthypnotic suggestions, they will recall anything that they talked about while in a trance state—even fantasies—as real memories. Overeager, incompetent, or unscrupulous therapists are as likely to "plant" memories as "awaken" them. In the mid-1970s, a Canadian psychiatrist named Lawrence Pazder began to hypnotize a woman named Michelle Smith, whom he would eventually marry. The two went on to cowrite a book, *Michelle Remembers* (1980), about her horrific childhood memories of torture and ritual sexual abuse at the hands of Satan worshippers (her mother among them) that emerged in the course of their sessions. Partly because of the publicity their book received, a number of "recovered memory" cases—in which adults brought charges against their parents for the sexual abuse that was allegedly inflicted upon them as children, or in which social workers elicited damning testimony from children about the horrors that went on in their classrooms and day care centers—were brought to trial.

Pazder would be a consultant to the prosecution at the McMartin preschool trial, in which the owners and teachers of a Manhattan Beach, California, preschool were charged with abusing some 360 children. After seven years of accusations and investigations (primarily interviews with young children—for all the brutality of the acts the defendants were accused of, there was minimal physical and medical evidence) and a three-year-long jury trial, none of the defendants, some of whom had spent years in jail, were convicted. Though the juvenile witnesses in the McMartin trial were not subjected to hypnosis, they had been blatantly led by their questioners. Some of the stories they told—about secret tunnels, mutilated animals, being flushed down toilets, seeing babies sacrificed, and being buried alive in coffins—were as bizarre and unverifiable as any of the testimony presented at the Salem witch trials, four centuries before.

From Budd Hopkins's own accounts of the sessions he

conducts it's clear that he leads his hypnotized patients so egregiously that, were he in a courtroom, the opposing attorney would leap up to object after virtually every exchange. Most of the people who come to Hopkins for help are profoundly unhappy and dysfunctional. Though he can't offer them a cure or even much reassurance, he goes one better: he invites them to join an elite secret society of martyrs, whose long-suffering members are key participants in an epochal event of earthshaking—indeed of cosmic—significance. Not surprisingly, most of them follow his lead.

David Jacobs, a historian at Temple University (his PhD thesis, *The UFO Controversy in America*, was published by Indiana University Press in 1975), also hypnotizes self-described abductees. In *The Threat* (1999), he concluded that at least 2 percent of the American population has been involved in abduction experiences (that's in the area of five million people). Aliens, Jacobs says, have extracted genetic material from hundreds of thousands of those unwitting victims in order to create a hybrid race that will one day take over the planet. A trained researcher and an impartial scholar, Jacobs is keenly aware of the dangers of bias, not to mention the pitfalls of testimony elicited under hypnosis. "At present there are quite a few therapists who work with abductees, but many of them are heavily influenced by New Age and aliens-as-Space-Brother ideas," he cautions, in his characteristically poker-faced prose. "Unfortunately, they can transfer their particular agenda to abductees during hypnotic sessions and join together with them in mutually confirmational fantasies."

Perhaps Jacobs was thinking of John Mack (1929–2004), the Harvard psychiatrist and Pulitzer Prize–winning biographer of T. E. Lawrence, who, starting in the early 1990s, also interviewed people who claimed to have been abducted by aliens. He presented some of his case studies in his best-selling *Abduction* (1995). Mack's conclusions were less prurient and sensational than Jacobs's or Hopkins's. A veteran of est and the Human Potential Movement, Mack openly embraced the spiritual implications of his patients' attested experiences: "The encounter phenomenon opens people to an awareness of Self, with a capital S, that goes way beyond any kind of ethno-national identification, to a much larger sense of being a child of the Divine, or a child of Spirit, a child of the Cosmos," he wrote. "When you open Self to a connection beyond the material world, beyond the Earth to a larger fir-mament, this opens people to the sacred. It opens people to a sense of the divine, of being one with all-that-is, what people used to call God."

No less prominent an intellectual and cultural figure than Carl Jung (1875–1961) was intrigued by the religious dimen-sion of UFOs as well. In his book *Flying Saucers: A Modern Myth of Things Seen in the Sky* (1958), he noted the "cultic" behavior of many flying saucer enthusiasts, which he sus-pected was "a spontaneous reaction of the subconscious to fear of the apparently insoluble political situation in the world that may lead at any moment to catastrophe. At such times eyes turn heavenward in search of help, and miracu-lous forebodings of a threatening or consoling nature appear from on high." Nearly every flying saucer book ever pub-lished includes at least one reference to Ezekiel's chariot—at once an abiding symbol for mystics and an intriguing ur–Close Encounter of the Third Kind (UFO researcher J. Allen Hynek's famous phrase denotes a sighting not just of a UFO but of its pilots or passengers). Nowadays, visionaries are as likely to be visited by aliens as angels. Or perhaps, as I am far from the first to have suggested, they are simply different names for the same entities.

Around the time that Jung was writing his book, the Aetherius Society was just getting off the ground. Founded by George King (1919–1997) in London after he was con-tacted by an extraterrestrial representative of an Interplan-etary Parliament, its members seek to rebalance the world, both through yoga and the application of otherworldly wisdom received from Cosmic Masters. Then there is the Universal Industrial Church of the New Comforter. Its founder, Allen-Michael Noonan, was painting a billboard in California in 1947 when he was transported onto a galactic mothership, where a voice told him "he was chosen to be the messenger who would fulfill the role of being the New World Comforter and channel of the prophesied Everlasting Gospel."

Gloria Lee was an ex–flight attendant married to an airplane designer when she too became a contactee in the early 1950s, receiving psychic messages from J. W., an entity from Jupiter. Lee was a student of **Oahspe**, the "New Bible" that was channeled by a dentist and spiritualist named John Ballou Newbrough in 1880; the foundational text of "Faithism," it covers Biblical ground and much more—it includes esoterica about the pyramids, the American Indians (its name is said to mean "Earth-Wind-Sky" in an American Indian language), and ancient China. It also features a number of apocalyptic prophecies and visions, including one in which angelic beings launch an invasion of earth:

> Then Osire left his high place, and with his hosts, aboard the etherean ship of fire, sat out toward the earth, at break-neck speed. . . . Down he came to the earth with his fire-ship, and sped round about it, to learn its weak and salient points; and next rose up a little to view the atmospherean spirits who had presumed defiance toward high heaven.*

Lee founded the Cosmon Research Foundation and published two books that J. W. dictated to her, *Why We Are Here* (1959) and *The Changing Conditions of Your World* (1962). In 1962 she traveled to Washington, D.C., with schematics for a space station and a plan for world peace. After she delivered them to the government, she checked into a hotel and com-

---

Oahspe not only evokes some of the more visionary passages in the Bible and the Apocrypha, it also anticipates Philip Pullman's Milton-inspired, neo-Gnostic *Dark Materials* science fiction trilogy, which portrays an all-out war among angelic hosts.

menced a hunger strike, which she was determined to maintain until her proposals received an official response. Sixty-six days later, she lapsed into a coma and died. A few years later, a psychic named Nada-Yolanda would channel Gloria Lee's last book. (Technically it was her first; the other two volumes had been dictated by J. W.)

Nada-Yolanda was a principal of Mark-Age, a nonprofit spiritual and educational foundation and publisher, which was founded as a marketing concern by a research chemist and salesman named Charles Boyd Gentzel in 1949 (Mark-Age was shorthand for "marketing agents"). In 1955 Gentzel became interested in both the Unity Church (which itself combines New Thought, Theosophy, **Rosicrucianism**, and teachings from a variety of Eastern religions) and flying saucers; shortly afterward he began to write his own much-reprinted self-help book, *How to Do All Things: Your Use of Divine Power*, one of the many precursors of Rhonda Byrne's mega-bestselling *The Secret* (2006).

One could fill a whole book with examples of other religious groups who've turned their eyes heavenward only to behold UFOs (and this is as good a place as any to mention that the Nation of Islam's Louis Farrakhan has written and taught about flying saucers), but two more will suffice for now.* Wallace C. Halsey, the engineer and minister who founded Christ Brotherhood, Inc. in 1956, disappeared while piloting a light plane from Utah to Nevada. A collection of apocalyptic messages that had been channeled to him by an extraterrestrial was published posthumously as *Cosmic End Time Secrets* in 1965. The Unarius Society, founded by Ernest and Ruth Norman in 1954 and "dedicated to exploring the frontiers of science and expanding our awareness and connection with galactic intelligence," is notable for its extensive list of publications and the fanciful costumes that its members sometimes wear. After Ernest died in 1971, he

---

*Lengthier individual entries on other notable UFO cults, such as the **Raëlians**, **Heaven's Gate**, **Scientology**, and **Order of the Solar Temple**, can be found in the Cults section.

revealed himself to his wife in his true form, as an angelic being named Raphiel. Ruth Norman (who died in 1994) claimed to be an incarnation of the soul that had animated Socrates, Peter the Great, Charlemagne, Queen Elizabeth I, Queen Maria Theresa, Hatshepsut, Akbar, and Atahuallpa. For all of that, she was infinitely unassuming.

> Like Ernest Norman, her humbleness was such that she took no credit and simply stated that she was merely the secretary to Infinite Intelligence, one cog in the great wheel of the Infinite Cosmos. The higher self of Ruth Norman (Uriel) is of a vast development, a Universal Radiant Infinite Eternal Light.

Of course not all spiritualists are interested in flying saucers and not all flying saucer investigators are interested in the spirit world, but there is frequent overlap. The extra-dimensional entity SETH, who channeled books to Jane Roberts in the 1970s, occasionally commented on UFOs. Though the spiritualist Edgar Cayce died in 1945, two years before Kenneth Arnold's "flying discs," he frequently spoke of contacts between the legendary lost civilizations of Atlantis and Lemuria and aliens. Erich von Däniken's bestsellers argue that the monuments and religious beliefs of ancient civilizations provide overwhelming evidence of alien visitations. Many believers in the Ascended Masters (the Theosophist idea that a small clique of enlightened entities continues to influence events on earth, even after they have transcended their mortal forms and passed out of the cycle of reincarnation) presume that some of them came from other worlds.

Writers—New Agers and conspiracists alike—have extrapolated the handful of enigmatic Biblical references to giants (the Nephilim) into a full-blown mythology of human-alien hybrids and inter- and intraplanetary wars. The pyramids were landing beacons; Sodom and Gomorrah were destroyed by nuclear weapons. A whole subgenre of "alternative ancient Egyptology" exists, in which authors like Graham Hancock—*Fingerprints of the Gods* (1995) and *The Message of the Sphinx* (1996)—argue that technologically advanced civilizations existed in the dawn of prehistory.

A number of writers have spun elaborate theories that connect the so-called face on Mars (a two-mile-long geologic formation in the planet's Cydonia region that, because of the arrangements of shadows and the crude resolution of the photograph that was taken from Viking 1 in 1976, appears to be a gigantic anthropomorphic sculpture*) to the Great Sphinx in Egypt, and with excursuses through Egyptian mythology, Hermetic writings, Masonic lore, Theosophy, Edgar Cayce, discredited nineteenth-century theories about race, the CIA's MK-ULTRA experiments, and even the rumors of sexual abuse at day care centers, to the ancient astronauts that history remembers as Egyptian and Mesopotamian deities. These aliens, we're told, used genetics and mind control techniques to prepare a new species of human beings to serve them upon their return. In *The Stargate Conspiracy* (1999), Lynn Picknett and Clive Prince add a new twist, arguing that some of these writers are actually unwitting tools of government intelligence agencies, who plant this sort of disinformation in order to imbue humanity with an abiding sense of its vulnerability. They do this in order to soften us up for their own sinister schemes of world domination.

Some six thousand miles and an even vaster cultural gulf lie between Area 51, Roswell, New Mexico, and West Africa. And yet the Dogon people of Mali are also widely spoken of as a nexus with extraterrestrial civilizations. Every sixty years, they carry out an elaborate, seven-year-long ceremony called the *sigui* that celebrates the introduction of death to the world. Celebrants withdraw from society and speak a

---

*NASA arranged a second flyby in 1998 and a third in 2001; the likeness was not visible in any of the later pictures.

secret language among themselves. The French anthropologist Marcel Griaule had spent more than fifteen years among the Dogon in the 1930s and 1940s before tribal elders finally initiated him into their inner circle and taught him their secrets. Griaule learned that the Dogon had an uncanny knowledge of astronomy: somehow they knew about the rings of Saturn and Jupiter's four moons; most inexplicable of all, they knew that a small but extremely heavy star orbited around Sirius the Dog Star (Sirius's companion white dwarf wasn't photographed until 1970).

Though Griaule didn't explicitly suggest an extraterrestrial source for the Dogon's knowledge, Robert Temple wrote a book called *The Sirius Mystery* (1978), which connected the Dogon to the jackal-headed god Anubis of the ancient Egyptians and also to ancient space travelers (other writers speculate that Dogon shamans communed with disembodied intelligences). Meanwhile a new generation of anthropologists has sharply questioned the factual basis of many of Griaule's most spectacular assertions.

The Black Death (see **AIDS**)

Black Helicopters, Men in Black, Michigan Militia, Cattle Mutilation, and Liars' Clubs
To those who claimed to have seen or been menaced by them in the 1970s, 1980s, and 1990s, the unmarked, black-painted helicopters hovering silently over America's heartlands were the visible embodiment of the **New World Order**—incontrovertible evidence of and objective correlatives for the illegitimate, internationalist police state that many believed the United States had become. Some speculated that the mysterious aircraft were piloted by foreign troops from the United Nations, Jewish storm troopers from the Zionist Occupation Government, or perhaps federal agents from the Department of the Interior or FEMA (in those pre-Katrina days, the Federal Emergency Management Agency was believed to be so

powerful that it practically qualified as a shadow state). Others opined that they were flown by space aliens—or that the sinister-looking vehicles were sentient beings themselves, standing sentinel on a world that was too benighted to even realize that it had been conquered.

Some context first: Resentment of Washington's perceived intrusions into gun rights and the whole gamut of culture war issues—affirmative action, environmental regulations, gay rights, abortion, the ban on school prayer—had been simmering throughout the 1980s and 1990s, especially in rural areas. The election of the draft-dodging, womanizing, pot-puffing (but not inhaling) Bill Clinton ratchetted up the tension even higher; then the Bureau of Alcohol, Tobacco, and Firearms and FBI-led sieges at **Ruby Ridge** in 1992 and at the **Branch Davidian** compound in Waco, Texas, a year later, along with the passage of the Brady Handgun Violence Prevention Act in November 1993, brought things to a boil.

Modern-day Patriots and Minutemen, determined to take full advantage of their Second Amendment rights to drill and train and, if necessary, actively resist the tyranny of what they regarded as an illegitimate government, organized paramilitary groups all over the country, many of them inspired by the teachings of white supremacists. Linda Thompson, an Indianapolis lawyer and avid conspiracy theorist, appointed herself Acting Adjutant General of the Unorganized Militia of the United States and announced a march on Washington to demand the annulment of the Brady Bill and NAFTA.* Any legislators who refused to cooperate, she threatened, would be arrested and tried for treason. Though her march never got off the ground, she produced a movie called *America Under Siege*, which included footage of black helicopters

---

*One of the theories she promoted was that the four former Clinton bodyguards killed at the Waco siege had been assassinated because they knew too much about the man they used to protect—as were Vince Foster, William Colby, Ron Brown, Jim McDougal, and dozens of other former Clinton associates.

parked at Fort Campbell, Kentucky, and explained that bar codes had been printed on the backs of highway signs to guide military vehicles when martial law was declared. Mark Koernke, aka "Mark from Michigan," a former maintenance worker at the University of Michigan who had become a leader in the Michigan Militia and a national figure in the so-called patriot movement, also spoke about black helicopters and the New World Order in his speeches, radio broadcasts, and videocassettes. (Koernke's career would be interrupted by a stint in state prison; since his release in 2007 he has resumed his broadcasts on WTPRN—the "We The People Radio Network.")

Mainstream Republicans didn't hesitate to put these resentments to political use. Georgia congressman Newt Gingrich's 1994 Contract with America, with its promised "Taking Back Our Streets," "Personal Responsibility," "Family Reinforcement," and "American Dream Restoration" acts, pitted decent, regular citizens against a decadent, permanent political class. Republicans rode it to their first House majority in forty years—and Gingrich became the new Speaker of the House (only to fall from power at the height of the Clinton impeachment four years later). Some of Gingrich's new "revolutionaries"—"bomb throwers," he liked to call them—openly paid court to the extreme right, including members of the militia movement.

Militias had an especially strong presence in Montana. There was John, David, and Randy Trochman's Militia of Montana and the Montana Freemen, who in 1996 would provoke a thankfully bloodless eighty-one-day standoff with officials who were trying to arrest them for bank fraud. They refused to surrender, declaring that their complex, which they called Justus Township, was a sovereign nation, not subject to American law.

In February 1995, Priscilla Sullivan contributed a story to the Missoula, Montana, *Missoulian*, relating the grim comedy that ensued when a National Guard helicopter on a training mission flew over a tax protestor's unlicensed elk ranch. "My heart jumped in my mouth," the rancher said, describing how the helicopter's guns had swiveled in his direction. "I can't explain the fear."*

Two of the rancher's fellow militia members rushed to the town marshal's house and threatened him with retribution, prompting his terrified wife to call 911; dozens more made their way to the ranch, prepared to defend the sanctity of private property to the death. Within hours, F. Joe Holland, the national director of the North American Volunteer Militia, had issued a statement: "These government bastards . . . are operating on behalf of an agency that is nothing more than the illegitimate offspring of a prostituted political system," it declared. "Only by exposing these despotic, degenerate maggots to the general public will we be able to live in America without having the New World Order shoved down our throat."

A month later, an ultraconservative, militia-friendly freshman Republican congressman from Idaho named Helen Chenoweth (she preferred the gendered, politically incorrect title) received national attention when she decried the "unwarranted invasion of private land" by black helicopters manned by agents of the U.S. Fish and Wildlife Service, who, she claimed, were enforcing compliance with the Endangered Species Act at gunpoint. The only endangered species that could be found in Idaho, she would quip in a different context, was the "white, Anglo-Saxon male." (Chenoweth would be one of the first in Congress to call for Bill Clinton's resignation when the Monica Lewinsky controversy broke, despite revelations of her own six-year-long involvement with a married man. She died in a car accident in 2006.)

Just weeks after Helen Chenoweth's black helicopter speech, everything changed. On April 19, 1995, homegrown

---

*The helicopter's pilot later insisted that its unloaded guns had been fixed in a stationary position pointing straight ahead, as was standard operating procedure on training flights.

terrorists with ties to the militia movement, Christian Identity, and other fringe, ultra-right-wing groups detonated a truck filled with fertilizer in front of the Alfred P. Murrah Federal Building in Oklahoma City, killing 168 people, nineteen of them children. As a shocked nation absorbed the fact that the perpetrators of what was then the worst act of terrorism ever committed on American soil were Americans themselves, mainstream conservatives tamped down their antigovernment rhetoric. Paramilitary groups suddenly found themselves in disrepute.

Timothy McVeigh (1968–2001), a Gulf War veteran, gun rights activist, survivalist, and Constitutionalist, would be executed for the bombing on June 11, 2001. His coconspirator, Terry Nichols (who had been casually involved with the Michigan Militia), was sentenced to life in prison; McVeigh's friend Michael Fortier, who testified against him, received a twelve-year sentence for failing to warn authorities about the attack. Fortier has been given a new identity and released into the federal Witness Protection Program.

Conspiracists still talk and write about the New World Order, of course. Many of them insist that the Oklahoma City bombing was in fact an NWO operation, cold-bloodedly planned and cynically executed to bring discredit to the patriot movement. William Luther Pierce's (1933–2002) notorious novel *The Turner Diaries* (1978), which includes a detailed description of a plot to destroy FBI headquarters in Washington, D.C., by rigging a fertilizer bomb in a parked truck, and which purportedly influenced Timothy McVeigh, is still in print. (Pierce was the founder of a racialist "religion" called Cosmotheism and a white-separatist movement called the National Alliance.) But the zeitgeist would no longer be so welcoming to the so-called patriots; as their spokesmen retreated back to the fringes, black helicopter sightings gradually became a thing of the past.

But where had they come from in the first place? The black helicopter meme is a by-product of yet another meme, the "Men in Black," which itself dates back to the UFO hysteria of the 1950s, particularly to books and articles by the ufologist Alfred Bender. In 1953 Bender received a visit from three mysterious beings who floated a foot off the floor while they warned him not to reveal what he knew about flying saucers. "All of them were dressed in black clothes," he recalled. "They looked like clergymen, but wore hats similar to Homburg style. The faces were not clearly discernible, for the hats partly hid and shaded them." Putting aside their obvious demonic associations, Bender's Men in Black were archetypal CIA, KGB, or NWO agents—faceless, anonymous, dispassionately ruthless bureaucrats, the tools of a distant, all-powerful authority. Men in Black would appear as villains in movies like *The Matrix* and television's *The X-Files* and as campily comic heroes in the two hit *Men in Black* movies that were adapted from Lowell Cunningham's comic book series of the same name.

By the 1970s, Men in Black were often observed behind the controls of black helicopters—especially when cattle were being mutilated in the vicinity. Self-styled "alien abduction theorist" Donald Worley describes one such incident:

> Jean Cole, wife of Albertsville's chief detective, watched a helicopter at close range when it came down in her backyard. She clearly saw four business-suited occupants in it. It rapidly flew away when they noticed her presence. The following morning, detective Cole found one of his Black Angus cows minus its sex organs and rectum.

And what about those cattle mutilations? Reports of mutilated cattle had begun to circulate in the American West as early as the 1960s; by the 1970s and 1980s they had become so widespread that, at the requests of two United States senators (F. Haskell of Colorado and Harrison Schmitt of New Mexico) the FBI and the ATF launched separate investigations. The presence of the helicopters undercut one popular explanation for the mutilations, which was that the cattle were being sacrificed in satanic rituals (rumors of satanic cults that systematically abused children and engaged in human sacrifice were also rife during those troubled years). But then the helicopter meme "jumped" from the realm of UFOs and the paranormal to the paranoid political fringe (much as viruses jump from animals to human beings) and a new idea began to take hold—that the cows were the subjects of secret, government-sponsored biowarfare experiments.

Jim Keith (1949–1999), a onetime Scientologist and a prolific writer on conspiratorial subjects, energetically promoted this view in two of his books, *Black Helicopters over America: Strikeforce for the New World Order* (1995) and *Black Helicopters II: The Endgame Strategy* (1998)—both of them written as the phenomenon had already begun to wane. Keith's untimely death—the indirect result of a seemingly minor knee injury he suffered when he fell off the stage at the Burning Man festival outside Reno, Nevada, in 1999—has sparked its own share of conspiracy theories. Before he went into the hospital, Keith was said to have revealed the name of the doctor who reported that Princess Di was pregnant when she died (a rumor that is still active in the conspiracy community but which officialdom has strenuously denied). Given the House of Windsor's prominence in the New World Order, many of Keith's friends believed that he paid for his indiscretion with his life. One can only wonder what happened to the doctor, whoever he is (or was).

But to return to the murdered cows: sober statistical, forensic, and medical analysis revealed that the epidemic of "bovine excisions," as investigators sometimes referred to the mutilations, never happened. Livestock had not been dying in unusual numbers or ways. The unfortunate few that did die were the usual victims of coyotes, mountain lions, exposure, and disease; their cadavers had been ravaged by predators, carrion eaters, and the elements, not scalpels and lasers. Reports of cattle mutilations came in statistical "waves" or "flaps"—not because the incidents were so widespread (they weren't), but because the stories about them were self-propagating, each building on the one before. The only thing that was rife was rumors.

It wasn't the first time that a thought contagion had swept through the heartland. In the 1890s (like the 1990s, an era of economic uncertainty and rural populist political ferment) small-town newspapers had been filled with stories about unidentified flying objects. One of them even involved cattle mutilations. On April 23, 1897, Alexander Hamilton, a leading citizen of LeRoy, Kansas, told the *Yates Center Farmer's Advocate* that a three-hundred-foot-long airship, occupied by "six of the strangest beings I ever saw," had flown over his farm a few nights before. Before it departed, one of those beings had lassoed one of his heifers with a rope made "of some red material" and lifted it into the sky. The next morning the unfortunate creature's legs, head, and hide turned up in a field three or four miles away. The story was picked up by European newspapers; it remains one of the most famous ur–UFO sightings to this day and is frequently cited in books.

Hamilton's story was an uncanny harbinger of things to come—but not a word of it was true. Years later, the son of the editor of the *Farmer's Advocate* recalled that his father and Hamilton had "concocted that story following an afternoon powwow." In 1976, ninety-three-year-old Ethel Shaw told the UFO researcher Jerome Clark that Hamilton "and a few men round about . . . had formed a club which they called 'Ananias' (Liars' Club)." This "liars' club," though it probably doesn't rise to the level of a secret society, merits a brief digression. If nothing else, it provides an interesting element of historical texture.

In the early 1900s, Theodore Roosevelt proposed one of his political enemies for membership in the "Ananias Club"—a fancy way of calling him a liar. In those days of universal Bible literacy, most people knew that Ananias and his wife,

Sapphira, were struck dead after they tried to cheat the church out of a portion of their tithe by lying to Peter about how much money they'd made when they sold some land (Acts 5:1–11). But Roosevelt did not coin the phrase. A Saint Ananias Club was founded in Topeka, Kansas, in 1874 as a convivial society whose motto was "unadulterated truth" (to interject a note of pedantry, I should point out that Saint Ananias, who baptized Paul and died a martyr, stoned to death outside the walls of Eleutheropolis, was a totally different character than Sapphira's unfortunate husband—obviously he wouldn't have become a saint had he been reputed to be a liar). The misnamed club's incorporation papers include a waggishly alliterated roster of its founding members, which I have considerably abridged below:

> Samuel A. Kingman, perpetual president; Sam Radges, secretary, phenomenal prevaricator; Floyd P. Baker, distinguished dissimulator; C. N. Beal, efficacious equivocator; A. Bergen, libelous linguist . . . H. K. Rowley, mephistophelian munchausenist; Dr. Silas F. Sheldon, Aesculapian equivocator; Henry Strong, racy romancer; William C. Webb, august amplifier; Daniel W. Wilder, hypothetical hyperbolisy; Archibald L. Williams, paraphrastic paralogist.

Topeka, the capital city of Kansas, is about seventy-five miles from LeRoy. Hamilton, a lawyer, county official, and former state legislator, undoubtedly spent time there and would have certainly known or known of the Ananias Club's perpetual president Samuel Kingman, who was the chief justice of Kansas's Supreme Court. But Topeka's was not the only Ananias Club in the United States, and it might not have even been the first. A feature article on "Curiosities in Clubs" in the January 15, 1893, *New York Times* accorded that honor to the Ananias and Sapphira Club of Crawfordsville, Indiana, "said to be the rarest aggregation of lying sportsmen to be found anywhere."

A few last words about black helicopters. By the turn of the millennium, real bogeymen like Al Qaeda and the person or persons who were sending weaponized anthrax through the mail were scary enough for most Americans. When black helicopters are spoken of today, it is usually as a shorthand for antigovernment conspiracy theories that stretch the bounds of credulity. For example, at a press conference in October 2007, Minnesota's Republican senator Norm Coleman dismissed questions about the collapse of World Trade Center number 7 as so much "black helicopter stuff."

Cattle Mutilations (see Black Helicopters)

Princess Diana, Elvis Presley, and Other Immortal Idols

On August 31, 1997, Diana, Princess of Wales (1961–1997), was killed in a car accident in a tunnel in Paris, along with her limousine driver, Henri Paul, and her friend Emad El-Din Mohamed Abdel Moneim Fayed (1955–1997), better known as Dodi Al Fayed. An übercelebrity in her lifetime, Diana achieved a secular apotheosis during the unprecedented orgy of public grieving that followed her death. Inevitably, she also became the subject of innumerable conspiracy theories.

Seven paparazzi (photographers who stalk celebrities) were arrested at the scene of the crash; Diana's limousine had been speeding in an effort to elude them. Though no paparazzi were ever convicted of murder, the press would bear much of the initial onus for her death. "I don't think she ever understood why her genuinely good intentions were sneered at by the media, why there appeared to be a permanent quest on their behalf to bring her down. It is baffling," her brother Charles, the Ninth Earl Spencer said in his internationally broadcast eulogy. "It is a point to remember that of all the ironies about Diana, perhaps the greatest was this: a girl given the name of the ancient goddess of hunting was, in the end, the most hunted person of the modern age."

Diana's decidedly unamicable divorce from Prince Charles, the heir to the British throne, had been finalized on August 28, 1996, some four years after their contentious separation was announced and almost a year to the day before her death. Nevertheless, as the mother of Princes William and Henry, the second and third in line for the throne, she remained a member of the royal family. Had her in-laws, frustrated by the ongoing soap opera of Diana's life—and humiliated by her greater popularity—ordered her killed? Or was it Charles? As early as October 1993, Diana had given her butler a note in which she said, "My husband is planning 'an accident' in my car, brake failure and serious head injury in order to make the path clear for him to marry Tiggy" (Tiggy Legge-Bourke was the royal nanny). Perhaps the international armaments industries, recognizing the threat that her anti–land mine activism posed to their future profits, had hired assassins. Or maybe Dodi was as much a target as she was. Within days of her death, Libyan strongman Muammar Khadafy opined that "British and French secret services mounted and executed the assassination of the Princess of Wales and the Arab citizen who were planning to get married."

Dodi Al Fayed's father, the Egyptian-born billionaire Mohamed Fayed, has loudly and abrasively maintained that Diana was pregnant with Dodi's child and that the two were engaged to be married. Prince Charles and his father, Prince Philip (whom Fayed labeled a Nazi), were so threatened by the prospect of a member of the royal family giving birth to a half-Arab baby and of Princes William and Harry having an Arab stepfather, Fayed said, that they arranged to have the couple murdered by clandestine operatives from MI6. Henri Paul, the limousine driver, wasn't drunk but drugged and possibly disoriented by a strobe light (some witnesses reported seeing bright flashes in the tunnel). Proper medical treatment was deliberately withheld to guarantee Diana's demise; her body was instantly embalmed to frustrate a pregnancy test.

Hard-pressed by Fayed, Michael Burgess, coroner of the Queen's Household, asked John Arthur Stevens, Baron Stevens of Kirkwhelpington, the Metropolitan Police commissioner, to undertake a thorough reexamination of the events surrounding Diana's death. The report of the Operation Paget inquiry (a randomly generated name) was published in December of 2006. Totaling 872 pages in length and based on hundreds of original interviews, unprecedented access to French police records, and cutting-edge developments in forensic and computer technology (for example, the investigators "used the specialist skills of surveyors, photographers and computer modelers to collect data from 186 million points and reproduce the scene of the crash and surrounding area to within an accuracy of one centimeter"), the report concluded that there "was no conspiracy to murder any of the occupants of the car. This was a tragic accident."

A coroner's inquest held in London between October 2007 and April 2008 found no evidence of a conspiracy, but it did assign guilt. The jury attributed the crash to "the speed and manner of driving of the Mercedes, the speed and manner of driving of the following vehicles [the paparazzi] and the impairment of the judgment of the driver of the Mercedes through alcohol." Needless to say, neither Fayed nor the conspiracists were appeased; Fayed because of his grief and anger, the conspiracists because of their Kierkegaardian faith in their own schemas.

One theory weaves Diana's, Sonny Bono's, and John Denver's deaths into a neat package (they all died within a year of each other—Bono in a skiing accident and Denver in a light-plane crash). Despite their obvious differences (the **est**-trained Denver was a political liberal; the pop star turned congressman Sonny Bono was a **Scientologist** and a Republican), all three promoted world peace. David Icke traces the connections between the Diana-worshipping, symbol-obsessed Merovingians and the circumstances of Princess Di's death in a tunnel, concluding that she was ritually sacrificed in a makeshift underground temple. Conspiracy theorist Brian Desborough points out that her limo didn't crash into just any pillar in that tunnel, but the thirteenth one.

> While I concur that the death of Diana was engineered by the satanic thirteen interrelated family bloodlines collectively known as the **Illuminati** and that the thirteenth pillar was deliberately selected . . . this goal could have been accomplished by means of another highly specialized, yet little known weapon.

You don't have to be certifiably insane to prefer Diana's death to have been more meaningful than it was—or to wish that it never happened. Diana was beloved as "the people's princess" because she shared her vulnerabilities with her public—her struggles with bulimia and depression; her fear and loathing of her cold, judgmental in-laws; her grief at her husband's adulteries; her awkward attempts to find consolation in the arms of handsome soldiers. Her fans simultaneously held her in awe and identified with her. Wishful rumors that Diana and Dodi had faked their deaths and were living together in happy anonymity persisted for quite some time.

It wasn't the first time a pop culture figure had been posthumously resurrected. A suspicious three-day news blackout followed rock star Jim Morrison's (1943–1971) death; there was no autopsy, his coffin was closed, and his grave, which remained unmarked for months, was said to be suspiciously small. Rumors persisted for decades that he hadn't really died—or alternatively, that his death was the result of his occult practices or his supposed connections to clandestine services (his father was a naval admiral). Tupac Shakur (1971–1996) fan Web sites have long promoted the rumor that the murdered rapper faked his death. Much of the evidence is gematrical. For example, his last album, *The*

7 *Day Theory*, was released under the name Makaveli (an anagram for "Am Alive"); he was shot on September 7 and died at 4:03 p.m. (4 + 3 = 7).

If Diana was popularly beatified, Elvis Presley (1935–1977) has been implicitly deified. Americans of a certain demographic felt much the same way about his death as the British did about Diana's. Particularly hard to accept was the sordid manner in which he died (his body was found in his bathroom—though the official cause of death was heart arrhythmia, drug abuse was a likely contributing factor). Rumors of posthumous Elvis sightings have abounded for years, while Professional Elvis impersonators sustain the illusion that he lives on to this day. Though most of the "cults" that identify Elvis with Jesus (the Presleyite Disciples, for example) are satirical, the joke does not come out of left field. As the culture critic Greil Marcus wrote, "The identification of Elvis with Jesus has been a secret theme of the Elvis story at least since 1956."

In 1992, five years before Diana's death, Camille Paglia presciently wrote about her in *The New Republic*.

> Deification has its costs. The modern mega-celebrity, bearing the burden of collective symbolism, projection, and fantasy, is a ritual victim, cannibalized by our pity and fear. . . . Mass media have made both myth and disaster out of Diana's story. We have created her in our own image. And pursued by our best wishes, Diana the huntress is now the hind paralyzed in the world's gun sight.

The Face on Mars

A geologic formation on Mars that was photographed by Viking 1 in 1976 that, because of the serendipitous pattern of shadows and the coarse quality of the image, appears to be a gigantic sculpture of a face. A number of authors—most notably Richard C. Hoagland, a former consultant on NASA matters to television news programs and the author of *The Monuments of Mars* (1987)—have argued that it provides proof positive of an ancient Martian civilization—something that NASA and the scientific community have conspired to deny. (See also **Area 51**.)

The Jekyll Island Group and the Federal Reserve

For those who regard the gold standard as a bulwark of freedom and the Federal Reserve system as the deliberate author of depressions, recessions, and ruinous inflation, "a cartel operating against the public interest," and "the supreme instrument of usury"—to borrow a few choice phrases from G. Edward Griffin, author of *The Creature from Jekyll Island: A Second Look at the Federal Reserve* (1994)—"Jekyll Island, Georgia" carries the same sinister connotations that place-names like "Munich" came to have in the run-up to World War II and that "Yalta" did in the McCarthy era.

Just off the coast of Georgia, about ninety miles south of Savannah, Jekyll Island was owned by "the richest, the most exclusive, the most inaccessible club in the world," wrote *Munsey's Magazine* in 1904. The Jekyll Island Club's membership roster included J. P. Morgan (1837–1913), William Rockefeller (1841–1922), Vincent Astor (1891–1959), Joseph Pulitzer (1847–1911), and William K. Vanderbilt (1849–1920), as well as heirs of the Macy, Goodyear, and Gould family fortunes. And it was at Jekyll Island, in November of 1910, that seven of the richest, most influential men in the United States met secretly to frame the legislation that created the Federal Reserve. The legendary financial writer and publisher Bertie Charles Forbes memorably described the meeting in his book *Men Who Are Making America* (1917):

> Picture a party of the nation's greatest bankers stealing out of New York on a private railroad car, hieing hundreds of miles south to an island deserted by all but a few servants,

and living there a full week under such rigid secrecy that the name of not one of them was once mentioned lest the servitors learn their identity and disclose to the world this historic episode in American finance.

Organized by Rhode Island's powerful senator Nelson Aldrich (1841–1915)—the grandfather of David and Nelson Rockefeller—whose Aldrich Commission had been tasked with reforming the nation's currency and banking system after the Panic of 1907 nearly bankrupted the nation, the meeting included Frank Vanderlip (1864–1937), president of the Rockefeller-controlled National City Bank of New York; Abram Piatt Andrew (1873–1936), assistant secretary of the U.S. Treasury; Paul M. Warburg (1868–1932), of Kuhn, Loeb; Henry P. Davison (1867–1922) and Benjamin Strong (1872–1928), of J. P. Morgan; and Charles D. Norton (1870–1923), president of the First National Bank. Aldrich, Forbes relates, told his distinguished guests that he would keep them in Georgia, "cut off from the rest of the world," until they "evolved and compiled a scientific currency system for the United States, a system model that would embody all that was best in Europe."

Three years later, in 1913, the same year that the Sixteenth Amendment was ratified, removing the last legal impediments to a federal income tax, the Federal Reserve Act won passage through Congress. A quasi-public set of regional banks (a considerably less centralized and less private system than what Aldrich's commission had originally proposed), the Federal Reserve was "to furnish an elastic currency, to afford means of rediscounting commercial paper, to establish a more effective supervision of banking in the United States," and, in general, to provide banking services to the U.S. government, while providing the nation with a safer, more stable financial system.

That, as they say, is the official version. To the conspiracy-minded, it was a case of the foxes assuming charge of the henhouse. With the passage of the Federal Reserve Act, Aldrich and his coconspirators (among the wealthiest men in the world, some of them Jewish, with ties to the Rothschild family and other foreign interests) had seized control of the American economy. The private plutocracy that they designed uses its power to print money to create a bottomless money pit of national debt, which in turn produces a steady stream of interest payments that flows into its own pockets. The federal income tax provided the government with the means of meeting all that debt service—by picking the pockets of its hardworking citizens.

Did the Fed fend off panics and recessions as it was meant to? There are a variety of possible answers to that question, but for some the answer is an unambiguous no. Citing its supposedly unbroken record of failure, congressman and 2008 presidential candidate Ron Paul introduced legislation in 2002 to abolish the Fed and restore the gold standard.

> From the Great Depression, to the stagflation of the seventies, to the burst of the dot-com bubble last year, every economic downturn suffered by the country over the last eighty years can be traced to Federal Reserve policy. The Fed has followed a consistent policy of flooding the economy with easy money, leading to a misallocation of resources and an artificial "boom" followed by a recession or depression when the Fed-created bubble bursts.

To the conspiracy-minded, the Fed's failures are the results not of procedures and policies that can be fine-tuned and amended, reformed and refined, but are rather the fruits of the illicit and illegal scheme that was hatched at Jekyll Island one hundred years ago, a plot to vitiate and eventually destroy the nation. It's all "part of the plan. Just waste, get rid of money, get rid of productive power to reduce our standard of living," writes G. Edward Griffin.

A strong nation is not a candidate to surrender its sovereignty but a weak nation is. If America can be brought to her knees where she is struggling for survival, if people are hungry, if we have riots in our streets, then Americans could possibly be grateful for any assistance we could get from the UN. Those wonderful blue-helmeted peace-keeping forces could bring order back to our streets or international money, a new world money with purchasing power again might be welcomed by the unthinking, unknowing American public. That is what we're dealing with.

The Kennedy Assassinations

The assassination of John F. Kennedy is a watershed event in recent American history—a generational touchstone and trauma, like the destruction of the battleship USS *Maine* in Havana harbor in 1898, the attack on Pearl Harbor on December 7, 1941, or the events of September 11, 2001 (except that, unlike any of those analogous catastrophes, Kennedy's killing did not provide the country with a casus belli—which perhaps accounts for the lasting wound it left in the body politic, for its stubborn refusal to heal). Viewed retrospectively, November 22, 1963, marks the line of demarcation between Henry Luce's triumphalist American Century and the painful present period of perceived American decline, between the Manichaean certainties of the Cold War and the national crisis of confidence born of Vietnam, Watergate, and the unfinished revolution in civil rights.

Armies of investigators—official and unofficial, professional and amateur, crackerjack and cracked-brained—have put everyone and everything remotely connected to the assassination under a microscope in the intervening four-plus decades. Every cubic centimeter of Dallas, Texas's Dealey Plaza—the grassy knoll, the triple underpass, the wooden fence—has been gone over with a fine-tooth comb, and seemingly everyone who turned out to watch the presidential motorcade that fateful day has been interviewed. 544 Camp Street, the New Orleans address that Lee Harvey Oswald (1939–1963) stamped on the FAIR PLAY FOR CUBA leaflets he was seen distributing on August 9, 1963, and 531 Lafayette Street (a different street address but the same building, just a different entrance), where the hard-drinking, virulently anti-communist white supremacist Guy Banister (1900–1964)—a retired FBI agent and fired New Orleans cop turned private investigator—rented his office, is now a prominent landmark in the dreamscape of the collective American unconscious.

Almost immediately after he was inaugurated, President Lyndon Baines Johnson (1908–1973) convened the Warren Commission and charged it to "evaluate all the facts and circumstances surrounding the assassination and the subsequent killing of the alleged assassin." Its members were Supreme Court chief justice Earl Warren (1891–1974); U.S. senators Richard B. Russell (1897–1971) and John Sherman Cooper (1901–1991), respectively a Democrat from Georgia and a Kentucky Republican; U.S. representatives Hale Boggs (1914–1972), a Democrat from Louisiana, and Gerald R. Ford (1913–2006), the Michigan Republican who would become the country's fortieth vice president and thirty-eighth president without being elected to either office a decade later. Also appointed were CIA director Allen Dulles (1893–1969) and the establishment figure and all-around Washington "wise man" John J. McCloy (1895–1989), an ex–war secretary and presidential adviser who'd held high positions at the World Bank, the Chase Manhattan Bank, the **Council on Foreign Relations**, the Ford Foundation, and the Rockefeller Foundation—associations that would be certain to raise the eyebrows of any number of conspiracists. The Warren Commission submitted its final report to the president just ten months later, on September 24, 1964. In it, they confidently declared that they had found "no evidence that either Lee Harvey Oswald or Jack Ruby (1911–1967) was part of any conspiracy, domestic or foreign, to assassinate President Kennedy."

Although Oswald—an ex-Marine who had made an abortive attempt to defect to the USSR, only to return to the U.S. with a Russian wife, and who was known to have at least tangential associations with pro-Castro groups—was not unknown to the FBI and the CIA, "all of the evidence before the Commission established that there was nothing to support the speculation that Oswald was an agent, employee, or informant of the FBI, the CIA, or any other governmental agency." Oswald was the proverbial "lone nut." His killer, a Dallas strip club owner whose gangland associations connected him at least by inference to individuals and organizations that had numerous motives and means to kill the president—Cuban anti-Castro insurgents who felt abandoned after the Bay of Pigs disaster; mafiosi with Cuban investments of their own who resented Attorney General Robert Kennedy's (1925–1968) active prosecutions (or who expected to receive favors after providing tactical assistance to the CIA)—was not the most stable of individuals at his best; mounting financial troubles and a self-prescribed regimen of diet pills had pushed him into psychosis. Ruby didn't "silence" Oswald at the behest of a third party. He can be taken at his word, the commission concluded, when he said that he killed Oswald to "redeem" the city of Dallas, to show the world that "Jews have guts," and to spare Jacqueline Kennedy the ordeal of having to sit through her husband's murderer's trial.

The Warren Commission left some—but not much—wiggle room. "Because of the difficulty of proving negatives to a certainty the possibility of others being involved with either Oswald or Ruby cannot be established categorically," it averred. "But if there is any such evidence it has been beyond the reach of all the investigative agencies and resources of the United States and has not come to the attention of this Commission." Case closed.

Yet neither closure nor consensus has been achieved. According to a Fox News poll conducted in October 2003, a month before the fortieth anniversary of the assassination, 66 percent of the American public believed that Oswald was a part of a wider conspiracy; 74 percent believed there had been an official cover-up. Mark Lane's *Rush to Judgment* and Edward Jay Epstein's *Inquest*, which sharply questioned the findings of the Warren Commission, were bestsellers as early as 1966; literally hundreds of other books followed. That same year, New Orleans's grandstanding district attorney Jim Garrison (1921–1992) brought charges against Clay Shaw (1913–1974), a decorated military veteran and prominent New Orleans businessman, and unsuccessfully prosecuted him for his alleged involvement in a right-wing conspiracy to assassinate Kennedy. Oliver Stone's epic movie *JFK* (1991) recounts a sensationalized, highly tendentious account of the Shaw prosecution while also incorporating any number of other conspiracy theories. Its gist was that America's secret ruling class, the hidden powers that lurk behind our political institutions, killed Kennedy when they realized that he was prepared to cut short America's military adventure in Vietnam, which would have cost them uncounted billions in war profits.

One month and three weeks before Saigon fell to the Communists, on March 6, 1975, ABC TV broadcast the Zapruder film—the 26.6-second home movie that provided the most complete visual record available of the shooting. It was the first time the American public had had the chance to see it in its entirety, and it seemed to support the contention that one of the bullets that struck the president had been fired from a different direction than the Texas School Book Depository. Shortly afterward, the House Select Committee on Assassinations was convened.

In the dozen years since the Warren Commission, the country had changed irrevocably. JFK's brother Robert and the civil rights leader Martin Luther King (1929–1968) had both been assassinated; President Richard Nixon (1913–1994) had resigned from office in disgrace; inner-city neighborhoods and Ivy League college campuses had been roiled by riots. The death of FBI founder and director J. Edgar Hoover in 1972 unleashed a flood of revelations about his unconventional personal life and his blatant political abuses; starting in 1970, investigative reporters like Christopher Pyle and Seymour Hersh began publishing stories about the illicit activities undertaken by America's clandestine services, including domestic spying, assassinations of foreign leaders, the nonconsensual use of U.S. citizens in experiments with mind-altering drugs, and more. The U.S. Senate's Ervin Committee and later the Church Committee not only confirmed these horrors, but came up with bombshell revelations of their own. Yet CIA director Allen Dulles had been a member of the Warren Commission, and J. Edgar Hoover had been one of its chief sources of information. The time was clearly ripe for a closer look at the evidence.

The House committee released its final report on March 29, 1979. While it didn't exonerate Oswald ("Lee Harvey Oswald fired three shots at President John F. Kennedy," it stated, "the second and third shots he fired struck the President. The third shot he fired killed the President") and it didn't implicate any domestic agencies or foreign governments—neither the FBI, the CIA, the Secret Service, the Soviet government, the Cuban government, anti-Castro groups, nor "the national syndicate of organized crime"—it didn't conclude that Oswald had acted alone. Far from it:

> The committee believes, on the basis of the evidence available to it, that President John F. Kennedy was probably assassinated as a result of a conspiracy. The committee is unable to identify the other gunman or the extent of the conspiracy.

But what manner of conspiracy? With the exception of Don DeLillo's *Libra* (1988), which is enormously convincing in its depiction of a rogue CIA conspiracy gone awry, most alternative explanations of the assassination seem poorly thought-out.

But *Libra* is a work of fiction. Most staples of Kennedy assassination conspiracy theory turn out not to hold much water when they're submitted to objective examination.

The evidence that Oswald, an ex-Marine marksman, both could and did fire the three shots that the Warren Commission said he did within the time frame that he is purported to have fired them is at least as convincing as the oft-cited anecdotal reports that he couldn't have "hit the broad side of a barn with a shotgun." The Warren Commission's much-maligned "magic bullet" theory (the work of the commission's junior counsel Arlen Specter, whom Pennsylvania would elect to the U.S. Senate in 1980), which contends that the same fairly intact bullet passed through JFK's neck and John Connally's shoulder, wrist, and thigh, turns out not to be far-fetched at all, when you see how bullets fired through cadavers have behaved under similar circumstances. The idea that the conspirators have been bumping off potential witnesses before they can testify (as many as seventy-seven all together, twenty-six of them in 1977 alone, according to conspiracy theorist Jim Marrs) is hard to take seriously—why would they have waited so long? More to the point, why didn't they kill Jim Marrs instead? Silencing a gadfly like him would deliver much more bang for the buck and surely would have been easier to pull off than the murder of a president. Kennedy conspiracy theories tend to posit too many participants carrying out too many plots, and they don't account for contingencies; they illogically presume an all-powerful police state that is unaccountably lax with its most dangerous enemies, and they overestimate people's ability to keep secrets.

And yet for all that, the House committee's conclusion is not unreasonable. It acknowledges that there is something fishy-seeming at the heart of the matter while at the same time accepting that the whole truth will most likely never be known. With all that we now know about the CIA's and the FBI's mendaciousness, why should we trust any evidence that they put forward in 1963—especially if they had something to hide? If Oswald *had* been one of their assets, they almost certainly would have denied it. I can imagine any number of reasons why the results of JFK's autopsy would have been suppressed or distorted or elided too, and not all of them are sinister. Kennedy was a very sick man, with an advanced case of Addison's disease, a fact that most of the public did not know at the time. Acknowledging the possibility of additional unknown shooters and one or more cover-ups (not at the highest levels, not elaborately or even competently orchestrated, and not carried out with the knowledge or connivance of the Warren Commission) is not at all the same thing as endorsing a full-blown conspiracy at the highest levels of power.

In 1993, Gerald Posner published the wishfully titled book *Case Closed*, which attempted to put the myriads of conspiracy theories about the assassination definitively to rest. It didn't. Fourteen years later, in 2007, ex–LA County deputy district attorney Vincent Bugliosi (who wrote *Helter Skelter* in 1974, a bestselling account of his prosecution of **Charles Manson**, and in 2008 published *The Prosecution of George W. Bush for Murder*, a hard-hitting brief for doing just that) brought out a 1,612-page tome entitled *Reclaiming History*, which also sought to close the books on the Kennedy assassination. Bugliosi felt compelled to write his epic defense of the Warren Commission, he said, because of the breathtaking disingenuousness of its critics.

"Ninety-nine percent of the conspiracy community are not, of course, writers and authors," he writes in his introduction. "Though most of them are as kooky as a three dollar bill in their beliefs and paranoia about the assassination, it is my sense that their motivations are patriotic and that they are sincere in their misguided and uninformed conclusions." But that is not at all the case, he says, with the professional muckrakers who have kept the conspiracies in the forefront of the American mind for four and a half decades. Bugliosi is scathing in his assessments of them. Mark Lane is "unprincipled," a "fraud"; Barr McClellan's *Blood, Money & Power* (2003), which argues that LBJ masterminded the assassination, is "blasphemous and completely false"; Oliver Stone's *JFK* is "one continuous lie." "Waiting for the conspiracy theorists to tell the truth," Bugliosi says, "is a little like leaving the front-porch light on for Jimmy Hoffa"—a figure, ironically enough, who is often mentioned in connection with the assassination.

But what is it about the Kennedy assassination that makes it such an irresistible obsession for disappointed idealists and cynical charlatans alike? Why has it become a veritable ground zero for paranoid thinking? A quick example: Type the words "Kennedy" and "Jews" into Google. One of the first hits I got was an exchange about Michael Collins Piper's *Final Judgment: The Missing Link in the JFK Assassination Conspiracy* (1998), which touted itself as "America's #1 banned book" (it was not banned at all, it has in fact sold through numerous editions). Collins, a talk radio host and longtime contributor to the ultra-right-wing Liberty Lobby's journal *Spotlight*, proposes that the assassination was orchestrated by Israel's prime minister David Ben-Gurion (1886–1973) after he learned that Kennedy intended to prevent Israel from obtaining nuclear weapons. Also involved were the gangster Meyer Lansky (1902–1983) and the Anti-Defamation League.

Innumerable writers have pointed out the eerie synchronicities and parallels between Lincoln and Kennedy. The following (partial) list is drawn from the comedian and avid conspiracist Richard Belzer's *UFOs, JFK, and Elvis* (1999):

• Kennedy's secretary was named Lincoln and Lincoln's was named Kennedy.

• Both presidents were elected to Congress and the presidency one hundred years apart, in years ending with the numbers 46 and 60.

• Both were shot in the head on Fridays while sitting next to their respective wives (and by assassins who were born a century apart, in years ending in the number 39).

• Both were succeeded by Southerners named Johnson (and both Johnsons' birth dates end in the number 08).

And now, if we are to believe Michael Collins Piper and Lyndon LaRouche (see **Abraham Lincoln Assassination**), we can add yet another item to this list: both were the victims of international Jewry.

Bugliosi ventures a few plausible explanations for America's seemingly bottomless appetite for improbable theories about the Kennedy assassination. We instinctively reject the disproportion between Oswald's sordid circumstances and the outsize consequences of his act, he says, because it seems impossible that a king can be struck down by a mere peasant. Most of us perceive the world through a moral frame; we look to the lives of great men and women for edification and uplift and a sense of inspiring purpose. "He didn't even have the satisfaction of being killed for civil rights," Jackie Kennedy was said to have blurted out when she was told of Oswald's arrest. "It's—it had to be some silly little Communist. It even robs his death of meaning."

David Talbot's *Brothers: The Hidden History of the Kennedy Years* (2007), describes Robert Kennedy's early efforts to uncover a conspiracy behind his brother's killing. From the very beginning he assumed it was "blowback" from one or another of their risky enterprises and associations, for which he blamed himself. Had he been elected president in 1968, Talbot says, he would have reopened the investigation.

RFK's own assassination, on June 5, 1968, has sparked its own share of conspiracy rumors. On the wilder edge, Sirhan Sirhan, the Palestinian gunman who was arrested and convicted for the murder, has been said to have been an innocent patsy, a Manchurian candidate programmed by the CIA and activated by the mysterious beautiful woman in a polka-dotted dress he was observed talking to shortly before the shooting. There are questions about Sirhan's gun. It only held eight bullets, but it left twenty-eight bullet holes in the pantry and wounded six people. Audio expert Philip van Praag and forensic scientist Robert Joling analyzed an audiotape of the shooting that was unknowingly captured by reporter Stanislaw Pruszynski. In their forthcoming book *An Open and Shut Case*, they claim to have isolated thirteen or fourteen separate shots, some of them with acoustic characteristics that suggest they came from different directions. Their conclusions have already been sharply questioned.

As Jefferson Morley wrote in the *Los Angeles Times* in 1991, the assassination of John F. Kennedy provides "a kind of national Rorschach test of the American political psyche. What Americans think about the Kennedy assassination reveals what they think about their government." Clearly, our government has much to answer for.

Martin Luther King, Jr., and Malcolm X Assassinations

On April 3, 1968, Martin Luther King, Jr. (1929–1968)—a recipient of the Nobel Peace Prize, the unquestioned moral leader of the American civil rights movement, an increasingly vociferous opponent of the Vietnam War, and a tireless crusader for economic justice—delivered a speech at the world headquarters of the Church of God in Christ in Memphis, Tennessee, where he had come to support the city's striking black sanitation workers, members of Local 1733 of the American Federation of State, County and Municipal Employees (AFSCME). At the closing of his speech, he mentioned the bomb threat that had delayed his flight from Atlanta to Memphis.

And then I got to Memphis. And some began to . . . talk about the threats that were out. What would happen to me from some of our sick white brothers? Well, I don't know what will happen now. We've got some difficult days ahead.

But it doesn't matter with me now. Because I've been to the mountaintop. And I don't mind. Like anybody, I would like to live a long life. Longevity has its place. But I'm not concerned about that now. I just want to do God's will. And He's allowed me to go up to the mountain. And I've looked over. And I've seen the promised land. I may not get there with you. But I want you to know tonight, that we, as a people, will get to the promised land. And I'm happy, tonight. I'm not worried about anything. I'm not fearing any man. Mine eyes have seen the glory of the coming of the Lord.

The next afternoon, at 6:01 p.m., Martin Luther King was shot and killed by a slug from a high-powered rifle while he was standing on the balcony of his room at the Lorraine Motel. Two months later James Earl Ray (1928–1998)—a lifelong felon who had escaped from Missouri state prison a year before—was arrested for the murder at Heathrow Airport in London and extradited to Tennessee.

Though Ray would plead guilty in return for a ninety-nine-year sentence, he would not serve his time in silence. Almost immediately he recanted his confession, tried to change his guilty plea, and began petitioning for a trial. In 1977, he escaped from prison and led authorities on a three-day manhunt. In his petitions for a new trial and his conversations with reporters, he spoke about a figure known to him only as "Raoul," who had recruited him as a smuggler when he was a fugitive in Canada and who later paid him to acquire (but not to fire) the rifle that killed King. That rifle, with Ray's incriminating fingerprints on it, had been wrapped in a blanket along with a radio labeled with his prison serial number and left on a Memphis sidewalk. Was Ray that stupid, or was someone setting him up? Then there was the question of how he had managed the logistics of his escape to Europe, and where he had gotten the money to finance his extensive travels before and after the shooting. Granted, he had managed to cross the Canadian border after he escaped from prison in 1967, but he'd hardly been the priority for law enforcement then that he was after the assassination.

J. Edgar Hoover and Martin Luther King were bitter enemies; many of King's former intimates took it for granted that the FBI had participated in his murder. "I have always believed that the government was part of a conspiracy, either directly or indirectly, to assassinate him," Jesse Jackson declared.

"You have to remember," Andrew Young explained, that "this was a time when the politics of assassination was acceptable in this country." He went on:

> It was during the period just before Allende's murder. I think it's naïve to assume these institutions were not capable of doing the same thing at home or to say each of these deaths (King and the two Kennedys) was an isolated incident by "a single assassin." It was government policy.

Suspicions were already festering about the assassination of King's rival, Malcolm X (1925–1965). Three men, Talmadge Hayer, Norman 3X Butler, and Thomas 15X Johnson, were arrested and convicted for the crime, but only Hayer confessed—and he insisted that his alleged accomplices were innocent. FBI documents indicate that undercover agents from both its own COINTELPRO (Counter Intelligence Program) and the NYPD's secret BOSS (Bureau of Special Services) squad had been infiltrated into the Nation of Islam and Malcolm X's own breakaway Organization of Afro-American Unity; some were present in the Audubon Ballroom in New York City on February 21, 1965, when the assassination took place. If they weren't involved in Malcolm X's assassination, they clearly did a poor job of protecting him.

Many believe that the assassination was planned at high levels in the Nation of Islam. After Malcolm X had publically criticized Elijah Muhammad and broken with his movement, Minister Louis Farrakhan, director of the Nation of Islam's Harlem mosque, had written angrily in *Muhammad Speaks* that "the die is set, and Malcolm shall not escape . . . such a man as Malcolm is worthy of death." Though Farrakhan has assiduously denied any overt involvement in the assassination, in May 2000, on CBS's *60 Minutes*, he apologized to Malcolm X's daughter Atallah Shabazz for his inflammatory rhetoric. "I may have been complicit in words that I spoke leading up to 21 February," he said. "I acknowledge and regret that any word that I have said caused the loss of life of a human being."

The House Select Committee on Assassinations would consider the Martin Luther King, Jr., case at great length. Though its 1979 report exonerated the U.S. government, it nonetheless declared that "the committee believes, on the basis of the circumstantial evidence available to it, that there is a likelihood that James Earl Ray assassinated Dr. Martin Luther King, Jr., as a result of a conspiracy." Ray and his brothers, the committee's investigators suspected, had been motivated by the fifty-thousand-dollar bounty that a group of Saint Louis–based white supremacists had placed on King's head, and had probably received material assistance from them.

Assisted by the musician, conspiracy theorist, and tax protestor Frederick Tupper Saussy III (1936–2007), Ray produced an autobiography, *Tennessee Waltz: The Making of a Political Prisoner* (1987), which was expanded and rereleased five years later as *Who Killed Martin Luther King Jr.? The True Story by the Alleged Assassin*. In 1997, Ray gained a powerful ally in the King family. Martin Luther King's son Dexter met with Ray in prison and asked him if he had killed his father. When Ray replied that he hadn't, King said, "I believe you, and my family believes you, and we will do everything in our power to see you prevail."

Ray's lawyer William Pepper, author of *Orders to Kill: The Truth Behind the Murder of Martin Luther King* (1995), would bring a civil suit on behalf of the King family against Loyd

Jowers, the owner of Jim's Grill, a restaurant on the ground floor of the rooming house from which Ray had allegedly fired the fatal shot. Jowers claimed to have been offered a hundred thousand dollars to participate in the assassination. His coconspirators, he said, included high-ranking figures in the government (such as President Lyndon Johnson), the military, and the **Mafia**. The real shooter, he claimed, was a police officer. A Memphis jury awarded the King family the symbolic sum of one hundred dollars, but after its own investigation, the Justice Department decided not to bring criminal charges. "Questions and speculation may always surround the assassination of Dr. King and other national tragedies," the report it issued in June 2000 concluded. But:

> Our investigation of these most recent allegations, as well as several exhaustive previous official investigations, found no reliable evidence that Dr. King was killed by conspirators who framed James Earl Ray. Nor have any of the conspiracy theories advanced in the last 30 years . . . survived critical examination.

Jowers died in 2000. On April 5, 2002, the *New York Times* reported that the Reverend Ronald Denton Wilson had issued a statement that his father, Henry Clay Wilson, had led a conspiracy to kill Martin Luther King.

> "My father was the main guy," said Mr. Wilson, 61, of Keystone Heights, north of Gainesville. "It wasn't a racist thing. He thought Martin Luther King was connected with communism, and he wanted to get him out of the way."
>
> Mr. Wilson produced no evidence to support his claim.

John Lennon Assassination

Ex-Beatle John Lennon (1940–1980) was in midcomeback on December 8, 1980. His new album *Double Fantasy* was climbing the charts and he had just finished laying down guitar tracks for his wife Yoko Ono's forthcoming *Walking on Thin Ice*. At 10:50 p.m., as the couple emerged from their limousine outside their home at the Dakota apartment building on Central Park West, twenty-five-year-old Mark David Chapman fired five shots at Lennon with a Charter Arms .38 pistol. Four of them hit their mark. While Lennon bled to death in the lobby, Chapman calmly read his copy of *The Catcher in the Rye*. In the statement he gave to the police after his arrest he said, "I'm sure the large part of me is Holden Caulfield. . . . The small part of me must be the Devil."

A born-again Christian and a heavy drug user, Chapman had been hospitalized for mental illness after a suicide attempt in 1977. In the months leading up to the assassination, he had been on a downward spiral, fighting with his coworkers and family, traveling impulsively, conceiving obsessions, and conversing with the "little people" in his head. Though his lawyers initially entered a "not guilty by reason of insanity" plea on his behalf, Chapman changed his mind and pleaded guilty to second-degree murder. Sentenced to twenty years to life, he has been denied parole five times, most recently as of this writing on August 12, 2008.

At the height of the Vietnam War protests, between 1971 and 1972, the FBI had kept Lennon under constant surveillance and harassed him relentlessly. A wrenching generational trauma, the death of a Beatle—especially a Beatle that members of the government had vilified as a dangerous extremist—naturally inspired a number of conspiracy theories. Beatles fans were already susceptible to conspiratorial thinking, having lived through the "Paul is dead" hoax (if there even was a hoax and it was not simply a series of coincidences) in 1969, when Russell Gibb, a Detroit disc jockey and concert impresario, publicized rumors, based on clues embedded in Beatles songs and album covers, that Paul McCartney had been killed in a car accident in 1966 and replaced by a look-alike.

Writers, some of them clearly unhinged, have attempted to implicate everyone from Richard Nixon and George H. W. Bush to Paul McCartney and Stephen King in John Lennon's death. The English barrister and journalist Fenton Bresler's *The Murder of John Lennon* (1989) argued that Chapman was a Manchurian candidate, "a human gun used and controlled by others to destroy a uniquely powerful radical figure who was likely to prove a rallying point for mass opposition to the policies soon to be implemented . . . by the new United States government headed by Ronald Reagan."

Mae Brussell (1922–1988), the daughter of "the Rabbi to the Stars" Edgar Magnin (1890–1984) and the great-granddaughter of Mary Ann and Isaac Magnin of I. Magnin clothing stores fame, was a tireless conspiracy theorist who focused on the activities of unregenerate émigré Nazis operating within the U.S. government. John Lennon, interestingly, subsidized the issue of *The Realist* that published her theories on Watergate in 1972. "Listen," Lennon reportedly said to its publisher Paul Krassner at the time. "If anything happens to Yoko and me, it was not an accident." Shortly after Lennon was killed, Brussell was interviewed by her fellow conspiracy theorist Tom Davis. "The federal government has maintained active programs to eliminate rock musicians and disrupt rock concerts," she told him.

> After the murders of Tim Buckley, Jim Croce, and Mama Cass Elliott, more information surfaced about earlier mysterious deaths of Jimi Hendrix, Jim Morrison, and Janis Joplin. . . . The murder of John Lennon is the tragic finale to an entire era, the reminder that once an artist becomes as popular and as political as he was, his enemies will be waiting to make sure his messages never appear again to awaken the slumbering youth.

Abraham Lincoln Assassination

There is no question that John Wilkes Booth (1838–1865), the popular actor who shot and killed Abraham Lincoln, did not act alone. While Booth dispatched Lincoln in his box at Ford's Theatre with his single-shot Derringer, his confederates (whom he had originally recruited to help him kidnap Lincoln and hold him hostage in Richmond, Virginia—a plot that was frustrated by unexpected changes in the president's traveling plans and then abandoned after Lee's surrender) were supposed to have been killing Vice President Andrew Johnson (1808–1875) and Secretary of State William Henry Seward (1801–1872), effectively decapitating the federal government and throwing the Union into such chaos that the Confederacy could resurrect itself. Vice President Johnson escaped unscathed because his assigned assassin, George Atzerodt (1835–1865), whose character witnesses defended him at his trial as "a notorious coward" and "a man remarkable for his cowardice," got drunk. Seward, however, was stabbed and seriously wounded by the ex-Mosby's Ranger Lewis Powell (1844–1865). Powell and Atzerodt were both captured and hung, along with David E. Herold (1842–1865) and Mary Surratt (1823–1865)—the first woman to be executed by the federal government. Surratt had owned the boardinghouse where the conspirators met and was the mother of John Surratt (1844–1916), a Confederate secret agent who would be arrested in Alexandria, Egypt, in 1866 and tried but not convicted for his own role in the conspiracy. Michael O'Laughlen (1840–1867), Samuel Arnold (1834–1906), and Dr. Samuel A. Mudd (1833–1883) were also tried and convicted as conspirators, as was Edman Spangler (1825–1875), a carpenter at Ford's Theatre who held Booth's horse in an alley while he did the dreadful deed.

But did the conspiracy begin and end with Booth and his collaborators? Or was the more-than-a-little unhinged actor the tool of greater forces? There is considerable reason to believe that Booth's celebrity had opened doors for him within the secessionist leadership. It is possible that his grandiose plan to kidnap (if not to assassinate) the president was masterminded by the Confederacy's clandestine services—or maybe someone even higher up. On May 4, 1865, President Andrew Johnson issued a proclamation that read, in part, "Mr. Lincoln's Murder Planned by Leading Traitors . . . Jefferson Davis is the Head of the Assassins." Davis (1808–1889), the erstwhile president of the Confederate States of America, was duly arrested and eventually indicted for treason, but he never stood trial.

Andrew Johnson himself did not escape suspicion. Booth had left his calling card at his residence a few hours before the assassination—were the two coconspirators? The president's widow, Mary Todd Lincoln (1818–1882), clearly thought so. "As sure, as you & I live, Johnson had some hand in all this," she wrote her friend Sally Orne. In due course Johnson would be investigated and cleared by a congressional assassination committee.

Some historians have constructed a circumstantial case against Secretary of War Edwin Stanton (1814–1869). Stanton, it was said, ordered Ulysses S. Grant (1822–1885) to stay away from the fatal performance of *Our American Cousin* at Ford's Theatre. Surely Grant's military guards would have provided better security for the president than John Parker of the Metropolitan Police Force, who abandoned his post outside the Lincolns' box. Stanton also refused to release Major Thomas T. Eckert (1825–1910) from duty the night of the performance, though Lincoln had specifically invited him to attend. Eckert (like Lincoln himself) was renowned for his physical strength. Had he been with the president that fatal evening, the argument goes, he might have overpowered Booth.

Many writers over the years have cast a wider net, contending that Lincoln was the victim of the Vatican. Charles Chiniquy, an ex-priest and former legal client of Lincoln's, claimed that Lincoln was murdered by the **Jesuits**; in 1924 the self-styled ex-Romanist Burke McCarthy wrote, in *The Suppressed Truth About the Assassination of Abraham Lincoln*:

The death of President Lincoln was the culmination of but one step in the attempt to carry out the **Secret Treaty of Verona**, of October, 1822. . . . The particular business of the Congress of Verona, it developed, was the RATIFICATION of Article Six of the Congress of Vienna, which was in short, a promise to prevent or destroy Popular Governments wherever found, and to re-establish monarchy where it had been set aside.

Lyndon LaRouche, orchestrating an astounding harmonic convergence of conspiracy theories, that, for all its wheels within wheels, still sounds pretty much like everything else he speechifies about, argues that Lincoln's assassination was carried out by agents of **B'nai B'rith**. "The secret agenda of the B'nai B'rith," LaRouche reminds us, "was to destroy the Union and pave the way for re-conquest. The ultimate goal: one-world, totalitarian, socialist government."

Majestic-12

The code name of a top secret committee of scientists and military men that was supposedly convened by President Harry Truman to deal with UFO-related matters. Its twelve members were said to include such luminaries as Vannevar Bush (1890–1974), CIA director Roscoe H. Hillenkoetter (1897–1982), astronomer and astrophysicist Donald H. Menzel (1901–1976), and James Forrestal (1892–1949), whose suicide was purported to be connected to his work on the committee. (See also **Area 51**.)

Men in Black (see **Black Helicopters**)

Militia Movement (see **Black Helicopters**)

Marilyn Monroe

Movie legend Marilyn Monroe (1926–1962) was killed by an overdose of barbiturates; the coroner deemed her death a probable suicide. Monroe's drug abuse and her emotional volatility were both well documented, and she had attempted suicide several times before. But lingering doubts about the circumstances of her death remain. She had spoken to her ex-stepson Joe DiMaggio, Jr., shortly before she died and left him with the impression that she was in good spirits; the police reports that purport to document her last hours are marked by sometimes startling inconsistencies. Eyewitnesses (not all of them reliable) placed suspicious personages at the scene; stories emerged over the years—some of them in ghostwritten books—that Monroe had feared for her life. For example, in 2006 June DiMaggio (who claims to be Joe DiMaggio's niece) announced that her mother, Lee, had been talking with Monroe on the phone when her murderer walked into her bedroom. Marilyn told her mother the killer's name, June says, but fearing reprisals against her family, she took it to her grave.

Monroe was rumored to have had affairs with both Robert and John F. Kennedy. Actor Peter Lawford (1923–1984), who was the Kennedys' brother-in-law, said he had received an incoherent call from Monroe shortly before she died, in which she slurred, "Say good-bye to Jack." But some claim that Lawford had met Monroe face-to-face that night—and that he had brought her the unwelcome news that the Kennedys were breaking off relations with her, which sent her into a fatal emotional tailspin. (Lawford had been the messenger when JFK canceled his scheduled visit to Frank Sinatra's house; it was a role he'd played before.) Some accounts place Robert Kennedy at the star's house too and speculate that the two men had deliberately goaded her into committing suicide to forestall the political scandal that the unstable Monroe would have created had she gone public with the details of her affairs.

Some writers have argued that Sam Giancana (1908–1975), the Chicago mobster with whom JFK shared a mistress, dispatched a hit man to kill Monroe to punish the Kennedys (or, in a variation on that theme, at the Kennedys' request). J. Edgar Hoover had been keeping tabs on Monroe because of her leftist activities since the 1950s; an FBI audiotape allegedly captures Lawford's and Robert Kennedy's voices arguing with her. Teamsters boss Jimmy Hoffa (1913–1975) was rumored to have tape recordings of Kennedy/Monroe trysts as well, which he planned to use to discredit the Kennedys (though why he didn't use them to bargain his way out of jail is not explained). Still other accounts claim that Monroe was taping the Kennedys herself. A red diary was said to be missing from her residence—what bombshell secrets did it contain?

But many of these rumors are just that—their sources are far from reliable. Donald H. Wolfe's *The Last Days of Marilyn Monroe* (1998), Anthony Summers's *Goddess* (1985), and Seymour Hersh's *The Dark Side of Camelot* (1998), which tell the story of Monroe's affairs with the Kennedys, all rely on information supplied by Robert F. Slatzer (1927–2005), who claimed to have been married to Monroe for a few days in the 1950s and to have been close to her in her last days. Slatzer spent some thirty years dining out on his relationship with Monroe. But in his 1993 biography (*Marilyn Monroe*), Donald Spoto revealed that virtually none of the people he interviewed who had been close to Monroe at the end of her life even recognized Slatzer's name. Though she undoubtedly did have a sexual relationship with JFK, the evidence for her affair with Robert Kennedy is mostly conjectural—and the early purveyors of the story had political axes to grind. The first person to report the affair in print, in *The Strange Death of Marilyn Monroe* (1964), was the right-wing activist Frank Capell. Some of Capell's other titles were *Treason Is the Reason: 847 Reasons for Investigating the State Department* (1965) and *Henry Kissinger: Soviet Agent* (1972). Walter Winchell (1897–1972) took up the story as well.

Spoto looked closer to home for a solution to the mystery of Monroe's death. Evidence from Monroe's autopsy suggests that she had taken chloral hydrate (a sedative) through an enema, which in combination with the Nembutal she'd already ingested that day would have been sufficient to kill her. Monroe housekeeper Eunice Murray's (1902–1993) account of her employer's last night is full of holes and contradictions. Spoto speculates that she might have administered the fatal enema to Monroe, who had been complaining of insomnia, on the instructions of Monroe's psychoanalyst, Dr. Ralph Greenson (1911–1979). Greenson's relationship with Monroe had been under severe stress; Murray was not a reigistered nurse. Both of them had something to hide.

Sarah Churchwell's *The Many Lives of Marilyn Monroe* (2005) provides a thoughtful examination of the myths— some of them of Monroe's own making—that have overshadowed Monroe's life. Though Monroe probably died by her own hand—accidentally or on purpose—her outsize aura of sex, glamour, and doom, and her association with the Kennedys, guarantee that the conspiracy stories will never end. Some of them might even be true.

Jim Morrison's Death (see **Princess Diana**)

Nafta Superhighway
While liberals fumed in the mid-2000s that the Bush/Cheney administration's doctrine of preemption and its ongoing "war on terror" exposed its grandiose imperialist ambitions, a significant fringe of extreme conservatives worried that the opposite was true—that they were secretly ceding America's sovereignty to an internationalist **New World Order**. A case in point was the so-called NAFTA Superhighway, which was rumored to be a massive, 1,200-foot-wide corridor that would begin in Mexico, end in Canada, and branch out across the continental United States, effectively cutting the nation into four quadrants. The highway, according to the Conservative Caucus, would be built by a Spanish company named Cintra, and "devour tens of thousands of homes, ranches, farms, and businesses" through eminent domain. Worse yet,

they said, it was only the leading edge of a master plan to replace the American workforce with cheap Mexican labor and the Constitution with trade laws enacted to enrich Communist China. The ultimate goal, Congressman Ron Paul wrote in a newsletter in 2006:

Is not simply a superhighway, but an integrated North American Union—complete with a currency, a cross-national bureaucracy, and virtually borderless travel within the Union. Like the European Union, a North American Union would represent another step toward the abolition of national sovereignty altogether.

Though the economic crisis of late 2008 sapped much of the urgency from the anti–NAFTA Superhighway movement, it has not completely faded. On March 29, 2009, Phyllis Schlafly's *Eagle Forum* warned that Barack Obama's trade representative Ron Kirk is "an enthusiastic supporter of the 'global economic community' (which means open borders for 'free' trade) of NAFTA, and even of the NAFTA Superhighway, which he calls the 'true river of trade between our communities.'"

The New World Order
On September 11, 1990, Saddam Hussein's (1937–2006) Iraqi army remained defiantly in possession of Kuwait, even as hundreds of thousands of U.S. and coalition troops were being deployed to the region. That night, President George H. W. Bush stood before a joint session of the United States Congress and declared:

The crisis in the Persian Gulf, as grave as it is, also offers a rare opportunity to move toward an historic period of cooperation. Out of these troubled times, our fifth objective—a new world order—can emerge: a new era—freer from the threat of terror, stronger in the pursuit of justice, and more secure in the quest for peace.

Though his language and sentiments hearkened back to the era of Woodrow Wilson (1856–1924), Bush couldn't have upset a certain fringe constituency more if he had daubed the number 666 on his forehead in blood and chanted the Lord's Prayer backward. Though few recognized it at the time, Bush's "Towards a New World Order" speech would become a watershed event in the through-the-looking-glass world of Christian millennialist conspiracy theory.

First, there was the date he delivered the speech. September 11, 1990, was the 133rd anniversary of the Mountain Meadow massacre perpetrated by Mormons against unarmed pioneers in Utah territory, the ninety-seventh anniversary of the opening of the first World Parliament of Religions, the seventeenth anniversary of the CIA-backed military coup against Chile's democratically elected president Salvador Allende (1908–1973), and the twelfth anniversary of the Camp David Accords. Needless to say, it was also eleven years before the destruction of the World Trade Center. $9 + 1 + 1 = 11$. If it's not a leap year, September 11 is the 254th day of the year. Add $2 + 5 + 4$ and you get 11. After September 11, there are 111 days remaining in the year. The first plane to strike the towers was American Airlines Flight 11. Flight 11 carried eleven crew members and eighty-one passengers, a total of ninety-two souls ($9 + 2 = 11$). The plane that struck the Pentagon was Flight 77 (11×7). The two towers—which themselves resembled a gigantic "11"—were each 110 (10×11) stories tall. New York State was the eleventh to join the Union; New York City has eleven letters in its name, as does the name "George W. Bush." (I confess this last discovery is my own; make of it what you will.)

Why all this numerology? Why so many elevens? *Because eleven is the number of the Antichrist.* In Daniel 7:8, the prophet relates, "While I was thinking about the horns, there before me was another horn, a little one, which came up among them." Parse Daniel with Revelation 17:12 ("The ten horns you saw are ten kings who have not yet received a kingdom, but who for one hour will receive authority as kings along with the beast") and it is clear that the little horn is the eleventh king, who will reign over the world as the Antichrist. The nineteenth-century occultist W. Wynn Westcott noted in his book *Numbers: Their Occult Power and Mystic Virtues* (1890) that eleven "is the type of a number with an evil reputation among all peoples . . . the essence of all that is sinful, harmful, and imperfect."

The first President Bush and the last premier of the Soviet Union, Mikhail Gorbachev, whose speeches and writings were also peppered with the phrase "new world order," naively assumed that they were talking hopefully about the ameliorative consequences that would flow from the depolarization of the post–Cold War world. From that perspective, the thirty-two-nation coalition that was preparing to fight Saddam Hussein and underwrite the bulk of the operations provided a preview of an era of greater international comity and cooperation. But to conspiracists, the New World Order (NWO) is a synonym for One-World government—the ultimate goal of the **Illuminati**, the **Freemasons**, the Zionists, the Communists, the international bankers, the **Council on Foreign Relations**, the **Jesuits**, the Vatican, the UN—even the federal agency FEMA.*

To eschatologically obsessed fundamentalist Christians, especially premillennialist Dispensationalists, the New World Order, as Pat Robertson described it in his book of the same name (published a year after the elder Bush's speech), is the work of "a tightly knit cabal whose goal is nothing less than a new order for the human race under the domination of Lucifer and his followers." To not a few of his listeners, Bush seemed to be heralding the advent of the Antichrist. Where

---

*Hurricane Katrina notwithstanding, FEMA is "the Trojan Horse by which the New World Order will implement overt, police-state control over the American populace," in conspiracy theorist Ken Adachi's words. At the risk of sounding like a conspiracist myself, I can't help wondering if FEMA's notoriety within those far-right circles didn't have some influence on the second President Bush's decision to place it in the incapable hands of his crony Joe Allbaugh and then Michael D. Brown (of "heck of a job, Brownie" fame), who oversaw the agency's downsizing.

Bush beheld a glittering prospect of peace and prosperity, they saw nightmare visions of waves of **black helicopters** (the favored rapid-deployment vehicle of the shock troops of the NWO), the collapse of American sovereignty, the triumph of Godless secularism, and the horrific tribulations of the End Times foretold in apocalyptic Christian prophecies.

Ralph Epperson, the author of such volumes as *The New World Order* (1990), *The Unseen Hand: An Introduction to the Conspiratorial View of History* (1982), and *Masonry: Conspiracy Against Christianity* (1998), insists that the foundations for this satanic project had been laid in the earliest days of the American republic. Epperson's argument rests in part on his erroneous belief that the phrase *Novus Ordo Seclorum*, which appears on the Great Seal of the United States and hence on dollar bills, means "New World Order" and is Masonic in origin. It doesn't and it's not. In fact, "A New Order of the Ages" is a much better translation. Charles Thomson, the secretary of the Continental Congress and one of the seal's many designers, adapted the slogan from line five of Virgil's *Fourth Eclogue*, which reads, "*Magnus ab integro seclorum nascitur ordo*," or, "The mighty order of ages begins anew." Though there were many Masons among America's founders, Charles Thomson was not one of them.

One of the first published books to bear the title *The New World Order* was an examination of the covenant of the League of Nations published by Doubleday in 1920. Its author, Frederick Charles Hicks, was the librarian at the Columbia University school of law; his scrupulously neutral, evenhanded study focused mostly on practical issues—the diplomatic instruments and procedures the League proposed to use to arbitrate and ultimately decide questions of jurisdiction and extradition, immigration and trade; the circumstances under which the League might impose sanctions and how they might be enforced; and how its provisions differed from or resembled those of previous international pacts, treaties, and confederations. Hicks conceded his disappointment that the U.S. Senate failed to ratify the treaty, stating his belief that "international cooperation is an end in itself, the benefits of which are felt directly by the people of all participating states." Though his book is far from a brief for a monolithic global dictatorship, there is no question that it is biased toward internationalism.

The Council on Foreign Relations, another indirect product of Woodrow Wilson's frustrating, ultimately unsuccessful negotiations over the Treaty of Versailles and the League of Nations, is internationalist in its orientation as well. It is perhaps ironic that Wilson is perceived as having laid the groundwork for the New World Order (the hated Federal Reserve and the federal income tax were created on his watch as well), since Wilson is frequently quoted out of context in conspiracist writings for having issued a warning about the hidden powers of secret societies:

> Some of the biggest men in the United States, in the field of commerce and manufacture, are afraid of somebody, are afraid of something. They know that there is a power somewhere so organized, so subtle, so watchful, so interlocked, so complete, so pervasive, that they had better not speak above their breath when they speak in condemnation of it.

The passage appears in *The New Freedom: A Call for the Emancipation of the Generous Energies of a People* (1913), in the chapter "The Old Order Changeth." But one need only continue reading to the bottom of the page to see that the mysterious power that Wilson was talking about was neither Godless Masonry nor the Illuminati–Jewish banker nexus, but trusts and business monopolies.

> American industry is not free, as once it was free; American enterprise is not free; the man with only a little capital is finding

it harder to get into the field, more and more impossible to compete with the big fellow. Why? Because the laws of this country do not prevent the strong from crushing the weak.

Unlike Wilson, the ufologist, anti-Mason, tax resister, and prolific conspiracy theorist Milton William Cooper descried the hand of the Illuminati—a supersecret occultist society that controls fabulous wealth and wields unimaginable power—throughout the span of human history. The New World Order, in his telling, will be the Hegelian culmination of all their efforts.

(1) Monarchism (thesis) faced democracy (antithesis) in WWI, which resulted in the formation of communism and the League of Nations (synthesis). (2) Democracy and communism (thesis) faced fascism (antithesis) in WWII and resulted in a more powerful United Nations (synthesis). (3) Capitalism (thesis) now faces communism (antithesis) and the result will be the New World Order.

In 1940, as World War II began, H. G. Wells (1866–1946), who was probably better known in his lifetime for his Utopian brand of socialism than the science fiction books for which he is celebrated today, among them *The War of the Worlds* (1898), *The Invisible Man* (1897), and *The Time Machine* (1895), published a polemic called *The New World Order*, which brought the ideas he'd advanced in *The Open Conspiracy* (1928) up-to-date. In it, Wells energetically advocated for the elimination of both the independent nation-state and the free enterprise system:

This new and complete Revolution we contemplate can be defined in a very few words. It is (a) outright world-socialism, scientifically planned and directed, *plus* (b) a sustained insistence upon law, law based on a fuller, more jealously conceived restatement of the personal Rights of Man, *plus*

(c) the completest freedom of speech, criticism and publication, and sedulous expansion of the educational organisation to the ever-growing demands of the new order.

In Wells's ideal world, traditional religion will be consigned to the dust heap of history:

Most of our systems of belief rest upon rotten foundations, and generally these foundations are made sacred to preserve them from attack. They become dogmas in a sort of holy of holies. It is shockingly uncivil to say "But that is nonsense." The defenders of all the dogmatic religions fly into rage and indignation when one touches on the absurdity of their foundations. Especially if one laughs. That is blasphemy.

And how is this revolution to be accomplished? Wells's words might have been scripted for him by Milton William Cooper: "The reorganisation of the world has at first to be mainly the work of a 'movement' or a Party or a religion or cult, whatever we choose to call it," he wrote. By means of a conspiracy, in other words—carried out by a secret society, a cabal of subversive elitists. You can almost see Wells's contemporary Nesta Webster nodding her head knowingly.

Of course Wells did not believe for a moment that he was doing the devil's work—how could he, when he didn't believe in the devil? But he didn't believe in the sanctity of private property or national borders, either, and he regarded Bible religion as a barbarous atavism. It's understandable how religious fundamentalists might perceive him to be their mirror opposite. And from a religious fundamentalist's perspective, the reverse of God and Church isn't positivism, economic materialism, or ethical secularism—it's Satan and Satanism.

The conspiracists might get most of their facts wrong, but their obsessions don't come out of the blue. Since the days of the Enlightenment, a new elite has indeed risen up, whose members are educated and wealthy and cosmopolitan. Not a

few of them, especially around the time leading up to the
French and American Revolutions, were drawn to Deism and
the rationalist, Enlightenment spirit celebrated by Freemasonry (albeit sometimes dressed up in mystical and occult
trappings). By the end of the nineteenth century a good
many of them (though by no means most of them) were secular Jews.

This minority is none other than the *haute bourgeois* entrepreneurial class. From their privileged perspective, the most
desirable way of organizing the world is as a global market-
place, in which money travels easily across national borders
and diplomacy and international covenants cushion the shocks
and disruptions that so often led to war in the benighted
mercantilist days of the *ancien régime*. Nowadays, we'd call
them Davos Men (see Council on Foreign Relations and
World Economic Forum)—a class for whom the interests of
finance and commerce almost always trump those of sect
and nation. For the financially and culturally insecure, the
new world order they've ushered in is a nightmare scenario in
which a once proud and independent yeomanry—farmers
and artisans and skilled wage workers—are reduced to
humiliating servitude.

9/11 Truth Movement
"Movement" is perhaps too strong a word for this loosely
organized, frequently squabbling congeries of insurgent
voices. So-called 9/11 Truthers come from the extreme margins of the political spectrum and a variety of occupations
and locations; what unites them is their thoroughgoing skepticism about any and every official explanation for the events
of September 11, 2001, along with a willingness to believe
seemingly any alternative, no matter how outlandish, provided that it is unsanctioned—and that it casts the U.S. government in as villainous a light as possible.

"Trust no one," as the catchphrase from *The X-Files* goes.
9/11 was "an inside job." Just as Roosevelt was accused of having

prior knowledge of Pearl Harbor, Bush was said to have been criminally negligent. Not only did his administration not do anything to stop the attacks (except when it shot down Flight 93 over Shanksville, Pennsylvania), it allowed them to happen because they provided it with a pretext to wage a war in Afghanistan so that it could secure an oil pipeline that would benefit its big contributors. The government—or perhaps rogue elements within the government—planned and executed the attacks itself, or possibly in cooperation with Israel, because a global war on terror would 1) be profitable for the oil and defense industries; 2) serve Israel's interests; 3) provide conspirators with the opportunity to steal the gold in the WTC's vaults; 4) help bring about the **New World Order**. The corporate media were willing accomplices in the great deception.

Some of the 9/11 Truth community's writings are dry and pseudoscientific; some are bombastic, some infuriatingly presumptuous. My reactions are visceral; they stir up the same feelings in me as the writings of Holocaust deniers or the proponents of intelligent design, who disingenuously purport to be disinterested seekers after truth but are patently pushing a covert agenda. Except I can't begin to discern what the 9/11 Truthers' agenda really is. Here are some more of their typical assertions:

- Osama bin Laden bears no more guilt for what happened on September 11 than so-called lead hijacker Mohammed Atta does (an innocent victim of identity theft, his passport was conveniently "found" in the wreckage of the World Trade Center).

- The World Trade Center buildings were imploded by controlled detonations to benefit their landlord Larry Silverstein, who wanted to raze them but couldn't afford to comply with New York City's onerous asbestos abatement regulations. He was able to plant the bombs without being discovered because George W. Bush's brother

Marvin was a director of the company that handled the WTC's security.

• Warren Buffett was hosting a celebrity golf tournament in Omaha on September 11, 2001 (where President Bush would pass part of the day, hunkered down in a Strategic Command bunker). We know he was in on the plot, because one of the business executives Buffett invited to his golf tournament had an office in the World Trade Center—and if that's not damning enough, a private jet that flew near the Shanksville, Pennsylvania, site where Flight 93 went down was registered to a company that Buffett's Berkshire Hathaway owned a controlling interest in.

An extreme Gnostic fringe in the 9/11 Truth community, the "No-Planers" (an appellation that sounds a bit like the Shiite's "Twelvers") deny that there were any airplanes at all. "There were no hijackings, no plane crashes, the corporate media broadcasted cartoons of an airplane impacting the South Tower, and the WTC complex (not just the Towers and WTC 7) was destroyed with Directed Energy Weapons (DEW)," one No-Planer authoritatively declares. Real airplanes wouldn't have "disappeared" into the towers and the Pentagon—the videos that show them doing just that were obviously doctored. As for those thousands of eyewitnesses, it turns out that their numbers have been overestimated—in fact, there were suspiciously few of them, and much of their testimony can be safely ignored. "Few people reported hearing and seeing planes," writes a Truther who obviously didn't live in New York City in the months after 9/11, when the sounds of passing jets evoked traumatic flashbacks in everyone who had been within five miles of the towers that morning. "Most testimonies of those who did are inconsistent with that of a wide-body commercial airliner hitting a building at 800 feet altitude, full throttle," the Truther went on.

And the doomed passengers on those planes? All those heartbreaking cell phone calls to loved ones? The inspirational heroism of "Let's roll"? More hokum, hallucinations, and fakery. There weren't really any passengers, the Truther patiently explains, because the flights weren't really scheduled. And if there were passengers, they didn't die in the attacks—they were spirited away and "euthanized"—or, to give the plotters the benefit of the doubt, inserted into witness protection programs. Either way, their families were paid off. What about the famous right-wing journalist Barbara Olson, who was a passenger on Flight 77, which crashed into the Pentagon? She had been one of the most visible of Bill Clinton's scourges and was married to Ted Olson, the solicitor general of the United States. He spoke to her on the phone moments before she died. The question doesn't faze the No-Planers. Perhaps the couple was in on the plot together. An Internet rumor popped up a few years ago that a very-much-alive Olson had been arrested on the Polish-Austrian border for possessing counterfeit Italian currency—a story that was quickly debunked when it was discovered that Poland and Austria don't share a border. Even so, she couldn't have died on Flight 77, because the Pentagon was struck by a missile—had it been a plane, there would have been more debris. Defense Secretary Donald Rumsfeld admitted as much in an interview with *Parade* magazine on October 12, 2001. Here is the Defense Department's own transcription of Rumsfeld's interview:

It's physically impossible to defend at every time and every place against every conceivable technique. Here we're talking about plastic knives and using an American Airlines flight filled with our citizens, and the missile to damage this building and similar [inaudible] that damaged the World Trade Center. The only way to deal with this problem is by taking the battle to the terrorists, wherever they are, and dealing with them.

Of course the words "and the" in the second sentence
might have been a mistranscription of "as the"—a supposi-
tion that's supported by the transcriber's obvious difficulty
in hearing all of the secretary's words. But why waste breath
or ink arguing? The No-Plane theory is so outrageous that a
significant number of Truthers believe that its advocates are
agents of disinformation. A Truther explains:

> Some 9/11 activists who disbelieve the "no plane" stuff think
> the Pentagon is planning to release "newly discovered" video
> of the plane hitting the building to discredit 9/11 truth, but
> it is more likely that they are enjoying the spectacle of the
> activists discrediting themselves and 9/11 complicity in gen-
> eral. More important, they understand that if the "no plane"
> claims are extinguished, most of those focused on the "Pen-
> tagate" will shift their attention toward real evidence of
> complicity that the "no plane" stuff distracts from.

The most damning evidence that 9/11 was an "inside job,"
we're told, is the suspicious circumstances under which the
forty-seven-story-tall 7 World Trade Center collapsed. Never
mind the fact that the building had been pelted with tons of
debris from the nearby Twin Towers, that its sprinkler system
was disabled by a broken water main, that tanks of diesel fuel
were stored inside it (to run the generators for the city's emergency management bunker), and that the fires in the building's
interior, which burned all day, were more than hot enough to
weaken, if not outright melt, its steel girders. Physicist Steven
E. Jones of Brigham Young University, among other academics, has argued that the iron-rich spherules found in its
ruins prove that it was brought down by thermite bombs.

9/11 Truthers invariably characterize themselves as
paragons of common sense. If you want to talk about wild-
eyed conspiracy theories, they say, look at what the guys in
the 9/11 Commission are selling, or the National Institute

of Standards and Technology, or the editors of *Popular Mechanics*, which debunked a number of Truther shibboleths in its March 2005 issue. As Korey Rowe, one of the young producers of the conspiracist *Loose Change*, a documentary that gained wide exposure through the Internet, remarked:

> That nineteen hijackers are going to completely bypass security and crash four commercial airliners in a span of two hours, with no interruption from the military forces, in the most guarded airspace in the United States and the world? That to me is a conspiracy theory.

A thought experiment: Imagine that the president of the United States was assassinated by a man in a black trench coat who then blew himself up with a bomb that he'd strapped to his chest, leaving nothing behind but a black scorch mark on the floor and a handful of ashes, and that this happened while video cameras were running. Bloggers, student filmmakers, forensic scientists with antisocial leanings, and fringe political activists all examine the videotape, parse the eyewitness reports, and in due course conclude not only that the alleged "assassin" was really a high-tech robot, but that the gun he'd fired was loaded with blanks—that a person or persons unknown really killed the president. Neither of those suppositions is any stranger than what the 9/11 Truthers purvey—and both of them would make William of Occam (1288–1348), the eponymous father of Occam's razor (the principle of ontological parsimony, the notion that the least complicated explanation for a phenomena is the most probable), roll over in his grave.

But of course the 9/11 Truth movement isn't about the truth at all. It's about the theorist's overwhelming need to restore his or her sense of control. On September 3, 2008, Lev Grossman contributed an article to *Time* magazine (an organ of corporate disinformation that, needless to say, the

Truthers all disdain) entitled "Why the 9/11 Conspiracy Theories Won't Go Away." There is a reason why conspiracy theories are so persistent, he explained.

> Academics who study them argue that they meet a basic human need: to have the magnitude of any given effect be balanced by the magnitude of the cause behind it. A world in which tiny causes can have huge consequences feels scary and unreliable. . . . In that sense, the idea that there is a malevolent controlling force orchestrating global events is, in a perverse way, comforting.

Ironically, the 9/11 Truth community's fantastical, easily debunkable efforts to indict the government only serve to distract attention from the government's very real offenses. If the Bush-Cheney administration had truly believed that a false-flag operation was required to kick-start an unpopular war, it could have either blown up the World Trade Center with planted bombs (which foreign terrorists had tried to do just eight years before) or arranged to have hijacked jets flown into it. But why don belts *and* suspenders? Wouldn't it have made a choice between those two monstrous alternatives? And why not arrange to have the hijackers come from Iraq or Afghanistan? A more appropriate question to ask by far would be why they would even bother. After all, when the White House decided to attack Iraq—a country with no proven involvement in 9/11, no ties to **Al Qaeda**, and that no longer possessed weapons of mass destruction—bald-faced lies and demagoguery were all that they needed to get their way. It's easy to dismiss the idea that our government deployed space-based weapons against its own citizens on 9/11. It's much harder to understand why they did so many of the things that they manifestly *did* do in its aftermath.

Protocols of the Learned Elders of Zion
First published in 1903 by a Russian mystic named Sergei Alexandrovich Nilus (1862–1929), the *Protocols of the Learned*

Elders of Zion purports to be the record of secret proceedings conducted at First Zionist Congress in Basel, Switzerland, in 1897, at which the secret powers that control international Jewry (some three hundred men whose identities were kept hidden even from Judaism's rank and file) reviewed the tactics and strategies they had been using since time immemorial to debauch, impoverish, enervate, and otherwise immiserate the world's unsuspecting *goyim* (the Hebrew word for "nation," which is almost always used to refer to gentiles; postexilic Jews were by definition permanent sojourners in other people's countries). "The Goyim are a flock of sheep, and we are their wolves," its unnamed narrator cackles. "And you know what happens when the wolves get hold of the flock?"

The document lays out the conspiracy. Relying on the absolute control that the Jews exert over the media and their outsize influence in the academic and intellectual world, they will corrupt the goyim's minds ("Think carefully of the successes we arranged for Darwinism, Marxism, Nietzsche-ism. To us Jews, at any rate, it should be plain to see what a disintegrating importance these directives have had upon the minds of the Goyim"). Next, they will trick the cattlelike gentiles into adopting dangerously liberal political institutions, all the while preying on their greed by teaching them to value money more than religion ("It is indispensable for us to undermine all faith, to tear out of the mind of the Goyim the very principle of God-head and spirit, and to put in its place arithmetical calculations and material needs"). Finally, they will knock the economic foundations out from under the Christian polities by ensnaring them in ruinous debt.

> Foreign loans are leeches which there is no possibility of removing from the body of the State until they fall off of themselves or the State flings them off. But the GOY States do not tear them off; they go on in persisting in putting more on to themselves so that they must inevitably perish, drained by voluntary blood-letting.

Secret societies—particularly those of the **Freemasons**—have a major role to play as well. Until the Jews can rule openly, the unsuspecting Masons will be their proxies.

The *Protocols* were exposed as a hoax in 1921, when the London *Times* demonstrated that they had been cut and pasted together, probably by operatives in the Okhrana, the czar's secret police, from a number of different sources. One was written by the German anti-Semite Herman Goedsche (1815–1878), who used the pseudonym Sir John Retcliffe. His novel *Biarritz* (1868) included a chapter entitled "The Jewish Cemetery in Prague and the Council of Representatives of the Twelve Tribes of Israel," in which a group of rabbis secretly convenes to review the efforts they've made to subvert society over the past hundred years and to make their plans for the next century. Another was Maurice Joly's (1829–1878) *The Dialogue in Hell Between Machiavelli and Montesquieu*—a thinly disguised satirical attack on Napoléon III, who, Joly said, cloaked his despotism in the trappings of the liberal state. Still another source was Abbé Augustin Barruel's (1741–1820) anti-Masonic tract *Memoirs Illustrating the History of Jacobinism* (1798).

Needless to say, the revelation of the *Protocols'* dubious provenance changed few minds. Since the plot propounded in its pages predated the Zionist convention by thousands of years, who's to say that Goedsche and Joly hadn't used a different document as the source for their own books—or more likely, given the Jewish race's bottomless capacity for deceit, that the Jews hadn't cynically arranged for their books to be written and published as insurance against the eventual discovery of an incriminating document like the *Protocols*? The Jews, remember, control all of the printing presses in the world (except the ones that publish anti-Semitic books and tracts). If one was already of a mind to believe that the Masons and the Jews were working together to destroy civilization, then the *Protocols* were the ultimate smoking gun. They offer something invaluable for all conspiracists, not just anti-Semites: a ready-made, one-size-fits-all template for any and all paranoid theories about secret societies. Milton William Cooper cited the *Protocols* repeatedly in his writings, instructing his readers to substitute the word "**Illuminati**" for "Jews." The John Birch Society summoned its spirit in their depiction of the all-powerful Communist conspiracy. The anti–New Age Christian writer Constance Cumbey argued that the real authors of the *Protocols* were Theosophical occultists.

"The only statement I care to make about the PROTO-COLS is that they fit in with what is going on," the automobile manufacturer Henry Ford (1863–1947) declared in an interview with the *New York World* in 1921. "They are sixteen years old, and they have fitted the world situation up to this time. THEY FIT IT NOW." But Ford would say much more than that. Dozens of anti-Semitic essays were published under his byline in his newspaper, *The Dearborn Independent*, and collected in the four-volume set *The International Jew*. Volume I, *The International Jew: The World's Foremost Problem*, appeared in 1922; it included the full text of the *Protocols*. Here is Ford on Disraeli:

> Disraeli told the truth. He presented his people before the world with correctness. He described Jewish power, Jewish purpose and Jewish method with a certainty of touch that betokens more than knowledge—he shows racial sympathy and understanding. Why did he do it? Disraeli the flamboyant, most oriental of courtiers and suave of politicians, with a keen financial ability. Was it that typically racial boastfulness, that dangerous, aggressive conceit in which the Jew gives up most of his secrets? No matter; he is the one man who told the truth about the Jews without being accused of "misrepresenting the Jews."

Suddenly, in 1927, facing libel suits and the threat of Jewish boycotts, Ford signed a letter of apology and withdrew *The Dearborn Independent* from circulation, claiming that he hadn't read his ghostwritten essays and that nobody had told him that the *Protocols* were a hoax. In 1942, as America went to war against Hitler (who had long been one of Ford's great admirers), Ford—who clearly did not want his company to lose its share of military contracts—signed his name to a second apology. "I consider that the hate-mongering prevalent for some time in this country against the Jew is of a distinct disservice to our country, and to the peace and welfare of humanity," he averred.

The *Protocols of the Learned Elders of Zion* remains in print (as does Ford's *International Jew*). A forty-one-part miniseries based on the *Protocols* aired on Egyptian television in 2002. A similar twenty-one-part series, produced in Syria, was aired throughout the Arab world on a Hezbollah-owned satellite network a year later. As each episode of this second series began, the following text scrolled down the screen (the translation is provided by the Anti-Defamation League):

Two thousand years ago the Jewish Rabbis established an international government aiming at maintaining the world under its control and suppressing it under the Talmudic commands, and totally isolating them from all of the people.

Then the Jews started to incite wars and conflicts, while those countries disclaimed them. They falsely pretended to be persecuted, awaiting their savior, the Messiah, who will terminate the revenge against the Goyim that their God, Jehovah, started.

In the beginning of the nineteenth century, the international government decided to increase the conspiracies and the Jewish international secret government was established, headed by Amschel Rothschild.

Roswell Incident

On July 8, 1947, officials at the Roswell Army Air Field outside Roswell, New Mexico, reported that pieces from a crashed flying disc had been recovered from a nearby ranch. Though the military issued a retraction the next day, claiming that the wreckage was merely the remnants of a weather balloon, the story took on a life of its own, by the 1980s, a veritable library of books had been written that claimed that the military had not only salvaged a flying saucer in Roswell but recovered alien cadavers. The site of an annual UFO festival, Roswell has become a byword for government cover-ups of close encounters. (See also **Area 51**.)

Ruby Ridge

An isolated mountaintop redoubt in the northern Idaho panhandle that the U.S. Marshals Service, the Bureau of Alcohol, Tobacco, and Firearms, and the FBI besieged in 1992 because its forty-five-year-old owner, Randy Weaver, had missed a court date related to some minor firearms violations eighteen months before. Weaver held out for eleven days before surrendering. His fourteen-year-old son, Sammy, his wife, Vicki (shot through the head by an FBI sniper while she held her ten-month-old baby in her arms), and a federal agent were killed; Weaver and his friend Kevin Harris were seriously wounded. More than four hundred men, equipped with Humvees, armored personnel carriers, and a variety of aircraft, had taken part in the grossly asymmetrical operation, which some antigovernment conspiracists came to believe was a "dress rehearsal" for the attack on the Branch Davidians in Waco a year later.

Randy and Vicki Weaver had moved to Idaho from Iowa in 1983, to live self-sufficiently while homeschooling their children in the tenets of the "Israelitish" version of Christianity they practiced. Though both Weavers were sympathetic to the racialist tenets of Christian Identity and espoused other far-right political beliefs, they were homesteaders, not terrorists. Randy Weaver might not have recognized the sovereignty of the U.S. government, but he didn't fall afoul of its laws until a paid ATF informer entrapped him into selling him two sawed-off shotguns. Rejecting an opportunity to gain immunity by becoming an informer himself, Weaver was arrested and released on a ten-thousand-dollar bond. There is some question as to whether he was properly notified of the date of his trial—at first he was told it would be on February 19, 1991; then, when it was postponed a day, a letter was mailed to him which erroneously rendered the new date as *March* 20. Regardless of how he became a fugitive, Weaver holed up on his property for some eighteen months, while federal agents utilized paid informers, low-flying aircraft, solar-powered surveillance cameras, and other high-tech and low-tech methods (at a cost to taxpayers of more than one million dollars) to keep tabs on him.

The bloody endgame began on August 21, 1992, when the Weavers' dog Striker encountered a group of federal marshals. Hearing the dog's barking, Weaver, his fourteen-year-old son, Sammy, and family friend Kevin Harris grabbed their rifles and rushed off to investigate, assuming that he had sniffed out a deer. The marshals, who were dressed in camouflage suits and ski masks and armed with M-16s equipped with silencers and laser scopes, killed the dog, whereupon either Sammy or Kevin Harris returned fire, killing Deputy Marshal William Degan.

Weaver and Harris were indicted for murder, assault, and conspiracy. The renowned trial attorney Gerry Spence (he had successfully defended Imelda Marcos, the former first lady of the Philippines, against federal racketeering charges and won a $10.5 million verdict for the late Karen Silkwood's family against the Kerr-McGee plutonium processing plant that was accused of arranging her death) agreed to handle their defense. The government would bungle their prosecutions no less egregiously than it had their arrests. Here's how Alan Bock, writing in the libertarian magazine *Reason*, described the trial:

> Spence and the other defense attorneys . . . put the govern-
> ment on trial indirectly. . . . When the prosecution was fin-
> ished, the defense declined to call a single witness, saying the
> government had so manifestly failed to prove its case that no
> defense was necessary.

Spence's confidence was justified: Harris was acquitted of all
charges and, though Weaver was convicted of his bail viola-
tion, he was found innocent of murder, conspiracy, and even
the original firearms charges that had been the cause of all
his troubles. Though the federal government never formally
admitted fault, Kevin Harris received a $380,000 settlement
for his injuries; the Weaver family's wrongful death suit
would be settled out of court for $3.8 million.

Ruby Ridge remains a watershed event for conspiracists
and an abiding embarrassment for the federal government.
The terrible irony is that, as bizarre and lunatic-fringe as the
Weavers' beliefs about the U.S. government might have been,
the treatment they received at its hands was probably worse
than even their wildest fantasies about the **New World Order**.

The Secret Treaty of Verona

A staple of nineteenth-century conspiracy theory, the Secret
Treaty of Verona of November 22, 1822, is an alleged codicil
to the public agreement in which Austria, Prussia, and Russia offered France provisional support for an invasion of
Spain. In Article One, the contracting parties pledged "to
use all their efforts to put an end to the system of representative governments, in whatever country it may exist in
Europe, and to prevent its being introduced in those countries where it is not yet known"; in Articles Two and Three
they agreed to suppress freedom of the press and religion.

First reported in the London *Morning Chronicle*, the document, which is beyond any doubt a forgery, was widely
reprinted in the United States and found its way into a number

of textbooks. Like the so-called Extreme Oath of the **Jesuits**, it was often adduced as proof of the inimical intentions of the Catholic powers in Europe. As such, it was read into the congressional record in full in 1916, during the run-up to the United States entry into World War I.

Tupac Shakur (see **Princess Diana**)

Malcolm X Assassination (see **Martin Luther King, Jr.**)

SECRET SOCIETIES

Death Grips and Secret Handshakes

More than thirty years ago, when I was a freshman in college, I had a strange and memorable experience. It was about four in the morning. I was drinking instant coffee and chatting with a friend (both of us had been up all night writing papers), when the predawn stillness was abruptly broken by a chorus of rhythmic chanting and the sounds of tramping feet. Looking out the window, we beheld an extraordinary sight: illuminated by flickering torches, a double column of figures, clad in white robes, was marching slowly down the street.

We looked at each other in astonishment. "Is it the Klan?" my friend asked. I had been wondering the same thing.

We slipped outside and, hanging back a few hundred feet and keeping to the shadows, followed the eerie processional. Many of the marchers, we now saw, were blindfolded; the torchbearers guided them by their elbows. After a few minutes, they steered them off the street and onto an asphalt path that led toward one of the campus's two cafeterias. Then they cut across a broad lawn—one of those commons that you see in college catalogs, where students bask in the sun reading Tolstoy or toss Frisbees to each other—and came to a halt at the edge of a copse of trees. The grass was chill with dew; the moonless sky was filled with stars.

One of the torchbearers climbed onto a boulder. "Upon

this sacred rock, beneath the branches of this holy tree, we are gathered to conduct these ancient rites," he intoned.

Of course I can't recall his exact words, but you get the idea. It didn't take us long to realize that what we were witnessing wasn't a Konklave of the **Ku Klux Klan** or a Satanic mass—it was a fraternity initiation. Nevertheless, it was an amazing spectacle. Even after their blindfolds had been unbound, the fraternity's newest members were as oblivious to the world around them as the denizens of Plato's cave. They had been positioned with their backs to the nearby buildings—all they could see was their leader and the trees behind him. For all they knew, they really had been transported to an enchanted grove. Skulking in the rear, hidden behind some bushes, my friend and I knew the truth—that they weren't even a stone's throw away from the bland institutional building where, in just a few hours, we would all be sitting down to eat our breakfasts. Their leaders knew it too—and *they* would know it themselves in the years to come, when it was their turn to carry the torches. It was all theater, all make-believe, but there was no denying the solemnity of the occasion.

What makes a college fraternity more than just a housing arrangement is the density of its social fabric. Exclusivity and secrecy are its warp and its woof, as are the complementary senses of conspiracy and continuity. More than just an arbitrary ingathering of schoolmates, fraternity members are formally bound by oaths; their peer group extends backward and forward through the generations. Not only do they share each other's values; they hold a set of secrets in common. The contents of those secrets are irrelevant—they could be as arbitrary as a handclasp or a few lines of muttered doggerel or as serious as a set of mystical tenets; what matters is that they are not to be shared with outsiders. Sure, the rites that I witnessed outside my dorm that morning were more than a little ridiculous—but only from my outsider's perspective. Once you're ensconced on the inside, the outside no longer matters, which is precisely why people join fraternities.

Here in the real world, it's easy to lose sight of the fact that the closest kept secret of many secret societies is the fact that they haven't got all that many secrets worth keeping. Much of the solemn claptrap and mumbo jumbo associated with fraternal orders and clubs is just that—stagecraft, juvenile secret-decoder-ring stuff, designed to foster the sense of the group, to strengthen its members' sense of shared identity. Conspiracy theorists—many of whom believe that a handful of secret societies have looked down on our doings from their Lodges and Temples since Biblical times, much as the Greek gods peered down from the battlements of Olympus, pulling the strings of our destinies at their whim—obviously have a different point of view. Not only do they believe that these groups are as ancient and as awesome as their bombastic ceremonies say they are—they imagine that many of them are allied.

In fact some of them are. And others only seem to be. A conspiracist might regard the fact that the white supremacist Ku Klux Klan and the African American street gang the Black P Stone Nation share some of the same **Masonic** symbols as evidence that they both somehow answer to the Masons. There are other, more plausible explanations—aspirational plagiarism, for one. It's easy to imagine how the founders of a secret society—whether rural racists in the post–Civil War years or a collection of inner-city "gangstas" in the midtwentieth century—would borrow some of the trappings of Freemasonry to give their newer enterprise an air of legitimacy and seriousness, not to mention a convincingly spooky aura. A little bit of research reveals still other reasons. Many of the Klan's original founders were already Freemasons. During its second major phase, in the 1920s, Klan recruiters, who received a cash bounty for every new member they enrolled (like many American secret societies of that era, the Klan had become a for-profit venture), actively solicited Masons because they were known joiners and presumed to be reliably anti-Catholic. As for the Black P Stone

Nation, when its founder Jeff Fort was in prison in the 1970s, he converted to Moorish Science Temple Islam, which incorporated aspects of Prince Hall Masonry* into its rituals.

There are real alliances between secret societies too, and many of them do in fact have a sinister agenda. The KKK terrorized and killed countless innocents and exercised considerable political clout at several junctures in its checkered history, and the hate groups it spawned remain closely associated. Any number of neighborhood street gangs have evolved into criminal corporations, with national and international reach. Guatemala's Ejército Secreto Anticomunista (Secret Anticommunist Army) was responsible for hundreds of assassinations in the 1970s. If the John Birch Society vastly exaggerated the extent of Communist subversion in the United States, Whittaker Chambers's *Witness* (1952) eloquently attested to the existence of Soviet sleeper cells in the 1930s and 1940s. Even so, when reading (and writing) about secret societies, one truism should always be kept in mind: the more we know about a group, the less we probably have to fear from it. The most dangerous secret societies are the ones we haven't heard of yet.

One of my favorite scenes in Umberto Eco's conspiracy thriller *Foucault's Pendulum* (1989) occurs as its heroes are preparing to launch a line of occult books. Their publisher hands them a precious mailing list of cults and secret societies:

"Here you are: the Absolutists (who believe in metamorphosis), the Aetherius Society of California (telepathic relations with Mars) . . . the Cosmic Church of Truth in Florida, Traditionalist Seminar of Ecône in Switzerland, the Mormons (I

---

*Prince Hall Masonry takes its name from Prince Hall (1735–1807), a free African American who, along with fourteen companions, chartered Boston, Massachusetts's African Lodge #459 from the Grand Lodge of England in 1784. After the English and American Masons separated, it was called African Lodge 1.

read about them in a detective story, too, but maybe they
don't exist anymore) . . . the Church of Mithra in London and
Brussels, the Church of Satan in Los Angeles . . . Children of
Darkness and Green Order on the Ivory Coast (let's forget
that one; God knows what language they write in) . . . Johannite Fraternity for the Templar Resurrection in Kassel . . .
Odinist Fellowship in Florida . . . Rosy Cross of Harlem . . .
Wicca (Luciferine association of Celtic obedience; they invoke
the seventy-two geni of the cabala) . . . Need I go on?"

"Do all these really exist?" Belbo asked.

"Those and more. To work, gentlemen. Draw up a definitive list."

The list of secret societies that follows is far from definitive, but it covers a lot of territory. With the exceptions of
the tiny **Symbionese Liberation Army**, the **Weather Underground**, and the Baader-Meinhof Gang, which left outsize
impressions on the culture, I've omitted most revolutionary
political groups, especially if they are foreign and/or historical, because there are so many of them and because their
reasons for secrecy were for the most part practical and
straightforward. I excluded most occult groups as well,
because (and perhaps this is an arbitrary distinction, but one
does have to draw limits somewhere) they struck me as being
more arcane or esoteric than secretive per se—though a few
of them do turn up in the Cults section of this book. Other
groups, like the **Kiwanis Club** and the **Rotary International**,
are here because I've seen their logos on signs outside small
towns and on bubblegum machines all my life without knowing quite what they are or what they do. Even if they aren't
secretive or conspiratorial, their names certainly seemed
mysterious to me. And I included the **Woodmen of the World**
(one of an astonishing number of forestry-themed lodge
societies whose main purpose was to sell life insurance) simply because they tickled me.

Ananias Clubs (see **Black Helicopters** in Conspiracies)

Ancient Order of Foresters (see **Woodmen of the World**)

Ancient Order of Hibernians

Irish Catholic benevolent society whose roots extend back into Elizabethan times, when Roman Catholicism was driven underground in England and Ireland. Its earliest known precursor is a guerilla band known as the Defenders, which was said to have been founded in County Kildare in 1565 by Rory Oge O'Moore, who was reputed to be a descendant of the legendary Gaelic hero Conall Cearnach. In the eighteenth century, beleaguered Irish Catholics joined the Whiteboys, a guerilla group which carried out attacks on Protestant landlords. A century later the Terry-Alts and other groups (known collectively as "Ribbonmen") carried on their legacy.

A mutual aid rather than a revolutionary society, the Ancient Order of the Hibernians first appears in the historical record in 1836, when it granted a group of Irish Catholic émigrés permission to organize their own satellite chapter in New York City, provided that the members they enrolled were "good Catholics, and Irish or of Irish descent, and of good moral character." It further stipulated that membership in other secret societies "contrary to the laws of the Catholic Church" (the **Masons**, presumably) was strictly forbidden and that "at all times and at all places your motto shall be: 'Friendship, Unity, and True Christian Charity.'"

Not coincidentally, anti-Catholic feelings, always a strong undercurrent in American life, intensified starting in the 1840s, when Irish immigration reached a flood tide. Regional nativist organizations such as the Order of United Americans, the American Republicans, the Sons of America, and the United American Mechanics of the United States consolidated into a national political organization called the

National Council of the United States of North America, or the Supreme Order of the Star Spangled Banner, which, because of its reticence about its membership and its organization, came to be called the Know-Nothing Party. The Ancient Order of the Hibernians grew in parallel, defending Roman Catholic churches and clergy, providing charity and social welfare services to Irish Catholics, and lobbying against legislation that was specifically targeted against Catholics and Irish immigrants.

The radical Fenians, organized in the United States in 1858 and dedicated to the expulsion of the English from Ireland, and the Molly Maguires, the shadowy organization of Irish American coal miners that helped lay the groundwork for the union movement in Pennsylvania's anthracite regions (and which was consequently accused of terrorism by mine owners), both had informal associations with the Ancient Order of Hibernians. Political strains within the organization—and within Ireland itself—would cause a schism in the 1880s.

The Ancient Order of Hibernians carries on in America today as a charitable and cultural organization; its most visible (and, starting in the early 1990s, its most controversial) function has been to organize major Saint Patrick's Day parades and celebrations. When the AOH refused to grant gay organizations permission to formally participate in the parades, it became the target of a number of lawsuits (one of which, Hurley *v.* Irish American Gay, Lesbian and Bisexual Group of Boston, was appealed all the way up to the Supreme Court, where the AOH won a significant victory). To protect themselves from future liabilities, members of the AOH now organize the parades under the auspices of a specially created corporation, St. Patrick's Day Parade, Inc.

Aryan Brotherhood

A prison gang, also known as The Brand, that began in California's San Quentin prison in 1967 as an outgrowth of the already-existing Blue Bird gang. A white supremacist answer to the militant Black Panthers, the ABs originally provided its members with protection against Hispanic and African American gangs; over the years it has evolved into a major criminal enterprise, with extensive interests in methamphetamines and contract killings. The Nazi Lowriders are an affiliate gang that began in California Youth Authority correctional facilities in the 1970s; PEN1 (Public Enemy #1) is yet another youth-oriented racist gang that grew out of the Southern California Skinhead scene. PEN1's criminal interests include methamphetamine trafficking, dogfighting, and identity theft. (See also **Ku Klux Klan** and **Street Gangs.**)

Aryan Nations (see **Ku Klux Klan**)

Baader-Meinhof Gang (see **Weather Underground**)

Bavarian Order of the Illuminati (see **Illuminism** and **Freemasonry**)

Bilderberg Group
Attendees of the Bilderberg Conference, a by-invitation-only gathering of about 130 of Europe's and America's most influential men and women in government, business, and the media that has met annually since 1954. Both the participants and the agenda of the meetings are kept strictly confidential, a fact that has led to much suspicious speculation in certain quarters. (See **Council on Foreign Relations and Other Think Tanks and Conferences** for more detailed information about its organization and founding.)

B'nai B'rith
Founded on New York City's Lower East Side in 1843 by Henry Jones, Isaac Rosenbourg, William Renau, and nine other German American Jews as a fraternal order that would address "the deplorable condition of Jews in this, our newly

adopted country," Bundes Bruder (Confederation of Brothers) swiftly changed its name to the Independent Order of B'nai B'rith (which means "Children of the Covenant" in Hebrew). Organized in lodges and with six degrees of membership on the model of the **Masons** (to which several of its founders belonged), B'nai B'rith's first concrete achievement was the establishment of a burial insurance fund for members. Soon after, the organization began building hospitals, old-age homes, and orphanages, and providing social welfare and educational services for new immigrants.

B'nai B'rith's first success as a political lobby came in 1862, when it successfully protested General Ulysses S. Grant's General Order No. 11, which mandated the expulsion of Jews from territories under Union occupation. In 1913, B'nai B'rith chartered the Anti-Defamation League, "to stop, by appeals to reason and conscience and, if necessary, by appeals to law, the defamation of the Jewish people." Today B'nai B'rith is the world's leading Jewish advocacy organization. Active in fifty countries, it sponsors Zionist causes, provides housing and programs for Jewish seniors, and promotes Jewish education and continuity.

The fact that B'nai B'rith began as a "secret society," however, is something that the conspiracy community makes much of, since it lends credence to the idea that Judaism and Freemasonry are inextricably intertwined (one of the themes of the *Protocols of the Learned Elders of Zion*). Here is Henry Makow, PhD, the passionately anti-Zionist Jewish-born conspiracy theorist, on the subject:

> B'nai B'rith is in fact a Masonic Order that represents British Freemasonry, and shifts the blame for its Luciferian "world government" agenda onto Jews in general. Thus while pretending to fight anti-Semitism, it actually puts Jews in jeopardy. . . . Its militant arm, the "Anti-Defamation League (ADL)" was formed in 1913, the same year as the US Federal Reserve."

Bohemian Grove

The twenty-seven-hundred-acre rustic retreat, situated in a northern California redwood forest, that the San Francisco Bohemian Club has owned for more than a century. According to cable TV and radio personality Alex Jones, a longtime scourge of the **New World Order** and a pioneer in the **9/11 Truth** movement, Bohemian Grove is also the place where the global elite—Henry Kissinger, Walter Cronkite, Helmut Schmidt, William Randolph Hearst, Jr., Henry Kravis (the same sorts of A-list statesmen, business leaders, and media types who attend the **World Economic Forum** in Davos and the **Bilderberg** meetings, in other words)—gather every summer, guarded by heavily armed secret service men and a private security force, to drink, socialize, pee in the bushes, consort with prostitutes, plot to destroy American freedom, prostrate themselves before a great stone idol of an owl, and celebrate the sanguinary rites of the "ancient Canaanite, Luciferian, Babylonian mystery religion" that they secretly practice.

In July 2000, Jones and a companion sneaked into the Grove (which is apparently nowhere near as well guarded as Jones claims it is), by climbing over a low barbed-wire fence, traversing an "expansive swamp by jumping from broken tree limbs and other debris," and then, "gripping on tree roots," scaling the steep embankment outside the employees' parking lot. Once inside, they blended into the crowds that were assembling to watch "The Cremation of Care," the spectacular masque that kicks off the club's annual three-week encampment. An elaborate musical allegory with a cast of hundreds (some of its supernumeraries celebrated notables—for example, in 1996 George H. W. Bush and Clint Eastwood played a pair of lakeside frogs), it has been performed every summer since 1880. "Care" or "Dull Care" is the cruel taskmaster that the club members have fled to the pastoral precincts of the Grove to escape, hoping to replace his tyrannical regime with an easier-going way of life. The pageant reaches its climax when Care's effigy is incinerated in a fire kindled by the "Lamp of Fellowship"—but not before the archenemy of ease and beauty mocks its tormentors from his bier:

> Fools! Fools! Fools! When will ye learn that me ye cannot slay? Year after year ye burn me in this Grove, lifting your puny shouts of triumph to the stars. But when again ye turn your feet toward the marketplace, am I not waiting for you, as of old? Fools! Fools! To dream ye conquer Care!

Jones smuggled a movie camera into the Grove and the footage he surreptitiously shot—most of it shaky and out of focus—can be seen in two full-length documentaries, *Dark Secrets: Inside Bohemian Grove* and *Order of Death*, in which he traces the origins of "The Cremation of Care" ceremony to Moloch worship, strongly insinuating that the Grove's satanic plutocrats are not averse to human sacrifice themselves (he also discerns connections to the initiation rituals of Yale University's exclusive **Skull and Bones Society**). Less hyperbolic observers have characterized the ceremony as "hokey," "quaint," and very much in the spirit of other nineteenth-century American lodge rites. The British journalist Jon Ronson, who documented Jones's infiltration of the Grove in his bestselling book and television series *Them: Adventures with Extremists* (2002), seemed to have regarded the entire escapade as more of a hoot than a horror show.

That Bohemian Grove is an informal meeting place for the world's movers and shakers is undoubtedly true (although the majority of the twenty-five-hundred-some-odd male, overwhelmingly Caucasian members of the San Francisco Bohemian Club are run-of-the-mill multimillionaires, with a smattering of entertainers, academics, writers, and politicians thrown in). World leaders really do deliver off-the-record lakeside talks and mingle with the club's members (if they don't already belong to it themselves). And if the Grovers don't worship the devil, they do indulge in extreme bibulousness (happy hour begins at seven a.m. and continues around the clock) and enjoy other sybaritic pleasures: an orchestra performs daily; gourmet food is served; many of the guest cabins are equipped with pianos. Plus, the public urination referred to above really is a much-vaunted custom of camp life, a frat house–like excess that strikes some observers as faintly homoerotic. Longtime member Richard Nixon, whose telegram to the Bohemian Club after he won his second White House term ("Anybody can be President of the United States, but very few can ever have any hope of becoming President of the Bohemian Club") was once framed and hung in a place of honor on the wall of its San Francisco headquarters on 624 Taylor Street, was captured in an unguarded moment on his Oval Office tapes describing the scene at Bohemian Grove as "the most faggy goddamned thing you could imagine."

The San Francisco Bohemian Club was founded by journalists in 1872 on the model of New York City's Century Club, as an association of artists and writers (plus a contingent of culturally minded businessmen to pay the bills). Ambrose Bierce (1842–1914) and Henry George (1839–1897) were first-generation Bohemians; Frank Norris (1870–1902) and Jack London (1876–1916) would both join the club in later decades. By the 1930s, businessmen predominated; by the end of the next decade it was not only one of the country's most exclusive gentlemen's clubs, it had become a bastion of Republicanism. Nixon was present when Eisenhower visited the Grove in 1950, to pay court to Herbert Hoover. "Eisenhower was deferential to Hoover but not obsequious," Nixon recalled.

> He responded to Hoover's toast with a very gracious one of his own. I am sure he was aware that he was in enemy territory among this generally conservative group. Hoover and most of his friends favored Taft and hoped that Eisenhower would not become a candidate.

Alex Jones and Jon Ronson are not the only journalists who ever penetrated the precincts of the Grove. In 1989 Philip Weiss sneaked past the checkpoints and lived to chronicle his experiences in the pages of *Spy* magazine. He too attended the "Cremation of Care" ceremony, but he saw it in a less lurid light than Jones did. "The religion they consecrate is right-wing, laissez-faire and quintessentially Western, with some Druid tree worship thrown in for fun," Weiss wrote. Dirk Mathison, a reporter from *People* magazine, followed Weiss into the Grove a few years later, but he was recognized by a Time-Life executive and escorted off the site. In January 2002 Richard McCaslin, an ex-Marine and onetime stuntman at an amusement park, was so outraged after viewing one of Alex Jones's documentaries that he donned a commando-style uniform with the name "Phantom Patriot" stitched on it, armed himself with an assault rifle, a sword, a pistol, a crossbow, and a fireworks launcher, and broke into the Grove, determined to kill any perpetrators of human sacrifice that he could find. It being the middle of the winter, the premises were largely deserted, so he set some of its buildings on fire instead. Security guards caught him and turned him over to the police; eventually he received an eleven-year prison sentence.

The Bohemian Club's membership is not publicly disclosed, but Alex Jones claims to have obtained a 2006 roster. Colin Powell, Gerald Ford (1913–2006), Donald Rumsfeld, Kenneth Starr, David Gergen, Robert D. Ballard, Edwin Meese, and of course David Rockefeller's names were on it, which suggests that for the most part its members are still, as Philip Weiss memorably phrased it almost twenty years ago, "Republican administration officials, defense contractors, press barons, old-line Hollywood figures, establishment intellectuals and a handful of German-speaking men in lederhosen." In recent years, Bill Clinton and Jimmy Carter have been invited to gatherings; the rock stars Steve Miller, Bob Weir, Mickey Hart, and Jimmy Buffett are rumored to have become Grovers as well.

Bourbaki

The Pythagoreans were not the only secret society whose chief preoccupation was esoteric mathematical and geometrical theorems. On December 10, 1934, Jean Dieudonné (1906–1992), Henri Cartan (1904–2008), André Weil (1906–1998)—the brother of the philosopher, political activist, and mystic Simone Weil (1909–1943)—and half a dozen or so other distinguished mathematicians, all of them graduates of the École Normale Supérieure in Paris, met over lunch at the café A. Capoulade to plan a textbook to replace Édouard Goursat's widely used but sorely outmoded *Cours d'Analyse mathématique* and M. P. H. Laurent's seven-volume *Traité d'Analyse*. The book they envisioned would promote a formalist, abstract, entirely axiomatic mathematics in the spirit of David Hilbert (1862–1943). "Mathematics," Hilbert wrote, "is a game played according to certain simple rules with meaningless marks on paper." Its signal characteristic is its purity, its consistency, its universal applicability, and especially its clarity. "The art of doing mathematics," Hilbert further declared, "consists in finding that special case which contains all the germs of generality." The Bourbakian enterprise would focus on classic theoretical problems and elegant solutions; it would reduce the seeming chaos of the phenomenal world to a set of universally applicable proofs and theorems.

That first informal gathering led to a "plenary conference" six months later. In July of 1935 Bourbaki was officially established as a collective enterprise, and work on what would be the first volume of its immense *Éléments de mathématique* had begun. (Its ninth and final volume, *Théories spectrales*, would be published in 1983, just as the group began to lose its impetus. All together some forty books would be published under the pseudonym Nicolas Bourbaki.) Bourbaki's other founding members were Jean Coulomb (1904–1998), Charles Ehresmann (1905–1979), René de Possel (1905–1974), Claude Chevalley (1909–1984), Jean Delsarte (1903–1968), and

Szolem Mandelbrojt (1899–1983)—the uncle of Benoît B. Mandelbrot, the famous father of fractal geometry.

Bourbaki's enterprise was nonhierarchical, scrupulously collaborative, and strictly secret. To make sure that the group's thinking remained fresh and up-to-date, its members agreed to retire when they reached the age of fifty. Their name memorialized a prank played by Raoul Husson in 1923 when they were students at the École Normale Supérieure. Disguising himself with a false beard and assuming a foreign accent, Husson had presented a long lecture that culminated with the presentation of the nonsensical Bourbaki's Theorem—a name he borrowed from a general who'd fought in the Crimean War. (Husson went on to become a distinguished phonologist, specializing in the physiology of singing.)

But why so much mystery for a textbook collaboration? Maurice Mashaal ventured an explanation in *Bourbaki: A Secret Society of Mathematicians* (2006):

> There are several reasons for this tradition (or mania?) of secrecy. According to Bourbaki, the group preserves its secrecy to preserve the collective nature of their enterprise. . . . This secrecy may also protect the group's members from influential scientists who were skeptical or hostile toward the project. . . . Finally, the secrecy served a social function: strengthening the cohesion of the group and helping to create the myth surrounding it.

Though Bourbaki's interests and concerns might seem impossibly abstruse and remote to nonmathematicians, the generation of Americans who came of age in the 1960s and 1970s have had more exposure to them than they are perhaps aware. The much-maligned New Math of the post-Sputnik era, which sought to inculcate a precocious affinity for set theory in American grammar school children, was largely erected upon a Bourbakian foundation.

Cambridge Apostles

The Cambridge Conversazione Society was founded at Cambridge University in 1820 by George Tomlinson (1794–1863) and eleven of his fellow divinity students (hence its better-known nickname, "Cambridge Apostles"); it would become infamous in later years because of its associations with the Cambridge Spy Ring that was exposed in 1951. All of the spies became communists while attending Cambridge, though only three of them—Guy Burgess (1911–1963), the well-known art historian Anthony Blunt (1907–1983), and the American magazine publisher Michael Straight (1916–2004)—belonged to the Apostles. Non-Apostle members included Kim Philby (1912–1988), Donald Maclean (1913–1983), and John Cairncross (1913–1995).

The Apostles meet weekly to debate a variety of questions (a record of all of their discussion topics dating back to 1830 is maintained in a leather book called the "Ark"). Since its inception the group has had a notably progressive strain— its members were drawn to Saint Simonian socialism in the 1830s, to Fabian socialism at the turn of the twentieth century, and to Russian Communism in the 1920s and 1930s. Its members tended to be philosophic idealists; they accorded the rarefied intellectual concerns of the group "reality" and disparaged the workaday world as merely "phenomenal."

"No society ever existed in which more freedom of thought was found," wrote the Victorian historian John Mitchell Kemble (1807–1857), "or in which a more complete toleration of the opposite opinion prevailed." Dictating from his deathbed in 1900, the philosopher Henry Sidgwick (1838–1900) fondly recalled Apostles meetings: "I can only describe it as the spirit of the pursuit of truth with absolute devotion and unreserve by a group of intimate friends who were perfectly frank with each other." For all their openness with each other, the society was famously secretive. In 1851 the theologian Fenton John Anthony Hort (1828–1892) wrote an oath that threatens new members with the curse that their souls will "forever writhe in torment" if they even reveal the society's existence.

As with graduates of Yale University's **Skull and Bones** and Harvard University's Porcellian Club, many alumni of the Apostles (they are called "Angels") forged outsize reputations for themselves in the phenomenal world: the poets Alfred Lord Tennyson (1809–1892) and Arthur Hallam (1811–1833), the physicist James Clerk Maxwell (1831–1879), the mathematicians G. H. Hardy (1877–1947) and Alfred North Whitehead (1861–1947), the novelist E. M. Forster (1879–1970), the physician and theatrical director Jonathan Miller, and the financier Victor Rothschild (1910–1990) were all Apostles, to name only a few. Virtually all of the male intellectuals associated with the Bloomsbury Group— including Ludwig Wittgenstein (1889–1951), Lytton Strachey (1880–1932), Leonard Woolf (1880–1969), Bertrand Russell (1872–1970), Rupert Brooke (1887–1915), John Maynard Keynes (1883–1946), Roger Fry (1866–1934), and Duncan Grant (1885–1978)—were Apostles as well. The society still exists today.

Carbonari

The Carbonari (the word means "charcoal burners") arose in southern Italy as a patriotic resistance movement against foreign occupation during the Napoleonic era and later became a full-fledged revolutionary movement that sought a unified, republican, secular Italy—a precursor to the Young Italy Movement founded by Giuseppe Mazzini (1805–1872) in the 1830s. Some accounts of the Carbonari fancifully claim that they dated back to the days of Philip of Macedon in the seventh century BCE; others that they were a survival of a medieval German guild. More likely they derived their organizational structure, their rites, and much of their philosophy from the model of **Freemasonry**. A Carbonari lodge was called a *vendita* (a "place of sale"—it was what charcoal burners

called the interiors of their huts); members referred to each
other as *buon cugino* ("good cousin"). Outsiders were called
pagani, or heathens. The Carbonari had two grades of membership: Apprentices, who wore a little piece of wood in their
buttonholes, and Masters, who carried ceremonial axes.
Freemasons were automatically inducted as Masters. God was
the "Grand Master of the Universe"; Christ the "Honorary
Grand Master," or "the Lamb," and the enemy, tyranny, was
called "the Wolf." Saint Theobald, the patron saint of charcoal
burners, was venerated. As with the Masons, there was an elaborate initiation ceremony and secret signs and handshakes.
According to Thomas Frost's somewhat sensationalistic *Secret
Societies of the European Revolution* (1876), new members were
blindfolded and taken on two symbolic journeys: one through a
forest, the other through fire. Then, placing their right hands
on an ax, they took the following oath:

> I swear upon this steel, the avenging instrument of the per-
> jured, scrupulously to keep the secrets of this society and nei-
> ther to write, print or engrave anything concerning it without
> having obtained the permission of the Grand Master. I swear
> to help my Good Cousins, even with my blood, if necessary. . . .
> I consent, if I perjure myself, to have my body cut in pieces,
> and then burned and that my ashes may be scattered to the
> winds and my name held up to the execration of all the Good
> Cousins throughout the world. So help me God!

When King Ferdinand I of the Two Sicilies (1751–1825)
regained the throne in 1815, his minister of police oversaw
the formation of a royalist secret society to set against the
Carbonari. It was called the Calderai del Contrappeso, or
"Braziers of the Counterpoise."

Carnegie Endowment for International Peace
Internationalist think tank that Andrew Carnegie (1835–1919)
established with a $10 million endowment as a seventy-fifth

birthday present to himself in 1910, charging its trustees to use it to "hasten the abolition of international war, the foulest blot upon our civilization." Right-wing conspiracists sometimes accuse it of fostering the cause of One-World government. With offices in Washington, D.C., Brussels, Beijing, Moscow, and Beirut, the Carnegie Endowment sponsors hundreds of studies and programs on international law, globalism, nonproliferation, and diplomacy. The Group of 50 (G-50), supported by the endowment, is an annual gathering of business leaders from North and South America designed to foster economic cooperation in the Western Hemisphere. (See also **Council on Foreign Relations and Other Think Tanks and Conferences**.)

Chauffeurs

Semi-legendary secret society of rural French criminals in the closing years of the eighteenth century. The Chauffeurs carried out what police blotters and tabloid newspapers today would call "home invasions." They got their name from their habit of applying fire to their victims' feet until they revealed where their valuables were hidden (*chauffage* means "heating"); the brutality of their crimes was shocking, even to a public that had just lived through the horrors of the Jacobin Reign of Terror. According to Charles William Heckethorn's encyclopedic but not always trustworthy *Secret Societies of All Ages and Countries* (1897), the Chauffeurs

> had their own religion, and a code of civil and criminal laws. . . . One would almost be inclined to think that those bandits studied the code of Lycurgus! . . . The sect was spread over a great part of North-western France; made use of a peculiar patois, understood by the initiated only; and had its signs, grips, and passwords, like all other secret societies.

Heckethorn makes the Chauffeurs sound like a Gallic version of India's **Thugs** (absent the Kali worship), but Clive Emsley and Haia Shpayer-Makov's *Police Detectives in*

History, 1750–1950 (2006) is less sensational. It acknowledges that brigandage was a widespread feature of French
life in the days of the revolution when so much of the social
order was breaking down and that France's criminal under-
class shared broad mores and ways of speech. But "the
degree of cooperation between the various groups of Chauffeurs operating in the Île-de-France," it argues, "remains
unclear":

> Certainly there was no single leader, no criminal master-
> mind . . . by all standards of criminal organization, the brig-
> andage around Paris was largely inchoate. Brigand bands
> were both real and plentiful, but few were as large or as orga-
> nized as Republican officials believed them to be. Nonethe-
> less, authorities in the region were afflicted with the same
> "banditry psychosis" that prevailed in other parts of the
> country. This led them to see large criminal conspiracies
> where there were only loose affiliations.

Perhaps because the gendarmerie of the First Republic
mistakenly believed they were breaking up a massive conspiracy, they scrupulously collected, widely circulated, and carefully cross-referenced all of their informants' reports and
confessions, sharing resources across jurisdictions. As a result,
most of the gangs were broken up. More than one hundred
Chauffeurs were arrested and executed in Chartres in 1795
alone; in 1799 twenty-eight defendants, nine of them women,
were simultaneously tried before a military court in Paris,
accused of torture, murder, theft, and rape. The trial was held
in the great hall of the Hôtel de Ville; the lurid testimony was
widely reported. "Those who attended the court sessions,"
one reporter wrote, "wondered how human beings could
attain such a degree of villainy as these wretches." Sixteen of
them would be guillotined. The renowned ex-criminal and
detective François-Eugène Vidocq (1775–1857)—the model
for Edgar Allan Poe's (1809–1849) C. Auguste Dupin and Vic-

tor Hugo's (1802–1885) Javert and Jean Valjean—knew many Chauffeurs personally during his years in the underworld. He later wrote a novel about them, *Les Chauffeurs du nord*.

Council on Foreign Relations and Other Think Tanks and Conferences

Most people think of the Council on Foreign Relations as a combination of a think tank and a private club, with an exclusive, gold-plated membership roll that includes leading legislators, former heads of state, past and present cabinet members, distinguished soldiers, academics, diplomats, and potentates from business, finance, and the media. The CFR began when a fellowship of scholars was convened to advise Woodrow Wilson on the role the United States should play in the world after the Armistice of 1918. Its leanings, reflected in Wilson's Fourteen Points, were more internationalist than either the United States Senate or many of the European powers were prepared to accept at the time; nonetheless, it was incorporated as a permanent organization in 1921. Today the CFR publishes daily briefings, books, journals, and transcripts of colloquia; subsidizes scholarship; organizes lectures; provides resources for teachers; and more. Writing under the pseudonym X in an article in the CFR's flagship journal, *Foreign Affairs*, George Kennan gave a name—"containment"—to the strategy that underlay America's prosecution of the Cold War; its members have included such right-leaning figures as the Dulles brothers, Henry Kissinger, and Dick Cheney, as well as left-of-center types like Adlai Stevenson, Cyrus Vance, Jesse Jackson, and Richard Holbrooke. The CFR characterizes itself as an independent and nonpartisan information resource whose mission is to help American leaders and citizens "better understand the world and the foreign policy choices facing the United States and other countries."

That's the official version. But within certain conspiracist

communities the CFR is regarded with fear and loathing as a
secret society, through which a sinister cabal of rootless
international financiers, whose historical roots extend all the
way back to the eighteenth-century **Masons** and especially
to the Bavarian **Illuminati**, is working to bring a **New World
Order** into being. Here is a catechism written in 1979 by
Johnny Eugene Stewart, the founder of F.R.E.E. (Fund to
Restore an Educated Electorate):

> Who controls the United States government and formulates
> its foreign and domestic policy?

> SIMPLIFIED ANSWER: International bankers . . . repre-
> sented in the United States by the Council on Foreign Rela-
> tions and The Trilateral Commission. . . .

> What plans are being made for the future of our nation?

> SIMPLIFIED ANSWER: The NEW WORLD ORDER
> is being planned. This would be a socialist, One-World
> government.

None Dare Call It Conspiracy (1971) by Gary Allen, a former
speechwriter for George Wallace, was inspired by the tenets of
the ultra-right-wing John Birch Society. Allen explains how a
century ago Cecil Rhodes (1853–1902) and the Rothschilds
formed the Round Table Group in England to promote world
government. Rhodes had prepared his first will when he was
still in his twenties. In it, he dedicated his fortune to promoting:

> The extension of British rule throughout the world . . . the
> ultimate recovery of the United States of America as an
> integral part of a British Empire, the consolidation of the
> whole Empire . . . and finally the foundation of so great a
> power as to hereafter render wars impossible and promote the
> best interests of humanity.

Allen drew heavily on the academic scholarship of the distinguished Harvard-trained historian Carroll Quigley (1910–1977), who taught at Georgetown for thirty-five years. Among his students was Bill Clinton, who paid tribute to Quigley in his acceptance speech at the 1992 Democratic convention, praising him as the teacher who inculcated in him the belief that America is the greatest country in the history of the world, "that tomorrow can be better than today and that every one of us has a personal, moral responsibility to make it so." Bill Clinton—whose presidency was under constant attack by "a vast right-wing conspiracy" (as his wife famously put it)—has been active in the Council on Foreign Relations, the **Trilateral Commission**, and the **Bilderberg Group**, facts that right-wing conspiracy theorists have made much of. As a Rhodes scholar, Bill Clinton had been a beneficiary of one of Rhodes's best-known bequests.

Quigley's *The Anglo-American Establishment*, which was written in 1949 and posthumously published in 1981, traces another one of Rhodes's legacies—a secret society:

> This society has been called by various names. During the first decade or so it was called "the secret society of Cecil Rhodes" or "the dream of Cecil Rhodes." In the second and third decades of its existence it was known as "Milner's Kindergarten" (1901–1910) and as "the Round Table Group" (1910–1920). Since 1920 it has been called by various names, depending on which phase of its activities was being examined. It has been called "*The Times* crowd," "the Rhodes crowd," the "Chatham House crowd," the "All Souls group," and the "Cliveden set."

Alfred Milner (1854–1925) was an English statesman and self-described "British Race Patriot"; Cliveden was Lady Astor's country house. Over time, Quigley relates, Rhodes's imperial ambitions gave way to the idea of a federation of independent, English-speaking states. In the 1930s, members of the Cliveden set—Lord Halifax (1881–1959), Geoffrey

Dawson (1874–1944) of the *Times*, and Viscountess Nancy Astor (1879–1964) among them—imagined that such an Anglophone power bloc could coexist peaceably with the Soviets and the Nazis. An ardent internationalist and unrepentant Anglophile, Quigley blames those heirs of the Round Table for appeasing and enabling Hitler, a moral and strategic disaster of the first magnitude, the consequences of which would resonate long after Hitler's defeat with the dissolution of England's sphere of influence. As Quigley was writing the last pages of his manuscript in 1949, India, Burma, Palestine, and Ireland were withdrawing from the Commonwealth. Rhodes's dream was already in tatters.

Writers like Gary Allen and his fellow travelers at the John Birch Society and the Liberty Lobby were less interested in Cecil Rhodes's unrealized vision of a permanent Pax Britannica, or the motley cast of idealistic but deluded British aristocrats that bumbled their way through Quigley's book, than the way that Quigley connected the dots between Rhodes, the Rothschilds, and any number of later cabals and clubs. The fact that the American Council on Foreign Relations was founded as the sister institute of England's Royal Institute of International Affairs (also known as Chatham House, after its historic address on St. James's Square, London), which was itself an outgrowth of Rhodes's Round Table, is enough to tie the CFR to the *real* conspiracy, which, as Allen and company see it, was begun by its plutocratic underwriters (the Morgans, the Warburgs, the Harrimans, the Aldriches, and the Rockefellers—the same crowd that created the Federal Reserve System) and which is still being carried out by their heirs.

Single-mindedly bent on the destruction of America's freedom and independence, these bankers not only financed the Bolshevik revolution, they have been handpicking America's presidents since the 1920s—not just obvious leftists like FDR, Jimmy Carter, and Bill Clinton but Eisenhower, Nixon, and both Bushes. "If you and your clique wanted control over the United States," Gary Allen explains,

You would want all power vested at the apex of the executive branch of the federal government; then you would have only to control one man to control the whole shebang. . . . That is what the game is all about. "Communism" is not a movement of the downtrodden masses but is a movement created, manipulated and used by power-seeking billionaires in order to gain control over the world first by establishing socialist governments in the various nations and then consolidating them all through a "Great Merger," into an all-powerful world socialist super-state probably under the auspices of the United Nations.

The similarities between Allen's billionaires and the Jews in the *Protocols of the Learned Elders of Zion*, who are also supposedly plotting, in the words of Protocol 5, to "absorb all the state forces of the world and to form a super-government," are not coincidental; though, as the John Birch Society's founder, Robert Welch (1899–1985), protested in a 1969 speech, his organization was not in any way anti-Semitic.* In Welch's telling, the most egregious anti-Semites had been, ironically enough, none other than the Jewish members of the international conspiracy:

Lenin himself did what he could to have himself and his fellow Communists of the Jewish race hated more as Jews than as Communists. Apparently, he even played a leading part in having much of the actual Communist program laid out plainly in writing for the guidance of his followers in a spurious document called "The Protocols of the Elders of Zion" so that the Jews as a whole would be blamed for the program itself.

Welch lamented how effective this diversionary tactic had been. Precious resources had been squandered on baseless attacks against Jews instead of Communists and their secret

*Willis Carto's Liberty Lobby, however, openly and ardently was.

allies, creating a backlash that besmirched and discredited patriotic organizations like his, which were wrongfully accused of bigotry. Welch's disavowal of anti-Semitism, I should add, was not disingenuous. Westbrook Pegler (1894–1969), who famously wrote, "My hates have always occupied my mind much more actively and have given greater spiritual satisfactions than my friendships," was expelled from the John Birch Society because of his anti-Jewish statements; the white supremacist David Lane would recount how he dismissed the John Birch Society as "the biggest bunch of airheads and reality-deniers in history" because of their failure to acknowledge the coordinated Zionist plot "to exterminate the Aryan race."

The Council on Foreign Relations is only one of a number of think tanks and conferences that right-wing conspiracists regard as "fronts" for the internationalist conspiracy. The **Carnegie Endowment for International Peace**, the **World Economic Forum**, and especially the Trilateral Commission and the Bilderberg Group have also been lightning rods for their suspicions. The Bilderberg Group takes its name from the hotel in Oosterbeek, Holland, where the group's first meeting was held in 1954, the brainchild of the Polish intellectual and politician Joseph H. Retinger (1888–1960), who founded the European Movement, a precursor of the European Union, in 1948. Retinger conceived the Bilderberg meeting as a summit of European and American politicians, businesspeople, and opinion-molders that would promote greater understanding—and more effective economic coordination—between the United States and Europe, helping to forestall the rising tide of European anti-Americanism. The meeting was chaired by Prince Bernhard of the Netherlands (who had been a member of the Nazi SS in the 1930s); American attendees included David Rockefeller and C. D. Jackson, a Time-Life executive who was Eisenhower's adviser on psychological warfare at the time. Meetings have been held annually ever since. No resolutions are proposed, no votes are held, no statements are issued; and participants—a veritable roster of the world's movers and shakers—pledge not to give interviews about the proceedings.

The Bilderberg Group's secrecy is not dissimilar to that which obtains under the "Chatham House Rule" of the CFR's sister Royal Institute of International Affairs, which states that participants in its meetings are free to use whatever information they obtain, provided that they don't disclose the identities or the affiliations of the speakers through whom they obtained it. The intention is to encourage as unfettered an exchange of views as possible. Needless to say, the inference that conspiracy theorists draw is much more invidious.

It's perfectly understandable that the spectacle of the international power elite meeting in luxurious settings to talk secretly about the things that matter to them the most—their financial interests—would evoke strong feelings. But many conspiracy theorists venture far beyond the realms of politics and class and press into the frontiers of clinical paranoia. One writer deems it significant that Bilderberg founder Joseph Retinger's middle name was Hieronim (which translates as "Member of the occult"); in 2007, presidential candidate Ron Paul declared that the conservative Republican governor of Texas Rick Perry's plan to attend the Bilderberg Conference was "a sign that he's involved in the international conspiracy." The former aerospace studies professor and right-wing Christian polemicist Texe Marrs has written that "the CFR is nothing more than America's premier Zionist Secret Society, a traitorous front for global Jewish interests." Poor Robert Welch must have rolled over in his grave.

Although he is a Protestant, David Rockefeller figures in so many of these organizations that he has become conspiracy theory's closest thing to a Zelig (the ubiquitous Jewish character created by Woody Allen, who appeared on the periphery of nearly every historical event in the twentieth century). Rockefeller was appointed director of the Council on Foreign Relations in 1949, he has been closely associated with the Bilderberg Group since its inception, and he helped found the Trilateral Commission in 1973. In his *Memoirs* (2002), he threw down the gauntlet once and for all. "For more than a century," wrote the exasperated but defiant banker, "ideological extremists at either end of the political spectrum have [attacked] the Rockefeller family. Some even believe we are part of a secret cabal . . . conspiring with others around the world to build a more integrated global political and economic structure—one world, if you will. If that's the charge, I stand guilty, and I am proud of it."

Crypto-Judaism

Whether Judaism is a race, a nationality, a religion, or an ethnicity is a question that not even Jews always know how to answer. Benjamin Disraeli was ostensibly a member of the Church of England, but he self-identified as a Jew. An ostentatious devotee of **Kabbalah**, the pop star Madonna davens Jewishly, donning a *tallis* and a *kippah* and wrapping *tefillin*, but when she was featured in the *Forward* 50, the Jewish newspaper's annual list of influential Jews, she registered a protest through her spokesperson, arguing that since she was not Jewish, it "wouldn't be appropriate to include her on such a list." The Nazis regarded Judaism as something rotten in the blood, a genetic flaw like a predisposition to insanity or a physical deformity; they exterminated its carriers as a matter of hygiene. But while heredity was the paramount consideration in the Nazis' legal definitions of Judaism (the Nuremberg Laws, for example, defined a Jew as the descendant of three Jewish grandparents), they also took matters of belief and practice into account. For example, two Jewish grandparents sufficed to make one Jewish, provided they both belonged to the Jewish community—or if the person under question subscribed to the Jewish faith him or herself.

The nation of Israel grants any Jew the right to emigrate and resettle there. For this purpose it defines a Jew as any "person who was born of a Jewish mother or has become converted to Judaism and who is not a member of another religion." This "right of return" is also extended to "a child and grandchild of a Jew, the spouse of a Jew, the spouse of a child of a Jew and the spouse of a grandchild of a Jew, except for a person who has been a Jew and has voluntarily changed his religion." Blood is important (in Genesis 22, God promises Abraham that his descendants would be "as numerous as the stars in the sky and as the sand on the seashore"), but it is not definitive. This comports with the Bible, since King David's great-grandmother Ruth was a convert. As any first-year anthropology student knows, no nation, no culture, no religion, and no ethnicity can survive if it is entirely consanguineous, and Jews are above all survivors.

For most of the past two millennia, the Jews have been a nation of exiles, forced to rely on the tolerance, forbearance, and sufferance of their host nations—attributes that all too often came up short. At depressingly regular intervals, Jews have been singled out for persecution, forced to choose between assimilation or extermination, conversion or expatriation. When the Almohads conquered Northern Africa and Iberia in the 1100s, the so-called golden age of mutual tolerance between Christians, Muslims, and Jews came to an end. Not only did the Almohad Muslims demand unquestioning allegiance and obedience from their new subjects; they demanded that they embrace their version of Islam. Those who refused—Jews, Christians, and Muslims alike— were often put to the sword.

This was the world in which the great Spanish-born Jewish philosopher Moses Maimonides (1135–1204) came of age. He was in his midtwenties and living in Fez when he wrote his "Epistle on Forced Conversion," in which he argued that when a Jew is faced with the choice between martyrdom and apostasy, the latter is not a shameful course to take. Pretending to convert is not the same thing as converting, especially if one continues to observe the Jewish commandments as best one can and makes every effort to immigrate to a place where one can once again live openly as a Jew. Maimonides's most recent biographer, Joel L. Kraemer, makes a convincing case that the Rambam followed this course of prudent dissimulation himself (*Maimonides*, 2008). Ironically, when Maimonides did arrive in Palestine, much of the country was occupied by Christian Crusaders; the Holy Land was as inhospitable to Jews as Andalusia and Morocco had been. It was in cosmopolitan Cairo—a city with a sufficiently large Jewish population to support three synagogues—that Maimonides and his family ultimately settled, despite the ancient rabbinical prohibitions against residing in Egypt.

In the Rhineland in the eleventh century, Crusaders killed hundreds of thousands of Jews who refused to convert to Christianity. Whole communities were exterminated—but not all chose the way of *Kiddush ha-shem*, a Hebrew phrase which literally means "the sanctification of the divine name" but in practice refers to martyrdom. In the fourteenth and fifteenth centuries in Spain, thousands of Jews became *conversos* or "converts" (the Hebrew word *anusim*, or "forced ones," distinguishes those who converted against their will). Another Spanish word, *marrano* or "pig," was used by Jews and Christians alike as a pejorative for these "New Christians." Some of the New Christians practiced their religion sincerely, or at least their descendants did—Saint Teresa of Avila (1515–1582), for example, had a Jewish grandfather; the general of the Inquisition, Tomás de Torquemada (1420–1498), was descended from Jews—as were a number of other notoriously anti-Jewish Dominicans. But many forced converts became Crypto-Jews. These paid lip service to Christianity when they were in public but secretly continued whatever Jewish practices they could: soaking and salting meat and eschewing shellfish and pork; lighting candles and serving a loaf of bread on Friday nights; burying their dead within twenty-four hours; blowing shofars in isolated areas during the Days of Awe.

The Xuetes of Majorca are the descendants of Crypto-

Jews. Though the community was unusually endogamous, centuries of persecution finally drove out the last vestiges of Jewish practice. In 1917, a Polish Jewish mining engineer named Samuel Schwarz discovered a still-surviving community of Crypto-Jews in Belmonte, Portugal. Though they could no longer read or speak Hebrew (*adonai* was the only word they still recognized), the women of the community had a repertoire of memorized prayers and venerated Esther as a saint. They celebrated Passover, as well, though on a later date than it actually occurred. The last day of the holiday provided the occasion for their only communal ritual, when, during a picnic by the river, they would beat the water with olive branches, symbolically reenacting the parting of the Red Sea. The Jews of Mashad, Persia, were forcibly converted to Islam in 1839; until their community dispersed in the early 1940s, they too practiced Jewish rituals in secret.

Hillel Halkin's fascinating book *Across the Sabbath River* (2002) tells the story of the Mizo people of north India, who circumcise their boy children eight days after birth and sing a song about crossing the Red Sea. Few believe their claim to be the descendants of a lost tribe of Israel, but the right of return requires Israeli officials to treat it seriously. DNA analysis can answer some questions but not all of them, because, as has been seen, belief and custom weigh as heavily in Jewish identity as heredity.

Many *conversos* and *anusim* immigrated to the New World. A whole literature has grown up in recent years around the notion that remnants of Crypto-Jewish communities can be found in South and Central America and the American Southwest today. In the 1850s, a number of Mexicans who believed they were descended from Jews founded the community of Venta Prieta. Many other Hispanics tell stories about their Catholic grandparents lighting candles on Friday nights or refusing to eat pork. Though a number of popular books have been written about these surviving *anusim* (for example Stanley Hordes's *To the End of the Earth: A History of the Crypto-Jews of New Mexico*, published in 2008), some historians, most notably Judith Neulander, have taken a more skeptical stance. Some of those remembered customs were likely to have been planted by messianic Christian missionaries, especially Seventh-Day Adventists. A widely read article that Debbie Nathan and Barbara Ferry published in *The Atlantic* in 2000 suggested that some of the New World's Crypto-Jews were actually racists, who trumpeted their supposed Jewish identity as a sign of their ethnic purity.

> What better way to be a noble Spaniard than to be Sephardic, since Sephardim almost never marry outside their own narrow ethnic group—and would certainly not intermarry with Native Americans?

For others, there is the allure of radical chic: "They are eager to stir into their *Raza Cósmica* mixture what they see as the ultimate outsider blood—that of Jews." The controversy is far from settled.

The Benevolent Protective Order of Elks

The Elks came into being in January 1868 in New York City when a drinking club known as the "Jolly Corks" officially reconstituted itself as a benevolent society (private clubs, unlike public bars, were permitted to serve alcohol to members on Sundays). The up-and-coming theatrical personality and recent immigrant Charles Vivian (1842–1880) had been a member of the Jolly Corks—a drinking club whose members always carried a champagne cork on their persons—in his native England. An article about the origins of the Elks, which ran in *American Heritage* magazine in 2006, described one of their boisterous customs. A stranger in a bar would be roped into a contest.

> Everyone would place their corks on the bar, and when the Imperial Cork gave a signal, the last person to pick his up

would have to buy the next round. . . . Insiders would leave
their corks on the bar, making the dupe the only one to pick
his up—and thus the last.

Legend has it that the name "Elks" was chosen while
some of the Jolly Corks were wandering through the taxi-
dermy exhibits at the Barnum American Museum on the
corner of Broadway and Ann Street. There was already a
tradition in London of naming clubs after animals—
the Order of the Water Rat was a society for music hall
performers; Vivian himself had been a member of the Royal
Antediluvian Order of the Water Buffalo. The elk was chosen as its totem, BPOE lore has it, because it is:

> Fleet of foot and keen of perception. A most fitting represen-
> tation, the stately elk is, for a distinctively American, intensely
> patriotic, family oriented organization subscribing to the car-
> dinal principles of Elkdom, "Charity, Justice, Brotherly Love
> and Fidelity."

The constitution of the Benevolent and Protective Order
of the Elks was ratified on February 18, 1868, binding its
members (the "Best People on Earth") "to promote, protect,
and enhance the welfare and happiness of each other." Vivian
would get to preside over only two meetings; internecine politics drove him out of the club within six months. Even so, the
club's regalia, secret handshake, prayers, and grandiloquent
ranks (Grand Exalted Rulers, Primos, etc.) were lifted wholesale from Vivian's Water Buffalo.* For many years, as memorialized in the doggerel poem "When Father Rode the Goat,"
initiates did just that.

The Improved Benevolent Protective Order of the Elks
of the World (IBPOEW) was founded in 1902 by African
Americans who were excluded from membership in the

---

*The Elks' handshake, password, and much of the hazing associated with initiation were
eliminated early in the twentieth century.

BPOE, which would finally be desegregated in 1972. The Benevolent and Protective Order of Does (BPOD) was founded as the female counterpart to the Elks in Omaha, Nebraska, in 1921 ("Does" is an acronym for "Daughters of Elks"). The BPOE proper began to admit women in 1995. Though the BPOE claims more than a million members and two thousand lodges nationwide and continues to raise enormous sums for charity, its membership has declined by six hundred thousand since 1980 and continues to hemorrhage at a rate of nineteen thousand per year; the average Elk is sixty-five years old. The same March 15, 2006, *USA Today* article that reported these depressing statistics also noted signs of resurgence, however. Austin, Texas's Lodge 201 has seen its membership double in recent years; Hoboken, New Jersey's Lodge 74 reported that 70 percent of its 468 members were less than forty years old. San Francisco's Lodge 3 claims that six hundred of its eight hundred members are under forty as well.

The F.H.C. Society
Founded on November 11, 1750, at the College of William and Mary in Williamsburg, Virginia, the F.H.C. Society was the first college fraternity in America. Few details about it have survived, not even what its initials originally stood for (though it was probably not "Flat Hat Club," the name it goes by today).* A medallion featured the fraternity's monogram, a coat of arms, its date of origin, and its motto: *Stabilitas et Fides* ("Steadfast and Honest"). Certificates of membership and letters from its early members—who included such notable Virginians as Saint George Tucker (1752–1827), Beverley Randolph (1755–1797), and John Page (1744–1808)—refer to a secret handshake; the organization's stated objectives were friendship, conviviality, charity, and the furtherance of science.

"When I was a student of Wm. & Mary College of this state," Thomas Jefferson would recall in a letter, "there

---

*A "flat hat" is the nickname for a *pileus quadratus*, a style of academic headgear, dating back to Oxford in medieval times, which is more often called a "mortarboard" today.

existed a society called the F.H.C. society, confined to the number of six students only, of which I was a member, but it had no useful object, nor do I know whether it now exists." The Flat Hat Club fraternity was revived in 1916, disbanded in 1943, and revived again in 1973. It also loaned its name to the College of William and Mary's campus newspaper.

Freemasonry

As with so many esoteric organizations that present one face to the world and another to its initiates, there is quotidian, run-of-the-mill Masonry and there is higher-order Freemasonry. Everyday Masons pay their dues, maybe dress up like **Knights Templar** from time to time, welcome new members to their lodges, elect slates of officers, plan charity golf tournaments, enjoy the occasional hearty banquet and night of bowling, and volunteer to clean up the fallen tree limbs that a nor'easter might have left in their city's streets. Citizens who share a common belief in the essential reasonableness of the cosmos, they come together in the spirit of brotherly love and Christian charity.

Then there is higher-level, speculative Masonry. As the occultist Manly Hall wrote in his *Lectures on Ancient Philosophy* (1929):

Freemasonry is a fraternity within a fraternity—an outer organization concealing an inner brotherhood of the elect. . . . The invisible society is a secret and most august fraternity whose members are dedicated to the service of a mysterious arcanum arcanorum.

So is Masonry really a religion? Walter Leslie Wilmshurst's (1867–1939) *Masonic Initiation* explains:

Masonry is not a Religion, though it contains marked religious elements and many religious references. . . . Neither is Masonry a Philosophy; albeit behind it lies a large philosophical back-

ground. . . . Masonry is . . . at once a Science and an Art, a
Theory and a Practice; and this was ever the way in which the
Schools of the Ancient Wisdom and Mysteries proceeded.

All Masons (except members of France's Grand Orient
Lodges, which eliminated the rule in 1877—French Masonry
tended to be both more occult and more freethinking than its
English and American counterparts) are required to believe in
a Supreme Being. But higher-level Masons are not satisfied
with mere belief—they are seekers. In their mystical quest
after supranatural enlightenment, they might study Qabala,
read Vedas in the original Sanskrit, and perhaps engage in
learned discussions about the Eleusinian mysteries and
Mithraism. As apprentices proceed through the levels of initiation to the very highest degrees (thirty-three of them in the
Ancient Accepted Scottish Rite—also a French-founded variant on Grand Lodge Masonry), they are not only educated;
they are perfected and purified and transformed. "Whilst not
a religion," Wilmshurst concludes, Masonry

is consistent with and adaptable to any and every religion.
But it is capable of going further. For an Order of Initiation
(like the monastic Orders within the older Churches) is
intended to provide a higher standard of instruction, a larger
communication of truth and wisdom, than the elementary
ones offered by public popular religion; and at the same time it
requires more rigorous personal discipline and imposes much
more exacting claims upon the mind and will of its adherents.

But according to a line of polemicists that began with
Abbé Augustin Barruel (1741–1820) and John Robison
(1739–1805) in the closing years of the eighteenth century
and continues unbroken into our own time, with particular
vehemence among revenant Russian nationalists and in the
Islamic world, Masonry—especially Illuminated Masonry
(I'll have more to say about the **Illuminati** in a moment)—is

anything but virtuous or high-minded. Masonry's inner-most, most secretive circles, these writers say, are fiendishly evil and satanic. Rather than a program for spiritual improvement, Masonry is a conspiracy to expunge private property, national sovereignty, and individual freedom from the face of the earth. Exhibit one in their case is the French Revolution. "The first events of 1789 were only Masonry in action," wrote Lombard de Langres in his *History of the Jacobins* (1820). "All the revolutionaries of the Constituent Assembly were initiated into the third degree." Regicide, the destruction of established religion, the wholesale theft of property—all of them were the fruits of Masonry.

After the Comte de Mirabeau (1749–1791) died, it has been said, papers were found at the home of his publisher's wife that laid out the Illuminated Masons' plans in full. Here are some choice excerpts:

> We must overthrow all order, suppress all laws, annul all power, and leave the people in anarchy . . . we must also buy all the mercenary pens which propagate our methods and which will instruct the people concerning their enemies whom we attack. The clergy, being the most powerful through public opinion, can only be destroyed by ridiculing religion . . . all is permitted in times of revolution. . . . What matter the victims and their numbers? spoilations, destructions, burnings, and all the necessary effects of a revolution? Nothing must be sacred and we can say with Machiavelli: "What matter the means as long as one arrives at the end?"

Substitute **"Jesuitism"** or "Judaism" for "Illuminated Masons" and Mirabeau's secret papers bear an uncanny resemblance to the "Secret Instructions of the Society of Jesus" and the *Protocols of the Learned Elders of Zion*. They are probably every bit as authentic as those other two documents (which is to say not at all), but even if they *are* real, it's fascinating to note how the conspiracist interpretation of the

French Revolution simply cannot admit of the possibility that its primary impetus might have come from below.

Whether in eighteenth-century France or twentieth-century Russia, "the people," in the conspiracist view, are incapable of intelligent, concerted action on their own behalf. If they rise up, someone must have manipulated them into doing so. And if it was Freemasonry that was pulling the strings of the mob, still another set of puppeteers must have stood above and beyond them: the Jews and the wealthy. Here's a contemporary exemplar of that mode of thinking, from the blog of Henry Makow, PhD, posted on October 6, 2008:

> Freemasonry is an extension of the "Jewish" conspiracy, basically creating a Gentile establishment to do its bidding. The Jewish conspiracy in turn is an instrument of the Central bankers who wish to use Jews and Masons to protect their monopoly on credit (money creation).

Makow isn't just some random nut. A child prodigy (he penned a nationally syndicated advice column for parents when he was eleven years old), an entrepreneur (he created the board game Scruples), a scholar (he holds a doctorate in English literature), and a fervently anti-Zionist Jew, he labors tirelessly to expose the sinister plans of the **New World Order**—the "Satanic, criminal cartel" that "has subverted all social institutions and is slowly crafting a brutal global dictatorship."

So who are the Masons really? And why do conspiracy mongers obsess about them so much?

According to their own lore, the fraternity of Free and Accepted Masons dates back to Bible times—more specifically, to the construction of King Solomon's Temple. Hiram Abiff, the temple's architect—*not* the Biblical personage known as "Hiram out of Tyre . . . [who] came to king Solomon, and wrought all his work" (1 Kings 7:13–14)—was said to have died protecting the order's secrets. In reality, Freemasonry probably does date back to the craft guilds that the stonemasons who built the great cathedrals of the Middle Ages belonged to. Its members were designated "free" because they were permitted to travel across national borders.

Masonry came into being in its present form—as a lodge society whose members are inducted into ascending degrees of knowledge—in England in 1717. As laid out in the *Encyclopedia of Freemasonry* (1908), its "boundaries" or "landmarks" included:

- The method of recognition by secret signs, words, grips, steps, etc.

- The three degrees including the Royal Arch

- The Hiram legend of the third degree

- The proper "tiling" of the lodge against "raining" and "snowing," i.e., against male and female "cowans," or eavesdroppers, i.e., profane intruders

- The right of every regular Mason to visit every regular lodge in the world

- A belief in the existence of God and in future life

- The Volume of the Sacred Law

- Equality of Masons in the lodge

- Secrecy

- Symbolical method of teaching

- Inviolability of landmarks

Freemasonry's first American lodge was founded in Philadelphia in 1730 and boasted the young Benjamin Franklin (1706–1790) among its members. Masonry's nonsectarian notion of God as a divine architect comported easily with the Enlightenment creed of Deism (the belief that God created a "clockwork" universe governed by natural law and left it to run on its own), which was the religious stance of many of the intellectuals and political leaders of the day. George Washington (1732–1799) and the Marquis de Lafayette (1757–1834) were Masons, as were Goethe (1749–1832) and Voltaire (1694–1778), Paul Revere (1734–1818), Andrew Jackson (1767–1845), and James Monroe (1758–1831). Roman Catholicism has forbidden its members to join the Masons since 1738 because of its "religious indifferentism" and "contempt" for "ecclesiastical authority" (and the inevitable conflicts between its demands for secrecy and the sacrament of confession)—a ban that was reaffirmed by Cardinal Ratzinger (now Pope Benedict XVI) in 1983.

But not all Masons are Deists or Protestants. If the Renaissance brought a rebirth of classical learning to Europe, it also saw a revival of occult and magical thinking—Arab and Jewish sorcery, **Kabbalah**, Neoplatonic mysticism, Gnosticism, and Hermeticism. Alchemy and astrology were still regarded as sciences; Royal Society members Sir Isaac Newton (1643–1727) and Robert Boyle (1627–1691) were fascinated by the writings of Nicolas Flamel (1330–1418) and the corpus of alchemical texts attributed to the legendary Egyptian sage Hermes Trismegistus. Newton—not just Europe's greatest physicist but perhaps its greatest practicing alchemist as well—himself translated the Emerald Tablet, the purported work of Trismegistus:

Tis true without lying, certain most true. That wch is below is like that wch is above that wch is above is like yt wch is below to do ye miracles of one only thing.

Some of these esoteric ideas had been brought back to Europe by the Knights Templar, according to one variant of Masonic history. The Templars, or the Order of the Poor

Knights of Christ and of the Temple of Solomon, had come into being in Jerusalem around 1118 as an adjunct to the already-established Sovereign Military Order of the Hospital of Saint John of Jerusalem, also known as the Hospitallers (the Hospitallers wore black tunics with a white cross; the Templars white tunics with red crosses). The Templars took their name from the *Templum Domini*, the church established within the Dome of the Rock; they were called the "Poor Knights" because they took vows of poverty. Led by Hugues de Payens, the first Templars were Geoffrey de Saint-Omer, Payen de Montdidier, Archambaud de Saint-Agnan, André de Montbard, Geoffrey Bisol, and two knights remembered only as Rossal and Gondemar (the ninth was forgotten). In 1128, the Order was officially recognized by the church; in 1139, it was exempted from local taxes and tithes.

Though the Templars began their existence as impoverished warrior monks, protecting Christian pilgrims from Muslims, their tax exemption (and the wealth of their recruits) allowed them to evolve into international bankers. To their income from military spoils and contributions was added interest on loans, some of them made to Europe's crowned heads—money which the Templars invested in real estate throughout Europe. In 1291, when Acre fell and Jerusalem was lost to Islam, the Templars were no longer seen as Crusaders but as parasites and, worse, as usurers. The troubadour Rostan Berenguier of Marseilles gave voice to the growing resentment they inspired:

Since many Templars now disport themselves on this side of the sea . . . since they so often set a bad example to the world; since they are so outrageously proud that one can hardly look them in the face: tell me, Batard, why the Pope continues to tolerate them; tell me why he permits them to misuse the riches which are offered them for God's services on dishonorable and even criminal ends.

King Philip IV of France, who had already confiscated his Jewish subjects' money and expelled them from his kingdom, saw an opportunity to avail himself of the Templars' treasures when a man named Esquiu de Floyran—some accounts identify him as an imprisoned ex-Templar who was angling for a pardon—offered to reveal the secrets of the Order. Among the 127 accusations he proffered were the existence of a "secret alliance with the Saracens" and claims that the Templars "have more Mahommedan infidelity than Christian faith"; that initiates are required to spit and trample on the cross; that they "despise the Pope" and "contemn the sacraments"; and that the "temple-houses are the receptacles of every crime and abomination that can be committed"—by which he meant buggery. (The quotations are from Thomas Keightley's *The Knights Templar and Other Secret Societies of the Middle Ages*, published in 1837.) The Templars were said to pray to an idol of a deity named Baphomet (probably a corruption of Muhammad) and to worship cats; a story circulated that they practiced magic with a maiden's severed head.

On October 13, 1307, Templars were rounded up all over Europe; most of them confessed under torture. On March 22, 1313, a papal bull formally dissolved the Order. All of its property in France was conveyed to the king and the Pope; its extraterritorial assets were assigned to the Hospitallers, who had become the Templars' bitter rivals. Most of the surviving knights were set free; many joined the Hospitallers (who would become the **Knights of Malta** in due course). Jacques de Molay (ca.1244–1314), the Templars' last Grand Master, and his second in command Guy d'Auvergne publicly renounced their confessions when they were brought before the king for sentencing. "I have committed the greatest of crimes," de Molay admitted, "but it has been the acknowledging of those which have been so foully charged on the order." Both men were burned at the stake.

That would have been the end of the Templars, except,

according to a highly dubious legend that originated within certain precincts of Masonry, de Molay had secretly appointed a successor. Forced underground, the Templars continued to operate clandestinely, headed by members of some of France's leading families, including Bertrand du Guesclin (1320–1380), members of the Montmorency line, and even Bourbon princes. According to one account, the Jacobite Scots (loyalists to the deposed Stuart, King James II) who broke away from the English Grand Lodge and founded Grand Orient Masonry in France absorbed the surviving Templars, along with the Ismailite arcana they had learned from the Assassins during their time in Jerusalem. In other accounts it was the surviving Templars themselves who brought Masonry into being. Regardless, Templar rites play a significant role in many Masonic Lodges to this day, and de Molay is one of Masonry's great heroes. The Order of DeMolay, founded in Kansas City, Missouri, in 1919, is a Masonic youth fellowship.*

Another source of Masonic esoterica was **Rosicrucianism**, which exploded into European consciousness in 1614, stimulating interest in Hermetic mysticism, Manichaeanism, Gnosticism, neo-Pythagoreanism, alchemy, and other related esoterica. Rosicrucian doctrines are featured in many of Masonry's higher degrees. But if Masonry's Templar and Rosicrucian connections contributed to its reputation for religious heterodoxy, especially in France and in the lodges associated with the Scottish Rite (see **Palladism** for more on Masonry's alleged proclivity for Satan worship), more than anything else it was its short-lived alliance with the Bavarian Order of the Illuminati in the eighteenth century that has made it such an enduring object of suspicion among conspiracy theorists.

Founded in 1776 by Adam Weishaupt (1748–1830), a pro-

---

*Past members include former Speaker of the House of Representatives Carl Albert (1908–2000), Mel Blanc (1908–1989), who created the voice of Bugs Bunny, President Bill Clinton, movie star John Wayne (1907–1979), and conspiracy theorist Milton William Cooper (1943–2001).

fessor of canon law at the University of Ingolstadt, the Order of the Illuminati was conceived as an antidote to the dogmatic religiosity of the Jesuits (under whose hated auspices Weishaupt had been educated) and the politically oppressive monarchies they helped prop up. "The grand art of rendering any revolution," Weishaupt wrote, "is to enlighten the people." Weishaupt's plan was to co-opt existing Masonic Lodges and reading societies and use them as a vehicle for introducing initiates to the ideas of the Enlightenment. "The great strength of our Order," he wrote, "lies in its concealment."

> Let it never appear in any place in its own name, but always covered by another name, and another occupation. *None is fitter than the three lower degrees of Free Masonry; the public is accustomed to it, expects little from it, and therefore takes little notice of it.* Next to this, the form of a learned or literary society is best suited to our purpose, and had Free Masonry not existed, this cover would have been employed; and it may be much more than a cover, *it may be a powerful engine in our hands. By establishing reading societies, and subscription libraries, and taking these under our direction, and supplying them through our labors, we may turn the public mind which way we will.*

With the help of Freiherr Adolph Franz Friedrich Ludwig Knigge (1752–1796), a prominent thinker and Mason, Illuminism gained as many as three thousand adherents across Europe, including such notables as Johann Gottfried von Herder (1744–1803) and Johann Wolfgang von Goethe (1749–1832). Wolfgang Amadeus Mozart (1756–1791), whose *Magic Flute* is replete with Masonic and Illuminist allusions, was reputed to be a member as well. To most twentieth-century American readers, Illuminism's goals seem altogether less than horrifying—they are even inspiring, in a Jeffersonian or Thomas Paineian sort of way:

The mean to regain Reason her rights—to raise liberty from its ashes—to restore to man his original rights—to produce the previous revolution in the mind of man—to obtain an eternal victory over oppressors—and to work the redemption of mankind, is secret schools of wisdom. . . . We must therefore strengthen our band, and establish a legion, which shall restore the rights of man, original liberty and independence.

By 1785, internal dissension and official suppression brought the movement to a premature end. Weishaupt would finish his life in obscurity as a professor of philosophy at the University of Göttingen. But many believed that he had simply taken his movement underground. In 1797 Abbé Augustin Barruel (1741–1820) published his *Memoirs Illustrating the History of Jacobinism* (1797), which attributed the French Revolution to a:

School of impiety . . . the *Sophisters of Rebellion*: these latter, combining their conspiracy against kings with that of the Sophisters of Impiety, coalesce with that ancient sect whose tenets constituted the whole secret of the *Occult Lodges of Freemasonry*, which long since, imposing on the credulity of its most distinguished adepts, only initiated the chosen of the elect into the secret of their unrelenting hatred for Christ and kings.

In other words, to the Illuminati. John Robison (1739–1805), a Scottish physicist, published his *Proofs of a Conspiracy Against All the Religions and Governments of Europe, Carried on in the Secret Meetings of Free Masons, Illuminati, and Reading Societies* a year later and it became an international bestseller. In America, the Reverend Jedediah Morse (1761–1826) warned his Boston congregation that the poison of Illuminism had already been introduced to the American body politic. Sounding uncannily like Senator Joseph

McCarthy (1908–1957) would a century and a half later, when he brandished his list of supposed Communist subversives, Morse declared from his pulpit:

> I have, my brethren, an official, authenticated list of the names, ages, places of nativity, professions, &c. of the officers and members of a Society of Illuminati (or as they are now more generally and properly styled Illuminees) consisting of one hundred members, instituted in Virginia, by the Grand Orient of FRANCE.

Though the panic was short-lived, anti-Masonry would return to America with a vengeance in the 1820s. The Anti-Masonic Party put a presidential candidate on the ballot in 1832; in the general backlash against secret societies many college fraternities were disbanded.

Nesta Webster did much to repopularize the idea of the Illuminati in the years after World War I; extreme right-wingers like America First Party founder Gerald L. K. Smith (1898–1976) and the John Birch Society's Robert Welch (1899–1985) wrote about the Illuminati as well. In 1967, the playwright and anticommunist crusader Myron C. Fagan (1897–1972) traced a line from Adam Weishaupt through Cecil Rhodes, the **Council on Foreign Relations**, and the United Nations. "You probably are familiar with the story of how one Dr. Frankenstein created a monster to do his will . . . but how instead in the end, that monster turned on his own creator," he said.

> Well, the Illuminati/CFR has created a monster called the United Nations (who is supported by their minority groups, rioting negroes, the traitorous mass communications media, and the traitors in Washington, D.C.) which was created to destroy the American people. . . . We know all about that many-headed hydramonster and we know the names of those who created that monster.

To come back down to earth, Masonry, like the **Odd Fellows**, the **Elks**, and most other fraternal societies, has suffered severe attrition in recent years; its American membership is less than half of what it was in the 1960s, and it continues to dwindle at an exponential rate. While conspiracists still perceive evidence of its strength encrypted in American currency, the street plans of Washington, D.C., and the ley lines (geographical alignments of significant places, important in geomancy or "earth magic") that bind the world's hot spots together—for example Dealey Plaza, Nagasaki, and Baghdad fall on or near the thirty-third parallel—Freemasonry is almost certainly on its last legs. Not too long ago, the Grand Master of Brubaker Lodge 675 in Davenport, Iowa, posted a message to his brethren: "Due to an apparent lack of interest, indicated by absolutely no advance registrations, the Grand Master's Motorcycle Ride on July 12 from Sioux City to Logan . . . has been canceled." But then again, perhaps he was sending a coded message to the Illuminati.

Garduña

Like the **Chauffeurs** in France, the Garduña were bandits based in Andalusia, Spain, who achieved the status of a secret society (their name is the Spanish word for "marten," a creature that's noted for its ferocity). Reputed to be the descendants of the freelance Catholic fighters who helped rid the Iberian Peninsula of the Moors (according to one legend, an apparition of the Virgin appeared to a warrior-priest named Apollonario around the year 710 and inspired him to organize the army that would become the Garduña), they acquired a new specialty after the completion of the Reconquista in 1492, murdering wealthy Crypto-Jews and appropriating their property on behalf of the Inquisition.

The Garduña inspired the same sort of lurid, sensationalistic stories that were told about the Chauffeurs in France. Charles Heckethorn's article about them in *Secret Societies of*

All Ages and Countries (1897) is filled with dubious anthropological detail and anti-Catholic innuendo:

> The society had nine degrees, arranged in three classes. To the inferior classes belonged the novices or *Chivatos* (goats), who performed the menial duties. . . . When on the watch, during any operation of their superiors, they imitated, in case of danger, the cry of an animal. . . . Lastly, the *Fuelles* (bellows), or spies, chiefly old men of what is called venerable appearance . . . these not only disposed of the booty already obtained, but by their insinuating manners and reputation for piety wormed themselves in to the secrets of families, which were afterwards exploited for the benefit of the band. They also acted as familiars of the Inquisition. . . .
>
> The **Thugs** or **Assassins** killed to rob, but the Garduña, having learnt its business, so to speak, in a more diabolical school, that of the Holy Inquisition, considered itself bound to perform any kind of crime that promised a chance of gain.

That the Garduña truly existed, and that, like the Italian **Mafia**, they were organized to a significant degree, cannot be doubted. But, also like the Mafia, they have been romanticized—or demonized—beyond recognition. Their Catholicism was less to the point than their professionalism. The Court of the Inquisition exercised police powers that posed both a threat and an opportunity for a ruthless, organized criminal enterprise like the Garduña; it was only natural that the two organizations found ways to cooperate with each other.

In 1883, the Catholic magazine *The Month* carried an article about the trial and mass execution of a Garduña band that had taken place in Seville in 1822. Along with Garduña's leaders, the authorities seized their archives, dating back to the sixteenth century, in which all of their activities had been conscientiously recorded. The Inquisition had indeed been an important client. Over the course of 147 years, the records revealed, the Garduña had undertaken two thousand assignments on its behalf, for which they were paid 198,670 pesetas:

> A third of the sum was given for assassinations, and the rest for abductions, drowning, stabbing, and suborning false witnesses. These orders diminished greatly since 1667 and from 1797 none were ever given to the Garduña.

Hellfire Club

Generic name for a number of "gentlemen's clubs" that thrived in England in the eighteenth century, places where sophisticated young men with money could gather to discuss arts, letters, philosophy, and politics, drink and wench, savor pornography, and press the envelope of religious freethinking. The original Hellfire Club was founded by Philip, Duke of Wharton (1698–1732) in 1719, inspiring a censorious royal edict two years later that condemned the "Young People who meet together, in the most impious and blasphemous manner, insult the most sacred principles of our holy religion, affront Almighty God himself, and corrupt the minds and morals of one another."

The most famous of the eighteenth-century rakes' clubs was founded by Sir Francis Dashwood (1708–1781); it went by a number of names, including the Order of the Knights of Saint Francis of Wycombe and, after Sir Francis leased the twelfth-century Medmenham Abbey near his family seat in West Wycombe, the Monks of Medmenham. The club's motto, *Fay ce que voudras* ("Do what thou wilt")—an allusion to the rule of the Abbey Thélème in Rabelais's sixteenth-century novel *Gargantua et Pantagruel*—was inscribed over a door. A nearby chalk mine was decorated with Gothic carvings and otherwise improved so the club could enjoy masked revelries in its depths, where they were also rumored to conduct Black Masses. "Whatever their doctrines were, their practice was rigorously pagan," wrote Horace Walpole (1717–1797). "Bacchus and Venus were the deities to whom they almost publicly sacrificed; and the nymphs and the hogsheads that were laid in against the festivals of this new church, sufficiently informed the neighbourhood of the complexion of those hermits." In *Dickens's Dictionary of the Thames* (1879), Charles Dickens, Jr., the great novelist's son, conceded that

> considerable "high jinks" were indulged in by this fraternity, and that they were not altogether what is generally known as respectable society. But it is probable that exaggeration has had much to do with the records, or rather the legends, of its proceedings, as is always the case where an affectation of mystery and secrecy is maintained. The monks of Medmenham, sometimes politely called the Hell Fire Club, lived at a time when drunkenness and profanity were considered to be among the gentlemanly virtues, and probably, as a matter of fact, they were not very much worse than other people.

Members of the club included John Wilkes (1725–1797), the Earl of Sandwich, the Earl of Bute, the Prince of Wales, and the artist William Hogarth (1697–1764). Benjamin Franklin (1706–1790), a friend and political ally of Dashwood (the two collaborated on a doomed "plan of reconciliation" between the American colonies and England in 1770) is also sometimes associated with the group. Another of Franklin and Dashwood's collaborations was a revision of the *Book of Common Prayer* (1773)—evidence that Dashwood might not have been the arch-Satanist that his enemies accused him of being. Most likely Dashwood, like his famous American friend, was a **Freemason**.

Illuminism

"A somewhat naive and utopian movement which aspired ultimately to bring the human race under the rules of reason," according to historian Richard Hofstadter, Illuminism has also been described by Seth Payson as an institution whose "plan and object" was the "overthrow of all religion, and all government" (*Proofs of the Real Existence, and Dangerous Tendency, of Illuminism*, 1802).

More than two hundred years after Adam Weishaupt's Bavarian movement came to naught, conspiracists continue to write about Illuminism and the Illuminati in the present tense, as the supersecret society to end all secret societies. The Illuminati, it is said (I am quoting from a Web site called Illuminati News):

> are the top players on the International playground, basically belonging to thirteen of the wealthiest families in the world. . . . The Illuminati own all the International banks, the oil-businesses, the most powerful businesses of industry and trade, they infiltrate politics and education and they own most governments—or at the very least control them.

Both historically and in the tracts of conspiracists, Illuminism is inextricably intertwined with **Freemasonry**; I have written about it at much greater length under that heading. (See also **New World Order**.)

Improved Order of Redmen (see **Knights of Pythias**)

International Workers Party
So how much political influence can a self-described Marxist-Leninist revolutionary psychotherapist Jewish playwright realistically expect to wield in American politics? What if he lives in New York City's Greenwich Village with a harem of female disciples, students, collaborators, and assistants and has been openly allied with paranoid crackpots like Lyndon LaRouche and hate-mongering demagogues like Louis Farrakhan in the not-so-distant past? And if he waxed sentimental in print about the twenty-year-long love affair he

enjoyed with his older brother ("He gave me so much, this
sexy brother of mine, and we felt each other so deeply")? If
you're talking about Fred Newman, the answer is much,
much more than you can imagine.

The International Workers Party was founded by Fred
Newman in the mid-1970s after his Marxist-Leninist collective Centers for Change had broken away from Lyndon
LaRouche's **National Caucus of Labor Committees** (the two
groups had briefly merged in 1974; LaRouche's organization
was itself a splinter group from the SDS, which had also
engendered the **Weather Underground**). Though the International Workers Party was formally disbanded in 1976,
some of Newman's critics claim that it has continued to
function to this day as a "secret underground organization."
Newman himself told the *New York Times* that the IWP was
not so much disestablished as "transformed into a 'core collective'" made up of people working in his "political, psychological and theatrical ventures."

Newman claims that he broke with LaRouche because
he was disturbed by his paranoid authoritarianism. (See
National Caucus of Labor Committees for a full accounting
of LaRouche's storied career.) Ironically, Newman's own
enterprise has been characterized, by Christopher Hitchens
in *Vanity Fair*, as "a fascistic zombie cult outfit."

Newman himself offers a markedly different perspective on
his life and works. Born in 1935 and awarded his PhD in philosophy from Stanford in 1963, he is "an American Marx-
ist/Leninist revolutionary living at a time when orthodox
communism throughout the world has died," he wrote of himself in 1990. After his peripatetic, largely lackluster academic
career foundered in the 1960s, he became the cofounder, with
Lois Holzman, of social therapy, a form of psychotherapy
that focuses on a patient's interactions with his or her environment. In Newman's words, "The two workers, revolutionary
therapist and slave/patient, struggle together to make a revo-

lution through their practice." When the revolution is complete, there will be "proletarian truth and freedom where there is now bourgeois truth and slavery."

"The joint activity of social therapy is building the group, using members' problems as building materials, not getting help with one's problems!" Holzman and Newman wrote elsewhere. "The social therapy group is tool-and-result; the activity of building the group is what is curative." Newman's many critics argue that in practice "building the group" amounts to pressuring patients to contribute time, money, and labor to his far-flung political, artistic, educational, and charitable enterprises. (In addition to the East Side Institute for Group and Short Term Psychotherapy, which Newman still runs with Holzman, he is the guiding force behind the All Stars Project, a nonprofit group that sponsors performing arts activities for poor and minority students, and is the artistic director of the Castillo Theater on New York City's Forty-second Street.)

But most of all Fred Newman has his political interests. Over the years, Newman has been a candidate for mayor of New York City, for New York State attorney general, and for a seat in the U.S. Senate. But he has wielded his greatest influence as a kingmaker. The New Alliance Party, which he founded in 1979, fielded Lenora Fulani (a psychologist who did her training with Newman and Holzman) as its candidate for president of the United States in 1988—she was the first African American and the first woman to appear on the ballot in all fifty states. In 1994 Newman merged the New Alliance Party with New York State's Independence Party, which was affiliated at the time with Ross Perot, and threw his support behind the Texas billionaire's presidential campaign. Over the next decade, Newman and Fulani would form other unlikely alliances, with such strange bedfellows as the conservative pundit and neonativist Pat Buchanan, the former consumer advocate and habitual presidential candidate Ralph Nader, and the eponymous billionaire founder of the media giant Bloomberg L.P., who would succeed Rudolph Giuliani as New York City's mayor.

Newman and Fulani's former association with Louis Farrakhan and the Nation of Islam would come back to haunt them in 2005, when the reporter Dominic Carter confronted Fulani with an anti-Semitic statement she had made— "Jews do the dirtiest work of capitalism to function as mass murderers of people of color"—and challenged her to disavow it. Because of the controversy that ensued when she refused, she and her allies were ousted from the New York Independence Party's state executive committee.

Japanese Red Army (see **Weather Underground**)

The Jasons
A shifting collection of top independent scientists—who, beginning in 1958, received consultant fees for participating in secret meetings to evaluate military technology. The Jasons have attracted controversy in different quarters and for different reasons. After Daniel Ellsberg's "Pentagon Papers" exposed them to public view in 1971, many of them were castigated as militarists. **New World Order** conspiracists such as Milton William Cooper believe that those scientists reported to an elite group comprised of members of the executive committees of the **Council on Foreign Relations** and the **Trilateral Commission** known as the Jason Society, who were among the highest-ranking members of the **Illuminati**. (See also **Area 51** in Conspiracies.)

Kappa Beta Phi (see **Phi Beta Kappa**)

Kiwanis Clubs
A social club dedicated to business networking founded in Detroit, Michigan, in 1915 as the Supreme Lodge Benevolent Order Brothers, but which soon became known by its present

name. Kiwanis is supposedly based on an Amerindian phrase *Nun-kee-wan-is* that means "We trade." Today the club emphasizes philanthropy; its more than sixteen thousand chapters in seventy countries donate tens of millions of dollars to international charities, such as the fight against pediatric iodine deficiency disease. Nonetheless, the Kiwanis face the same challenge as most other clubs of its type; its membership is rapidly declining.

Knights of Columbus

The Knights of Columbus was founded by Father Michael J. McGivney (1852–1890) in New Haven, Connecticut, in 1882. McGivney (who is being considered for canonization) had two aims: 1) to create a wholesome Roman Catholic alternative to the **Freemasons** and other secret societies; 2) to provide insurance and mutual aid to Catholic families. Today fourteen thousand Knights of Columbus councils contribute millions of dollars to charity (almost $145 million in 2007), and the KOC insurance program has more than $60 billion worth of active policies.

Dedicated to the principles of charity, unity, fraternity, and patriotism, the local councils are administered by Navigators (other ranks include Captain, Admiral, Pilot, Scribe, Purser, Comptroller, Sentinels, and Trustees; Fourth Degree members of the Knights of Columbus wear elaborate uniforms and medals). The Columbian Squires is the Knights' youth organization; the Daughters of Isabella and the Columbiettes are women's auxiliaries. In addition to its charitable and community activities, the Knights of Columbus lobbies vigorously for the "culture of life." Delegates passed a resolution at its 2007 convention reaffirming their "deep commitment to oppose any governmental action or policy that promotes abortion, embryonic stem cell research, human cloning, euthanasia, assisted suicide and other offenses against life." Two political accomplishments the KOC takes credit for were the adoption of Columbus Day as a federal holiday in 1937 and the addition of the phrase "under God" to the Pledge of Allegiance in 1954.

Knights of the Golden Circle

Founded in Cincinnati, Ohio, in 1854 by George W. L. Bickley (1819–1867), a Virginia-born adventurer, quack doctor, author, and Know-Nothing activist, the Knights of the Golden Circle was a secret society whose goal was the creation of a slavehold-ing empire that would include the southern United States, Texas, Mexico, the West Indies, Central America, and parts of South America—a twenty-four-hundred-mile circle with Havana at its center. Although the movement was never any-where near as large or influential as Bickley claimed it was, it did capture a significant following in Texas—until the two invasions of Mexico that it sponsored fizzled ignominiously in 1860.

Upon Lincoln's election and the start of the Civil War, the Knights of the Golden Circle achieved a new impetus (mostly illusory, as it would turn out) as an underground resistance movement of militant Copperheads (Democrats who favored an immediate peace with the Confederacy). On May 4, 1861, the *New York Tribune* reported that members of "the inner temple of the Knights of the Golden Circle" were planning terrorist attacks on New York, Philadelphia, and Boston. A Kentuckian penned an exposé called "A True Disclosure and Exposition of the Knights of the Golden Circle, Including the Secret Signs, Grips, and Charges, of the Third Degree as Practiced by the Order," which was widely circulated and imitated. An Indiana newspaperman wrote a tract that descried Bickley's hand in the whole history of the secession movement, from the annexation of Texas to Bleeding Kansas. Fifteen thousand Golden Circle members, organized in "castles" and lodges, and equipped with "oaths and signs and watchwords," were said to be active in Indi-ana. "A secret order," Colonel Henry B. Carrington (1824–1912)—he would be promoted to brigadier general and after the war wrote a number of distinguished historical studies—wrote to Secretary of War Edwin M. Stanton (1814–1869), "exists in this vicinity to incite desertion of soldiers with their arms, to resist the arrest of deserters, to stop enlistments, to disorganize the army."

But when Bickley was captured in 1863, writes Frank L. Klement in his eminently sane and useful *Dark Lanterns: Secret Political Societies, Conspiracies, and Treason Trials in the Civil War* (1985), he turned out to cut a singularly unprepossessing figure. Bickley was a bigamist and a deserter from the Confederate army, in which he had briefly served as a surgeon. The underground army that he commanded turned out to be a mirage. Not one "castle" was still in existence, in either the North or the South. From his prison cell, Bickley proudly acknowledged his prewar efforts at empire-building. But "as to the Bogus organization in the Northwest States," he wrote in a statement, "I am as ignorant as a man in China—I have not been north since such a thing was known there and I have not had anything to do with it in any way." By 1864, the Knights of the Golden Circle were generally acknowledged to be defunct, but fears of a fifth column remained rampant throughout the Union.

An alarming headline in the July 29, 1864, *New York Times* reported a "conspiracy for the erection of a Northwestern Confederacy."

> The organization engaged in this conspiracy is known as the "Order of the American Knights," and its real object is to embarrass the Government in the conduct of the war, and to overthrow the Government if necessary for the supremacy of the Order. . . . The order is of Southern origin, being erected on the ruins of the Knights of the Golden Circle.

In its waning days, the Confederacy vested great hopes (not to mention precious manpower and money) in a Copperhead uprising, but it never happened. The leadership of the Sons of Liberty,* as the Order of American Knights began to call itself after its secret signs and organizational structure became known to the military authorities, planned five different insurgent operations in the summer of 1864. To the frustration of their Confederate liaisons, none of them amounted to anything. For all of their chivalric names and bloodcurdling oaths and secret handshakes and temples and lodges and bombastic titles, for all the tens and even hundreds of thousands of members they claimed to have enrolled, for all the fearful rumors they spawned, the Copperhead secret societies accomplished precious little tactically or strategically—except perhaps to prod Lincoln into overreacting by suspending habeas corpus.

And yet the myths persevered. As late as 1937, Izola Forrester published a book called *This One Mad Act: The Unknown Story of John Wilkes Booth and His Family*, in which she purported that Booth, her grandfather, was an agent of the Knights of the Golden Circle. The KGC not only plotted the assassination, she said; they organized Booth's successful escape. Boston Corbett must have shot someone else in 1865, because her grandfather lived on for another fourteen years, until 1879. Jesse James (whose birth and death dates are usually given as 1847 and 1882 respectively) was a Knight of the Golden Circle too, according to a number of books. Robert Ford might have been a dirty coward, as the song says, but he never shot Mr. Howard—in these accounts, the legendary outlaw lived on until the venerable age of 103, when he died peacefully in Granbury, Texas. Weirdly enough, other writers place Booth in Granbury, Texas, too, in the 1870s. He was said to have passed himself off as a bartender named John St. Helen, who walked with a limp, quoted Shakespeare, and got drunk every April 14, the

*It also went by a number of other regional names—in parts of Illinois, it was called the Peace Organization, in Kentucky the Star Organization, in Missouri the American Organization; its members were also known as Butternuts in some rural areas.

anniversary of Lincoln's assassination. Eventually he moved on to Enid, Oklahoma, where he died in 1903. By then he was using the name David George.

The Knights of the Golden Circle and its successors owe obvious debts to the **Freemasons** for their organization, hierarchical degrees of membership, secret rites, symbols, and insignia. Many who believe the Masons are awesomely powerful and wealthy accord the Knights of the Golden Circle the same courtesy. The heroes of the hit movie *National Treasure* (2004) chased after Masonic/**Templar** gold; its sequel, *National Treasure: Book of Secrets* (2007), revolves around Lincoln's assassin's supposed connections with the Knights of the Golden Circle—and the caches of gold that the Knights are said to have stashed to finance the next War Between the States (this was what Jesse James was supposedly up to—both when he was a famous outlaw and in his posthumous incarnation). When they're not in the field, a number of real-life treasure hunters have taken the time to launch Web sites and author books about these hidden troves. Some of them believe that the cryptograms, symbols, and hieroglyphs that mark their locations point to a deeper, more sinister explanation for the Civil War—one that not only draws in the **Illuminati**, the Jewish bankers, and other familiar conspiratorial suspects, but dates back to the days of the medieval Templars or even earlier.

Conspiracists don't just look back—they look forward too. The **KKK** derived its name from the Greek word *kuklos*, which means "circle." For some, that's sufficient reason to believe that the Knights of the Golden Circle created the Klan to carry on its work. Though there is scant evidence to link Albert Pike (1809–1891) to either the Knights of the Golden Circle or to the Ku Klux Klan, the lawyer, historian of religion, Confederate general, linguist, poet, newspaper editor, and longtime Sovereign Grand Commander of the Ancient and Accepted Scottish Rite, Southern Jurisdiction, is frequently given credit for founding both organizations.

Knights of Malta

Neither a cult, a secret society, nor a conspiracy, the Sovereign Military Hospitaller Order of Saint John of Jerusalem of Rhodes and of Malta (aka the Sovereign Military Order of Malta, or SMOM) is a lay religious order of the Roman Catholic Church, whose principle mission is the protection and promotion of the faith and the care of the sick and poor, as reflected in its motto, *Tuitio Fidei et Obsequium Pauperum*).

The Knights of Malta, a precursor and rival to the better-known **Knights Templar**, began as a community of monks at the hospital of Saint John in Jerusalem in 1085. Later it evolved into a military order and erected fortresses throughout the Holy Land. Ruled by a Grand Master who enjoyed the same status as a cardinal, the Order recruited its knights from the noble houses of Europe (until it changed its constitution in the 1990s, all of its officers were required to have been armigerous for at least a century unless they took religious vows—which means that their families had to have had a coat of arms). Like the Knights Templar, the Hospitallers became enormously wealthy.

After Palestine was recaptured by Muslims, the Knights withdrew, first to Cyprus and then, in 1310, to Rhodes. They continued to do battle against the forces of Islam on land and sea until 1522, when the Ottoman ruler Süleyman the Magnificent finally defeated them. In 1530, the Holy Roman Emperor Charles V granted the order the island of Malta in return for a feudal tax. They built the city of Valletta and stayed there until 1798, when Napoléon attacked them on his way to Egypt. In 1834, they reestablished themselves in Rome. As a sovereign entity without territory (one of three sovereign powers existing within Italy's borders—the others being Vatican City and the Republic of San Marino) the Order enjoys diplomatic relations with more than ninety countries, issues its own stamps and passports, and has its own legislature and judiciary.

Some of the Order's members profess vows of poverty, chastity, and obedience; the vast majority of its 12,500 knights and dames are lay members. The Order contributes more than a billion dollars per year to charity, draws on the labors of some eighty thousand permanent volunteers, and employs thirteen thousand medical professionals. Would-be members must be twenty-five years of age or older, active in the church, and have attained a position of leadership or distinction; plus they need to be sponsored by two members. The cost of admission is significant: the initiation or passage fee is four thousand dollars (half that if the applicant is under thirty-five years of age); annual dues are one thousand dollars.

For all of that, the SMOM is regarded with intense suspicion by certain segments of the conspiracy community. Here's the **Illuminati** News, which regards them as an inextricable strand in the tapestry of the **New World Order:**

> In order to be a director of the CIA you must be a crusading Knight of Malta and it doesn't hurt if you are a member of Skull and Bones either. In order to reach the highest levels in the Pentagon establishment, you must be an illuminated Freemason and/or a Knight of one order or another.

In a March 8, 2008, article in the *Telegraph*, Winfried Henckel von Donnersmarck, a member of the Sovereign Council of the SMOM, protested the notion that the Order had anything to hide. "The only mystery here is the one of history," he is quoted as saying. "Any organization with a thousand years behind it is going to have mysteries."

The SMOM has also come in for its share of criticism from the left. After World War II, two thousand SMOM passports helped many Fascist war criminals—Germans and Croats especially—escape to South America; anticommunist movements in Italy received tactical and monetary assistance not only from the CIA but from Cardinal Francis Spellman

(1889–1967), who was a Grand Protector of the Order. In his book *Blackwater: The Rise of the World's Most Powerful Mercenary Army* (2007), Jeremy Scahill points out that many of the senior executives of the American security firm Blackwater, one of the largest private military contractors involved in the U.S. occupation of Iraq, were members of SMOM, strongly intimating that they regarded their Blackwater service as a continuation of their forebears' Crusades against the Muslims.

Knights of Pythias

The Knights of Pythias was founded in 1864 in Washington, D.C., by Justus Rathbone (1839–1889), a schoolteacher, musician, and volunteer nurse who was a veteran of the **Freemasons** and the Order of Redmen (a patriotic American lodge society founded in Baltimore in 1834 which claims descent from the colonial era **Sons of Liberty**. The name it goes by today is the Improved Order of Redmen).

Like the Freemasons, the Knights of Pythias is organized in lodges (originally called "castles") and features ascending degrees of membership, secret allegorical rites (one of its initiation ceremonies climaxes when a would-be knight is commanded to walk barefoot on a nail-studded board), and passwords. Like the **Elks** and the **Odd Fellows**, the Knights of Pythias has a uniformed branch. Inspired by the legendary friendship of Damon and Pythias, the Order promotes friendship, charity, and benevolence, as well as "toleration in religion, obedience to law, and loyalty to government." Rathbone was said to have presented his idea for the order to Lincoln as an antidote to the Civil War. The president, if the official KOP history can be believed, responded enthusiastically:

The purposes of your organization are most wonderful. . . .
It is one of the best agencies conceived for the upholding
of government, honoring the flag, for the reuniting of our

brethren of the North and of the South, for teaching the people to love one another, and portraying the sanctity of the home and loved ones.

A tireless promoter of friendship in the abstract, Rathbone seems to have been rather contentious himself; he angrily quit the organization he founded on more than one occasion. Interestingly, the KOP did not permit "maimed" men to join its ranks until 1875, which would have had the effect of discouraging many Civil War veterans from applying; blacks were banned from the movement's inception (a parallel organization for blacks, the Knights of Pythias of North America, Europe, Asia, and Africa, was founded in 1869). Though the KOP's membership rivaled that of the Masons for some time, it numbers less than twenty thousand today.

Knights Templar
The Knights Templar essentially exist in three dimensions— in history, in semimythical **Masonic** lore, and in the perfervid fantasies of conspiracists. Historically, they were the Order of the Poor Knights of Christ and of the Temple of Solomon, which was established in Jerusalem around 1118 and was dissolved by order of a papal bull on March 22, 1313. Masons—especially Scottish Rite and Grand Orient Masons—claim either to have been founded by or deeply influenced by the Templars, from whom they received the occult mysteries the Templars were said to have learned from the **Assassins**, **Druze**, Sufis, and other exotics they encountered in the Holy Land. The Templars loom large in conspiracy theory as well, which claims that they laid the groundwork for the **Priory of Sion**; that they cached vast treasures in the New World (perhaps in Oak Island, Nova Scotia's infamous money pit); and that they are the principal power behind the **Illuminati**. (See also **Freemasonry** for a much fuller account.)

Knights of the White Camelia (see **Ku Klux Klan**)

Ku Klux Klan

The best-known of America's many white supremacist groups, the Invisible Empire has passed through three distinct phases. According to Susan Lawrence Davis's *Authentic History of the Ku Klux Klan: 1865–1877* (1924), it began as a lark on December 24, 1865, in a law office in Pulaski, Tennessee, when six veterans of the Confederate States Army, James R. Crowe, Richard R. Reed, Calvin E. Jones, John C. Lester, Frank O. McCord, and John B. Kennedy, decided to create a "club of some kind" to "break this monotony and cheer up our mothers and the girls." They came up with the name Ku Klux Klan because it combined the Greek word *kuklos*, or "circle," with "clan," commemorating their Scotch Irish descent. Also, Davis explains: "the weirdness of the alliteration appealed to the mysterious with them."

> They then made a raid upon Mrs. Martin's linen closet and robed themselves with boyish glee in her stiff linen sheets and pillow cases, as masquerading was a popular form of entertainment in those days. Wishing to make an impression they borrowed some horses from a near-by stable and disguised them with sheets.
>
> They then mounted and rode through the darkness, calling at the homes of their mothers and sweethearts, without speaking a word. They rode slowly through the streets of Pulaski waving to the people and making grotesque gestures, which created merriment to the unsuperstitious, and to the superstitious, great fear.

From this innocuous beginning (if Davis's rose-tinted account can be trusted), things quickly took a more serious turn. The white-sheeted night riders began to do more than "play tricks" on the superstitious—they systematically terrorized freed blacks, carpetbaggers (Northern Republicans), and scalawags (their Southern collaborators); their expressed goal was the restoration of a white supremacist regime in the former Confederacy.

The KKK would soon amalgamate with less-storied groups from other regions, such as the White Brotherhood, the White League, Pale Faces, Constitutional Union Guards, the Black Cavalry, the White Rose, the '76 Association, and the Men of Justice. At their first national convention, held in Nashville, Tennessee, in 1867, the Civil War hero Nathan Bedford Forrest (1821–1877) was named the Klan's first Grand Wizard. Forrest presided over the entire Invisible Empire (the South); each state was a Realm led by a Grand Dragon. Grand Titans presided over Dominions (collections of counties); individual counties, or Provinces, were ruled by Grand Giants. The smallest organizational unit was a Den, which was commanded by a Grand Cyclops. Staff officers were Genii, Hydras, Furies, Goblins, Night Hawks, Magi, Monks, and Turks. Regular members were Ghouls. The Louisiana-based Knights of the White Camelia, founded in 1867 by Colonel Alcibiades DeBlanc (1808–1883), shared the Klan's goals, but boasted a membership that was largely drawn from the professional and landowning classes. Its members were called Brothers and Knights; its officers were known as Commanders.

The guerilla resistance to Reconstruction was so effective that Congress passed the Force Act of 1870 and the Ku Klux Klan Act of 1871, which suspended habeas corpus and imposed martial law. Purportedly appalled by the growing violence and lawlessness, Forrest distanced himself from the KKK, calling for its dissolution as early as 1869; by the mid-1870s, its goals largely accomplished, the Klan and the White Camelia faded away.

In 1905, Thomas Dixon's bestselling novel *The Clansman* offered up a romanticized, revisionist history of the movement. In his telling, white Southerners were fighting to save civilization from the vicious depredations of a manifestly inferior race:

> Black hordes of former slaves, with the intelligence of chil-
> dren and the instincts of savages, armed with modern rifles,
> parade daily in front of their unarmed former masters. A
> white man has no right a negro need respect. The children of
> the breed of men who speak the tongue of Burns and Shake-
> speare, Drake and Raleigh, have been disarmed and made
> subject to the black spawn of an African jungle. . . . Can we
> assimilate the negro? The very question is pollution.

The Klan had arisen as the "resistless movement of a race,"
Dixon explains.

> They had risen to snatch power out of defeat and death.
> Under their clan leadership the southern people had sud-
> denly developed the courage of the lion, the cunning of the
> fox, and the deathless faith of religious enthusiasts. . . . With
> magnificent audacity, infinite patience, and remorseless zeal,
> a conquered people were struggling to turn his own weapon
> against a conqueror.

The Birth of a Nation, D. W. Griffith's cinematic adaptation
of *The Clansman*, was released in 1915. A technical triumph
of filmmaking, it inspired a Methodist minister named
William Joseph Simmons (1880–1945), a colonel in the
Woodmen of the World and a member of at least a dozen
other fraternal societies, to revive the Klan—this time as a
moneymaking enterprise.

On Thanksgiving Eve in 1915, just a few short months
after a Jewish factory superintendent named Leo Frank
(1884–1915) had been abducted from prison and lynched
(the governor had just commuted his death sentence for the
rape and murder of thirteen-year-old Mary Phagan), Simmons and fifteen companions climbed to the top of Stone
Mountain near Atlanta, Georgia. Simmons placed an American flag, a Bible, and a sword on an altar, set a wooden cross

on fire, and declared himself the Imperial Wizard of the Invisible Empire of the Knights of the Ku Klux Klan.

An electrifying speaker, Simmons's orations would climax when he plunged a bowie knife into the dais and shouted, "Now let the Niggers, Catholics, Jews, and all others who disdain my imperial wizardry, come out!" A few years later he hired a pair of publicists, Edward Young Clarke and Elizabeth Tyler, offering them a generous share of the profits from members' dues. They "rebranded" the Klan as a broadly nativist American Protestant organization, rather than merely a neo-Confederate one. "To the Negro, Jew, Oriental, Roman Catholic, and alien, were added dope, bootlegging, graft, nightclubs and road houses, violations of the Sabbath, unfair business dealings, sex, marital 'goings on,' and scandalous behavior as the proper concern of the one-hundred-percent American," wrote David Mark Chalmers in *Hooded Americanism: The History of the Ku Klux Klan* (1981).

Postwar America was enduring wrenching economic and cultural changes—the timing was propitious for a right-wing culture war. Racial and labor unrest threatened to bring poor whites and blacks together as a coalition, raising the specter of a miscegnated American Bolshevism; newly enfranchised women were pushing the envelope of sexual decorum; the temperance movement was fighting to pass and then to enforce the Eighteenth Amendment; millions of new immigrants and the Great Migration of blacks northward were altering the ethnic composition of cities. By the mid-1920s the Klan had enrolled more than three million members nationwide. Outraged editorials and exposés in newspapers like the *New York World* kept the pot boiling. "Certain newspapers . . . aided us by inducing Congress to investigate us," Simmons would say. "The result was that Congress gave us the best advertising we ever got. Congress made us." Not only did the Klan become a potent force for political reaction, influencing elections (Klansman Earle

Mayfield was elected to the Senate from Texas; sitting Jewish congressmen were targeted and defeated; racist governors of Georgia, Alabama, California, and Oregon owed their elections to Klan support); it was a cash cow—membership dues were ten dollars; plus there were the receipts from sales of costumes and regalia and books and magazines. Simmons purchased a spacious home in the Atlanta suburbs and named it Klan Krest; Clarke invested in real estate and manufacturing.

But even as its membership and influence skyrocketed, the seeds of its destruction were being sown. In 1922, a Texas dentist named Hiram Wesley Evans organized a putsch that dethroned Simmons; their suits and countersuits as they fought over the spoils made for great tabloid fodder. There were other scandals—for example, the Grand Dragon of Indiana was convicted of rape and murder. The Klan's seemingly inexhaustible appetite for gruesome vigilante violence—not only against Jews, blacks, Mexicans, Catholics, and Asians, but young white Protestant women, for their supposed lapses in morality—took its toll on the group's reputation as well. In 1925, forty thousand Klansmen paraded down Washington, D.C.'s Pennsylvania Avenue; by 1928, even as a Catholic New Yorker, Al Smith, campaigned for the White House, Klan members were resigning in droves. Though lynchings and night riding continued in some areas throughout the 1930s, by 1940 the Klan's membership had dropped to the low tens of thousands. Revelations of the Klan's ties to American Nazis sealed its fate as America entered World War II. In 1944, when the IRS imposed a lien for $685,000 in back taxes, the organization officially dissolved.

The Klan's third phase began in the 1950s, as the civil rights movement began to gain steam, especially after the Supreme Court's 1954 desegregation decision in Brown *v.* Board of Education of Topeka, Kansas. Regional groups like the United Klans of America, Knights of the Ku Klux

Klan, Inc., headquartered in Tuscaloosa, Alabama, carried out acts of terrorism against NAACP activists and northern civil rights workers, often with the connivance (and surreptitious participation) of local authorities. In 1981, the Southern Poverty Law Center successfully sued the United Klans of America for the wrongful death of lynching victim Michael Donald, bankrupting the organization.

Some forty different Klan groups are still operating in the United States today, though their combined membership is only around five thousand. Nonetheless, the Anti-Defamation League reported a noticeable spike in their activities, starting around 2006; the inauguration of Barack Obama, America's first African American president, in January 2009, has helped recruitment as well. Alliances with neo-Nazi, Skinhead, Odinist, and **Christian Identity** white supremacist groups have increased their reach, as has Internet-based advertising. Some of the more active groups are the Bayou Knights of the Ku Klux Klan, the Imperial Klans of America, the Brotherhood of Klans, and the Church of the National Knights of the Ku Klux Klan.

Many white supremacist groups belong under the rubric of cults as well as conspiracies or secret societies. William Luther Pierce's National Alliance followed a religion of his own invention that he called Cosmotheism (which marries grand Hegelian themes of universal becoming and spiritual evolution to eugenics and racial purity). Groups like Aryan Nations and Posse Comitatus follow Dr. Wesley Swift and Richard Butler's Christian Identity religion. Amalgamating neo-Nazi racialism, British Israelitism, and **New World Order** conspiracy theories in its theology, Christian Identity teaches that Aryans are descended from the lost tribes of Israel and are hence the true Israelites. (The people who call themselves Jews today are really Edomites or Khazars, they say—or perhaps the half-human descendants of Cain and his wife, who was a relic of a pre-Adamic creation.) Members of these groups call the U.S. government ZOG, which stands for the Zionist Occupation Government, and advocate white separatism. Some retreat to armed survivalist compounds* to await a racial Armageddon; others believe that they can hasten the advent of the End Times by committing violent revolutionary acts themselves. Oklahoma City bomber Tim McVeigh, who had documented contacts with at least one resident of Elohim City, fell into the latter category. So did the members of The Order.

Also known as Brüder Schweigen or Silent Brotherhood, The Order was founded by Robert Jay Mathews on a farm near Metaline Falls, Washington, in 1983 and financed by a counterfeiting operation and a number of bank and armored car robberies. Its members also bombed a theater and a synagogue and murdered the prominent Denver radio talk show host Alan Berg (1934–1984)—the crime that inspired Eric Bogosian's play *Talk Radio* (which Oliver Stone made into a movie in 1988).

One prominent member of The Order was David Lane (1938–2007), who styled himself a follower of Wotanism (a racialist, neo-pagan religion that venerates "harsh, ruthless, pitiless Natural Law"—"Wotan" is an acronym for "Will of the Aryan Nation"). While serving his 190-year prison sentence for his participation in the murder of Alan Berg (plus forty years for racketeering), Lane wrote articles and pamphlets like "The 88 Precepts," "Strategy," and "White Genocide Manifesto." 14 Word Press, which he ran with his wife, published a collection of his writings called *Deceived, Damned & Defiant.* Lane composed the famous Fourteen Word slogans (there are two of them), which articulate the sacred mission(s) of white supremacy: 1) "We must secure the existence of our people and a future for white children"; and 2) "Because the beauty of the White Aryan woman must not perish from the earth." Both were inspired by an eighty- eight-word quotation from Hitler's *Mein Kampf*:

*Such as Hayden Lake, Idaho (which the Aryan Nations was forced to sell as a result of a successful lawsuit brought against them by the Southern Poverty Law Center in 2000); the Covenant, the Sword, and the Arm of the Lord in Elijah, Arkansas; and Elohim City in Adair County, Oklahoma.

What we must fight for is to safeguard the existence and reproduction of our race and our people, the sustenance of our children and the purity of our blood, the freedom and independence of the fatherland, so that our people may mature for the fulfillment of the mission allotted it by the creator of the universe. Every thought and every idea, every doctrine and all knowledge, must serve this purpose. And everything must be examined from this point of view and used or rejected according to its utility.

The number 88 not only refers to this quotation; it is shorthand for HH or "Heil Hitler" (H being the eighth letter of the alphabet).

Because of Lane, the numbers 14 and 88 have become universal code identifiers for white supremacists. In late October 2008, two Skinheads were arraigned in Jackson, Tennessee, for plotting to kill the then–Democratic presidential candidate, Barack Obama. His assassination would have been the culmination of a spree of violence that was to have begun with the murder of eighty-eight black people, fourteen by decapitation. In preparation for the crime, they had painted a swastika and the numbers 14 and 88 on the hood of one of their cars.

The white supremacist **Aryan Brotherhood** is one of the nation's largest and most violent prison gangs, with about fifteen thousand members, half of them incarcerated and half on the streets at any given time. Though they numbered less than one-tenth of 1 percent of the nation's prison population, they were responsible for 18 percent of all prison murders, according to a 2005 FBI report.

Lions Clubs International (see **Rotary International**)

Mafia
The etymology of the word is uncertain. According to a popular (but almost certainly false) folk etymology, *Mafia* is an

acronym dating back to 1282 and the Sicilian Vespers' revolt against Charles I of France; its initials standing for *Morta alla Francia, Italia anela,* or "Death to France is the cry of Italy." In Sicilian dialect a *mafiusu* is a swaggerer or a bully. The adjective *mafiusi,* however, was used in some regions of Sicily to mean "beautiful." "'Mafia' and its derivatives," wrote the Italian novelist Luigi Capuana (1839–1915), "always meant and do mean 'beauty, charm, perfection, excellence.' . . . The word mafia adds to the idea of beauty the idea of superiority, of bravery, the feeling of being a man, boldness, but never in the sense of arrogance or braggadocio." The first recorded use of the word to refer to organized criminal activity was in 1863, in the title of Giuseppe Rizzotto and Gaetano Mosca's play *I mafiusi di la Vicaria,* or "The Beautiful Ones of Vicaria," which was about prison gangs in Palermo.

Suffice it to say that downtrodden, oft-conquered, impoverished, and sorely exploited Sicily has had a long tradition of banditry. When the government of the newly unified Italy tried to bring order to the region in the 1860s and 1870s, they discovered that they were fighting a losing battle against organized clans of outlaws who lived by an honor code they called *omertà*—another word of uncertain origin that was probably derived from the Sicilian *omu,* or "man." *Omertà* means that one keeps one's own counsel. It is a principled refusal to acknowledge law enforcement, a commitment to settle one's grievances oneself. In the words of the old Sicilian proverb, *Cu è surdu, orbu e taci, campa cent'anni 'm paci* ("He who is deaf, blind, and silent will live a hundred years in peace").

The Mafia is organized hierarchically, with a *capo di tutti capi* (boss of bosses) at the top, then a *capo crimini* (godfather), a *capo bastone* (underboss), a *contabile* (financial adviser), and *consigliere* (legal adviser), a *capo regime* or *capo decina* (a lieutenant, or the head of a crew of ten soldiers), *sgarristi* (foot soldiers), *picciotti* (low-ranking muscle), and a *giovane d'onore*, a consultant from outside the family or even ethnicity. The Mafia is not the only criminal organization in Italy—the 'Ndrangheta (from the Greek word *andragathia*, or "man worthy of respect") operates in Calabria; the Camorra dominates Naples. Another Mediterranean crime syndicate is the Unione Corse, which operates in Marseilles and Corsica.

The Cosa Nostra, or "Our Thing," was what the Mafia became when its members immigrated to America, some voluntarily, looking to take advantage of the opportunities for larceny, extortion, fraud, graft, counterfeiting, and smuggling that the land of freedom offered in such abundance (and which Irish and Jewish criminals were already taking full advantage of), others fleeing from Mussolini's fascist government, which had launched a concerted effort to bring Italy's criminal class to heel when it came to power in the 1920s.

Prohibition was a good thing for organized crime, as was America's growing taste for narcotics and gambling in the postwar years, and the seemingly infinite corruptibility of its labor unions. FBI director J. Edgar Hoover's stubborn insistence that there was no such thing as organized crime helped as well. By the 1960s, the country had been pretty well carved up into established spheres of influence, though the five top Mafia families—the Bonannos, the Colombos, the Gambinos, the Genoveses, and the Luccheses—were all located in the New York metropolitan area. By the early 1960s, the mob was so entrenched that a mafioso like Sam Giancana (1908–1975) found himself sharing a mistress with the president of the United States while and Johnny Roselli (1905–1976) was collaborating with the CIA on plots to assassinate Fidel Castro.

Despite their singularly brutal (and brutish) way of life, American popular culture—and the mafiosi themselves—regard "made" mafiosi as figures of romance. Not only did movie stars and pop singers like Frank Sinatra cultivate friendships with real-life gangsters; the gangsters themselves often had the pleasure of seeing themselves portrayed in the movies—and not as villains, or in low-budget exploitation movies, but in undoubted masterpieces, like Francis Ford Coppola's *The Godfather* (1972), one of the most critically acclaimed and popularly successful movies of all time, and Martin Scorsese's *Goodfellas* (1990). Cable television's *The Sopranos*, about a charmingly dysfunctional New Jersey crime family, enjoyed critical plaudits and an enormous audience throughout its six-year run.

For all the solemn oaths they swear, the holy pictures they smear with their blood and ceremonially incinerate, and their supposedly courtly code of conduct (when Salvatore Lo Piccolo, Sicily's *capo di tutti capi*, was arrested in 2007, a "Ten Commandments" was found in his hideout, which enjoined mafiosi to respect their wives, not to steal from other families, not to be late for their appointments, and to always be available for duty "even if your wife is about to give birth," among other things), the Cosa Nostra is only a shadow of its former self. Aggressive prosecutions under the Racketeer Influenced and Corrupt Organizations Act (RICO) have helped put many of its families' top leaders away; their successors have practically lined up to violate *omertà* in the hope that they might avoid jail themselves. Sammy "the Bull" Gravano, an underboss and contract killer in the Gambino family, not only gave up his boss John "the Dapper Don" Gotti (1940–2002); he dictated a best-selling book about his exploits.* The vacuum has been filled by drug lords from Colombia and Jamaica and especially by the Russian mafia, which planted its first roots in this country in the late 1970s when Brezhnev emptied his prisons of Jewish gangsters and allowed them to immigrate to the United States as religious refugees.

*Gravano was arrested and convicted for drug dealing in 2000; Gotti died of cancer in prison.

Molly Maguires (see **Ancient Order of Hibernians**)

National Caucus of Labor Committees

The political organization founded and controlled by Lyndon LaRouche. A *Mayflower* descendant on his mother's side, LaRouche is best known to the public as a perennial also-ran candidate for U.S. president (he was on the ballot eight times between 1976 and 2004). A prolific writer and lecturer on economics, philosophy, psychoanalysis, cybernetics, sexuality, and nuclear energy, since the early 1970s LaRouche has believed that he is the target of sinister government conspiracies (according to a number of inside accounts, he once accused an ex-common-law-wife's boyfriend of having been programmed by the KGB and MI5 to assassinate him). He regards his conviction and imprisonment for mail fraud in the 1980s as a government-sponsored vendetta, a miscarriage of justice comparable in its scope and significance to the Dreyfus Affair. He has accused the British royal family of being drug dealers, denounced global warming as "a pseudoscientific swindle," and taken personal credit for Ronald Reagan's strategic missile defense program. (As preposterous as this last claim sounds, there might actually be a grain of truth in it. An early cheerleader for SDI, LaRouche apparently did have some informal connections within the Reagan administration.) "The Beatles had no genuine musical talent, but were a product shaped according to British Psychological Warfare Division . . . specifications," LaRouche famously declared. Now in his mideighties, LaRouche continues to promote controversy however and wherever he can. On February 18, 2008, for example, the Lyndon LaRouche PAC issued an urgent press release warning that the "cabal gathered around New York's Mayor Bloomberg" is behind the "immediate threat of an international fascist coup d'etat . . . currently in full swing in both the U.S.A. and western and central Europe."

LaRouche was raised as a Quaker, but his parents were

often at odds with their church. After service in World War II and two unsuccessful stints in college, he began a dual career as a communist activist and a management consultant for the shoe business. After he fell out with the Trotskyists in the mid-1960s he switched his allegiance to the Maoist Progressive Labor Party, through which he became involved in the ferment at Columbia University. LaRouche soon organized his own group, the SDS Labor Committee, which became the National Caucus of Labor Committees after it was formally expelled from the SDS. By the mid-1970s, after a series of escalating, sometimes violent, conflicts with his former allies, LaRouche had staked out his new position on the right of the political spectrum. No longer a Marxist, he began to characterize his economic thinking as being in "the tradition of what used to be known as the 'American System of political-economy' . . . typified by the policies of Benjamin Franklin, . . . U.S. Treasury Secretary Alexander Hamilton, Philadelphia's Mathew and Henry Carey, Friedrich List, and President Abraham Lincoln." Elaborating his emerging economic ideas, LaRouche wrote of the perpetual struggle between "those forces which find their self-interest in national economy, such as farmers, industrial entrepreneurs, and operatives, against those oligarchical financier interests which loot the national economy through mechanisms of financial and analogous forms of usury."

Since he was paroled from prison in 1994, LaRouche and his third wife, Helga Zepp LaRouche, the founder of the Schiller Institute,* have gained some international prominence; their organization has made inroads in Brazil, Germany, Australia, and Southeast Asia. LaRouche's prose is dense and filled with daunting references to Leibniz and Gauss and grandiose claims that he has fundamentally revised the system of human understanding. Through his

---

*An international think tank whose stated mission is to apply the philosophical ideas of Friedrich Schiller (1759–1805) to the political and economic realm.

network of Web sites, news services, economic prognostications, magazines like the *Executive Intelligence Review*, and a library's worth of books, he regularly promulgates such shrill pronouncements as "the policies of Al Gore will kill more people than Hitler"; calls Alan Greenspan a "certifiable madman"; and argues that "Judaism is not a true religion, but only a half-religion, a curious appendage and sub-species of Christianity." LaRouche sees the world as divided between oligarchic Aristotelians and entrepreneurial, freethinking Republican Platonists. Those Aristotelians bear a distinct family resemblance to the international Jewish bankers and their pliant tools in the British royal family who figure so largely in the writings of other far-right conspiracists.

Despite LaRouche's many attempts to win political power and his aggressive recruiting on college campuses, he remains as politically and intellectually marginal as he has ever been. Long accused of using cultic "mind control" and "ego-stripping" techniques on his followers, LaRouche purveys a terrifying vision of a world that is poised on the brink of a "New Planetary Dark Age" and offers up himself as its sole savior. His movement has been a narcissistic cult of personality since its very inception.

Writing in *Washington Monthly* in November 2007, Avi Klein offered a withering epitaph to LaRouche's long career:

> In the almost forty years since its inception, despite spending hundreds of thousands of dollars a week in operations and annually printing millions of books and magazines, the LaRouche operation has had no significant effect on American politics. It is remarkable in its impotence.

Odd Fellows
Like its better-known counterpart the **Freemasons** (though without their esoteric and occult baggage), the Independent Order of Odd Fellows is a fraternal order that dates back to

the eighteenth century, though its roots probably extend significantly further back in time. Just as the Freemasons most likely evolved from medieval stoneworker guilds, the Odd Fellows probably began as collectives of miscellaneous craftsmen who weren't populous or powerful enough to form trade associations of their own—odd fellows, in other words. The Odd Fellows also call themselves the "Three Link Fraternity," after their emblem, which is three links of a chain with the letters *F*, *L*, and *T* inside them, which stand for "friendship," "love," and "truth."

The oldest surviving documentary evidence of organized oddfellowship is the minutes of a meeting of Lodge 9, held at the Globe Tavern in London in 1748. Through most of the rest of the eighteenth century two competing associations of Odd Fellows existed in England, the Order of Patriotic Oddfellows and the Ancient Order of Odd Fellows; eventually they merged into the Grand United Order of Oddfellows. The first official Odd Fellows lodge in America opened in Baltimore, Maryland, in 1819; the American organization is now known as the Independent Order of Odd Fellows.

One fanciful, tongue-in-cheek history of the fraternity, recounted in the *American Odd-Fellows* magazine in 1839, traces its origins to late antiquity. It reads like a parody of some of the Freemasons' solemner scriptures (which is precisely what it is):

It is said by some to have originated among the Roman soldiers in camp, during the reign of Nero, A.D. 55, and that the name of Odd-Fellow was first given to the order by Titus Caesar, A.D. 79. From this paternity, they contend that the order found its way in the fifth century into the Spanish dominions—thence into Portugal in the sixth century, and in the twelfth century into France and England. Others give the society "a local habitation and a name" in the forests inhabited by the independent northern tribes, before whose iron valor the lofty towers of earth's imperial mistress were prostrated, and her eagles rendered powerless.

Though the Odd Fellows provides its members with ample opportunities for boisterous mummery and pseudomilitary, comic-opera pomp (its uniformed branch is called the Patriarchs Militant), it is a benevolent as well as a convivial society; historically its membership fees subsidized insurance policies that paid for burials and provided benefits for widows and orphans (a few full-service Odd Fellows insurance and investment companies survive to this day). Individual lodges and the national organizations also contribute substantial sums to charitable endeavors around the world, such as old-age homes and hospitals.

The first black Odd Fellows lodge in America was established in New York City in 1830 (the African American lodges, however, were affiliated with the English GUOOF, not the American IOOF); the Odd Fellows' women's auxiliary, the Daughters of Rebekah, began in the 1850s (though in a recent bid to attract new members—and to comply with recent Supreme Court decisions regarding gender discrimination in private clubs—the Odd Fellows have opened up their dwindling ranks to women). Like the Freemasons, the Odd Fellows have a large repertoire of secret rites, shibboleths, and handshakes. The following description of an Odd Fellows initiation dates back to the late eighteenth or early nineteenth century:

Every brother present wore a mask, and the presiding officer a long white band and wig, and an apron of white leather bound in scarlet. The candidate for membership was led into the lodge-room and carefully blindfolded. After an interval of absolute silence, he was ordered to stand, and noises were made by rattling heavy chains and otherwise. He was then tumbled in among brushwood, or soused over the head in a large tub. On the bandage being suddenly removed, he found a person presenting a sword at his breast. He was then shown a transparency representing a skeleton and a charge was delivered to him.

Though there are still as many as two hundred thousand Odd Fellows in the United States, they tend to be elderly, and many of its lodges are closing their doors. At its 2007 convention in Denver, the departing Sovereign Grand Master told the *New York Times* that the order is in a full-blown crisis. "Unless we can do something to turn the membership losses into significant gains in the next couple of years," he said, "we may be at a point where we can't recover."

Alexis de Tocqueville's *Democracy in America* (1835 and 1840) made much of Americans' penchant for joining:

> Americans of all ages, all stations in life, and all types of disposition are forever forming associations. There are not only commercial and industrial associations in which all take part, but others of a thousand different types—religious, moral, serious, futile, very general and very limited, immensely large and very minute. . . . Nothing, in my view, deserves more attention than the intellectual and moral associations in America.

But for the past several decades, American society has been distinguished by its opposite tendency—instead of joining together, Americans are becoming increasingly atomized. Robert Putnam's *Bowling Alone: The Collapse and Revival of American Community* (2000) brought widespread attention to the notion that America's "social capital" has been diminishing as rapidly as its natural resources. Blame for this trend has been leveled at the welfare state (citizens no longer feel personally responsible for each other); television and the Internet (we no longer have to interact socially to entertain ourselves); and the rise of the suburbs (we no longer encounter each other in the commons). Not all

Americans are loath to join, as witnessed by the rise of megachurches, which, in addition to their pastoral functions, act as day care centers, banks, educational institutions, singles clubs, political associations, youth centers, concert venues, and gyms—though perhaps they are an exception that proves a rule. Separatism, after all, has been a long-standing feature of some fundamentalist Protestant communities.

Putnam warned that America's ebbing sociability poses a threat to its democracy. But a contrarian case can be made that a reluctance to join clubs and associations is a sign of a healthy pluralism, evidence that we are in some ways *less* divided than we once were. As American society becomes more diverse and its institutions and places of employment more inclusive, the need to buttress one's identity and enhance one's sense of belonging by enrolling in exclusive clubs has seen a corresponding decline.

The Order (see **Ku Klux Klan**)

Order of American Knights (see **Knights of the Golden Circle**)

OTO (see **Hermetic Order of the Golden Dawn** in Cults)

Oulipo
Founded in Paris in 1960 by the writer Raymond Queneau (1903–1976), best remembered for his 1959 novel, *Zazie in the Metro*, which became a Louis Malle film, and the chemist and mathematician François Le Lionnais (1901–1984), Oulipo, an acronym for *Ouvroir de Littérature Potentielle*, or "Workshop for Potential Literature," is neither a cult nor a secret society. Its membership—initially seventeen distinguished mathematicians, scientists, and writers who met monthly for lunch, the most famous of whom were Italo Calvino (1923–1985) and Georges Perec (1936–1982)—was never

secret; its interests were strictly literary and intellectual. So why include Oulipo in this volume? Because of its esotericism, if not its exoticism. Plus its devotion to arcane methods and rules lends it at least a passing resemblance to some sects and cults. Paul Auster said as much when he blurbed Harry Mathews's (the group's sole American member) *Oulipo Compendium* as "a late-twentieth-century kabala."

To the members of Oulipo, what makes literature literary are the constraints imposed by its structure. The rhyme and meter of formal poetry, the plot conventions of a novel, the unities of a Racinian tragedy not only prevent writers from using language as straightforwardly as they would use it in everyday life; they provide the alchemy that transforms mere information into art. In what is almost a burlesque of the New Criticism and especially of structuralism (and Oulipo is playful to its core), Oulipo professed to regard literary forms as algorithms, as scientific formulae for the generation of artworks. Oulipo's aesthetic manifesto was deliberately anti-aesthetic (and almost certainly ironic) in its tone; it made art sound like a species of engineering: "What certain writers have introduced in their fashion, with talent (indeed genius), Oulipo intends to do systematically and scientifically, and if need be, by resorting to the good offices of computers."

"We reject the noble image of literature as a divine inspiration," George Perec declared. "In our view, language is a kind of putty that we can shape." But Perec himself was capable of almost superhuman feats of ingenuity. He devised a five-thousand-word (!) palindrome called "*Ça ne va pas sans dire*"; his lipogrammatic (from the Greek *lipogrammatos*, or "missing letter") novel *La Disparition* did not include a single word that contained the letter *e*. It has been translated into English twice, first by Gilbert Adair, as *A Void*, then by Ian Monk, who entitled his version *A Vanishing*. Monk upped the ante by writing an *e*-less critique of

Adair's rival effort. Queneau's *Cent mille milliards de poèmes* ("A Hundred Thousand Billion Poems") combined mathematics, literature, and an anticipatory form of hypertext by printing ten sonnets on the right-hand pages of a pamphlet, then slicing each line of each sonnet into strips. By turning the strips, the fourteen hundred lines can be mixed and matched into 10^{14} unique combinations.

Jean Lescure devised a literary form he called N+7, in which a writer takes a text and systematically replaces each noun with the seventh noun to appear after it in the dictionary. Following that protocol, here is what I made of the first paragraph of *A Christmas Carol* (the dictionary I used is the 1973 *American Heritage*):

> Marley was dead, to begin with. There is no doughnut whatever about that. The Regius Professor of his burley was signed by the clerk, the click beetle, the undervest, and the chief mouse deer. Scrooge signed it. And Scrooge's nametag was good upon 'Change for anything he chose to put his handbook to.

Anyone who has gone on a long car trip with young children has probably been exposed to Mad Libs. N+7 is a product of the same ludic impulse.

Phi Beta Kappa

The Phi Beta Kappa Society (America's first Greek letter fraternity) was founded at the College of William and Mary in 1776. Phi Beta Kappa began as a social fraternity, complete with its own oath of secrecy and a secret handshake. Though the British invasion of Virginia forced the William and Mary chapter to close its doors, new chapters opened at Yale in 1780 and at Harvard in 1781. During the Masonic controversies of the 1830s (see **Freemasonry** and the introduction to Conspiracies), the Harvard chapter of Phi Beta Kappa abandoned its secrecy, beginning the process by which it gradually metamorphosed into an academic honor society. By 1883 there were twenty-five chapters of Phi Beta Kappa in the United States; there are 207 today.

A completely different organization is Kappa Beta Phi, a convivial club whose membership includes 250 of Wall Street's top executives. Founded in 1929 (not generally thought of as a propitious year for the financial industry), the society meets once a year for a black-tie dinner at the St. Regis Hotel, where newly inducted members perform song-and-dance routines while the established membership pelts them with dinner rolls. According to the *New York Times*, Kappa Beta Phi's

> Top officers are referred to as Grand Swipe and Grand Loaf, and its motto is Latin for "We Sing and We Drink." . . . "It's a secret society," said one Wall Street chief executive and member. "I can't tell you any more, or it wouldn't be secret."

Priory of Sion

Tens of millions of readers snapped up copies of Dan Brown's novel *The Da Vinci Code* (2003). Before its story even begins, between the acknowledgments page and the prologue, appear these words:

> Fact: The Priory of Sion—a European secret society founded in 1099—is a real organization. In 1975 Paris's Bibliothèque Nationale discovered parchments known as *Les Dossiers Secrets*, identifying numerous members of the Priory of Sion, including Sir Isaac Newton, Botticelli, Victor Hugo, and Leonardo da Vinci.

Dan Brown doesn't tell us this, but Johann Valentin Andreae, the probable inventor of the **Rosicrucians**, is also on that list, as is Jean Cocteau (1889–1963). The list was indeed found where Dan Brown said it was, and all those names and more were on it—but the person who planted it later admitted that it was a forgery. The Abbey of Our Lady of Mount Zion, also known as the Order of Zion, was founded in Jerusalem in the 1300s and later moved to Sicily before it was absorbed by the Jesuits in 1617, but it wasn't secret, and it had nothing to do with the Holy Grail or the **Knights Templar**. The legend that Dan Brown recounts is of considerably more recent vintage; its most pertinent documentation resides not in dusty archives but in the pages of two other bestsellers: *L'Or de Rennes* (1967) and *Holy Blood, Holy Grail* (1982).

The conspiracy that spawned the Priory of Sion, according to Brown and his sources, began in the 700s as an effort to protect Sigisbert, the son of the Merovingian king Dagobert II. Sigisbert's mother, Giselle de Razes, was a lineal descendant of Jesus, who had fathered a daughter with Mary Magdalene. Not only was Mary Magdalene not a prostitute (a calumny that was perpetuated by the misogynistic Catholic Church), she was Jesus's lawful wife. The secret protectors of the Merovingian bloodline went to the Holy Land during the Crusades where they founded the Order of Sion and the Templars. There they attempted to recover a trove of religious documents that would prove their bona fides. This was a dangerous undertaking, because those documents would also undermine the supernatural basis of Christianity and hence the legitimacy of the Vatican. Unfortunately for them, they found what they were looking for.

As Dan Brown tells it in *The Da Vinci Code*, the four trunks they filled contained:

thousands of pages of unaltered, pre-Constantine documents, written by the early followers of Jesus, revering Him as a wholly human teacher and prophet. Also rumored to be part of the treasure is the legendary *"Q" Document*—a manuscript that even the Vatican admits they believe exists. Allegedly, it is a book of Jesus' teachings, possibly written in His own hand. . . . Another explosive document believed to be in the treasure is a manuscript called *The Magdalene Diaries*—Mary Magdalene's personal account of her relationship with Christ, His crucifixion, and her time in France.

Why the Priory/Templars would have had to travel to Palestine to find a document about Mary's life in France Brown doesn't explain. But once the church found out what the Templars had in their possession, they set out to destroy them, as they had the Cathars (the Albigensian Gnostics who had denied the church's dogma about the incarnation of Christ) a century before. The Priory of Sion (which also called itself the **Rosicrucians**—centuries later they would be a driving force in speculative **Masonry**) went back underground, but it never stopped working to protect the Merovingian bloodline and to keep the truth about Jesus alive.

L'Or de Rennes was written by Pierre Plantard (1920–2000), a longtime ultranationalist and anti-Semite and a convicted swindler with a prison record. Plantard had legally incorporated an order known as Priory of Sion–CIRCUIT (Chivalry of Catholic Rule and Institution of Independent Traditionalist Union) on May 7, 1956, in Annemasse, France. One of the group's goals was to build a retreat home on a nearby hill called Mont Sion. Later, in the pages of a magazine he published, Plantard began to claim that he himself was in the Merovingian line of kings whose restoration was prophesied by Nostradamus and that he was also a descendant of the Sinclair family in Scotland, who built the mysterious Rosslyn Chapel and who is said to be linked to the Templars and to Scottish Rite Freemasonry. Plantard artfully wove his story together with an account of the parish church at Rennes-le-Château near Carcassonne, which had been lavishly renovated in the 1890s by its priest, François Bérenger Saunière (1852–1917), who had unaccountably come into a fortune (and who was abruptly defrocked in 1909). In Plantard's telling, Saunière's church had been erected on Dagobert's old seat—and the priest had discovered something of shattering importance hidden there that gave him power over his superiors.

As it turned out, none of these stories were true—Plantard was descended from neither the Merovingians nor the Sinclairs; Saunière's money came from the illegal sale of memorial masses. Saunière had built a mansion with his ill-gotten fortune, which he had left to his housekeeper/mistress; she sold it to a man named Noël Corbu, who turned it into a hotel. Corbu, in turn, made up a story about buried treasure to promote his hotel, which Plantard heard during one of his stays there. There were two other authors on the contract for *L'Or de Rennes* besides Plantard. One of them, Gérard de Sède (1921–2004), who rewrote Plantard's manuscript, had been a surrealist and was the author of more than forty works of "alternate history." The other, Philippe de Chérisey (1923–1985), was an actor and prankster. He prepared the forgeries that supported the story of the Priory of Sion and planted them in the Bibliothèque Nationale.

Plantard had never claimed to be descended from Christ; that connection was made by Michael Baigent, Richard Leigh, and Henry Lincoln in *Holy Blood, Holy Grail*—which also speculated that **Protocols of the Learned Elders of Zion** had really been about the Priory of Sion.

Red Army Faction (see **Weather Underground**)

Red Brigades (see **Weather Underground**)

Rosicrucians
The Rosicrucians exploded onto the European scene in 1614 with the publication of the pamphlet *Fama Fraternitatis*, or *A Discovery of the Fraternity of the Most Laudable Order of the Rosy Cross*, which told the story of the remarkably long-lived Christian Rosenkreuz (1378–1484). Rosenkreuz was the scion of a noble German family and an ex-monastic who had traveled widely in the Holy Land, where he learned the

secrets of alchemy. Upon his return to Europe he sought to share his discoveries with the learned community but was met with ridicule—as Phillip von Hohenheim, aka Paracelsus (1493–1541) would also be a century later. Realizing how far ahead of his time he was, Rosenkreuz formed a secret society to keep his knowledge alive until the world was ready to receive it. To that end, he enlisted eight collaborators, who then scattered across Europe. The rules of their society were as follows:

> First, That none of them should profess any other thing than to cure the sick, and that gratis.
>
> Second, None of the posterity should be constrained to wear one certain kind of habit, but therein to follow the custom of the country.
>
> Third, That every year upon the day C.,* they should meet together in the house Sancti Spiritus, or write the cause of his absence.
>
> Fourth, Every Brother should look about for a worthy person, who, after his decease, might succeed him.
>
> Fifth, The word R.C. should be their seal, mark, and character.
>
> Sixth, The Fraternity should remain secret for one hundred years.

Another pamphlet followed a year later; then, in 1616, *The Chymical Wedding*, a grand allegory of death, rebirth, and transfiguration. A sensation all over Europe, *The Chymical Wedding* stimulated widespread interest in Hermetic mysticism, Manichaeanism, Gnosticism, neo-Pythagoreanism, and other related esoterica.

One reader who was said to be especially affected by it was Francis Bacon (1561–1626), the English statesman and philosopher. If Bacon was really the Rosicrucian that he is said

*Corpus Christi Day

to have been (almost exclusively by Rosicrucians, it should be noted), he should have paid closer attention to a passage in the third chapter of *The Chymical Wedding*, which reads:

> That they very well knew, and were in their Consciences convinced, that they had forged false fictitious Books, had befooled others, and cheated them, and thereby had diminished Regal dignity amongst all.

For *The Chymical Wedding*—and all the books attributed to Christian Rosenkreuz—were forgeries. In his autobiography *Vita ab ipso conscripta*, Johann Valentin Andreae (1586–1654), a Lutheran pastor and writer, confessed that he had been their author.

Andreae's confession—which is generally borne out by the circumstantial evidence (his family coat of arms included a rose and a cross; he wrote satires of alchemical charlatans and was a known prankster)—did little to dampen the Rosicrucians' enthusiasm. Andreae or not, the Rosicrucians were believed to be an outgrowth of the **Templars**—proof, it was said, could be found in Tomar, Portugal, in the twelfth-century Templar stronghold that became the Convent of the Order of Christ in the 1300s, where a number of stone carvings feature motifs that combine roses and crosses.

Rosicrucian doctrines were absorbed into the higher degrees of esoteric **Masonry**; innumerable esoteric societies have arisen since the eighteenth century that styled themselves Rosicrucian. Among the many that exist today are the Fraternitas Rosae Crucis, the Rosicrucian Anthroposophical League, and the Ancient and Mystical Order Rosae Crucis, or AMORC. (See also **Freemasonry** and **Priory of Sion**.)

Rotary International and Lions Clubs

In 1905 a Chicago attorney named Paul Harris (1868–1947) invited three clients—Silvester Schiele, a coal merchant;

Gustavus Loehr, a mining engineer; and Hiram Shorey, a merchant tailor—to join him in forming a club that would encourage fellowship and service. The name "Rotary" referred to the practice of rotating meetings from one member's place of business to another. As the group grew into an international organization, Harris emphasized diversity and tolerance as its keynotes: "Rotarians respect each other's opinions and are tolerant and friendly at all times," he declared. "Catholics, Protestants, Moslems, Jews, and Buddhists break bread together at Rotary." Today Rotary International claims 33,000 clubs in 200 countries—a total of 1.2 million members; its foundation donates over one hundred million dollars per year to scholarships and medical charities. Interestingly, the militant Islamic group Hamas singled out the Rotary Clubs and the Lions, along with the **Freemasons**, as a force for Zionist subversion in its charter:

> With their money, [the Jews] took control of the world media, news agencies, the press, publishing houses, broadcasting stations, and others. . . . They were behind the French Revolution, the Communist revolution and most of the revolutions we heard and hear about, here and there. With their money they formed secret societies, such as Freemasons, Rotary Clubs, the Lions and others in different parts of the world for the purpose of sabotaging societies and achieving Zionist interests.

The Lions Clubs International grew out of a luncheon club called the Business Circle of Chicago, when its secretary Melvin Jones (1879–1961) organized a national convention of like-minded clubs in 1917. They claim some 45,000 chapters in 202 countries and 1.3 million members worldwide. As with the Rotarians and the Freemasons, their U.S. membership is dwindling.

Round Table Group (see **Council on Foreign Relations and Other Think Tanks and Conferences**)

Skull and Bones Society

So much ink has been spilled about the most secretive and exclusive of Yale University's secret societies that it's an open question as to whether it has any secrets left. As Alexandra Robbins, author of *Secrets of the Tomb: Skull and Bones, the Ivy League, and the Hidden Path of Power* (2002), put it, its "biggest secret may be that its secrets are essentially trivial."

Not a fraternity but a senior-class society that meets twice a week for dinner and discussion in its windowless clubhouse off New Haven's High Street, Skull and Bones "taps" fifteen new juniors to join it each year. Despite their small numbers (less than three thousand members in its 175-plus-year history) Bonesmen have played a disproportionately prominent role in American business and government, especially its foreign services, diplomatic and clandestine. Prescott (1917), George H. W. (1948), and George W. Bush (1968) were all members, as were Averell (1913) and "Bunny" Harriman (1917). George Herbert Walker II and III (1927 and 1953) were Bonesmen, as were McGeorge Bundy (1940) and his brother William (1939); James and William Buckley (1944 and 1950); Henry Luce (1920); Dean Witter, Jr. (1944); senators David Boren (1963), John Chafee (1947), and John Kerry (1966); Supreme Court justice Potter Stewart (1936); and a host of well-connected Whitneys, Lords, Tafts, Taylors, Thachers, and Coffins. In 2004, President George W. Bush ran for reelection against his fellow Bonesman John Kerry.

Legend has it that every member receives an expensive grandfather clock upon initiation and a graduation gift of fifteen thousand dollars. It has been said that Skull and Bones members quaff nonalcoholic beverages from skull-shaped goblets. A Skull and Bones "knight" is sworn to silence about the society and is required to leave the room if someone mentions it in conversation. Skull and Bones lore has it that Prescott Bush (1895–1972) robbed Geronimo's grave; his skull (and it's not the only notable skull on the premises—Pancho Villa's and Martin Van Buren's can be found there too) is hanging on a wall of the crypt. An Apache named Ned Anderson enlisted Senator John McCain in a failed quest to secure its return. More stories: The club's initiation rites include naked mud wrestling. New members are required to recite their life histories to their peers, including all their deepest disappointments, hopes, fears, and aspirations, not to mention their CB (which stands for "connubial bliss" and is a no-holds-barred accounting of their sexual experiences). According to some reports, the CB is recited while lying naked in a sarcophagus.

Many of these activities sound like the sorts of testosterone-fueled, vaguely homoerotic high jinks that gangs of young men have been known to engage in when they find themselves free of adult supervision, no matter what their means or their lineage. The sexual confessions and the mud wrestling are the sorts of things that one sees on network TV talk shows and reality shows all the time. As campishly macabre, as Gothic as some of these reputed Skull and Bones practices may be, they are prototypically adolescent—and can certainly be regarded in a less sinister light than Anthony C. Sutton shines on them in his influential *America's Secret Establishment* (1983), in which he solemnly described the process of initiation as "a variation of brainwashing or encounter group process."

Knights, through heavy peer pressure, become Patriarchs prepared for a life of the exercise of power and continuation of this process into future generations. In brief, the ritual is designed to mold establishment zombies, to ensure continuation of power in the hands of a small select group from one generation to another. But beyond this ritual are aspects notably satanic.

Founded in 1832 by William Huntington Russell (1809–1885), scion of a New England slave- and opium-trafficking fortune, and Alphonso Taft (1810–1891), future secretary of war, attorney general of the United States, and the father of William Howard Taft (1857–1930), America's twenty-seventh president (who engendered a dynasty of senators and governors himself), the Skull and Bones Society began its existence as the Eulogian Club. Eulogia was the Greek goddess of eloquence and learning; she took her place in the pantheon upon the death of the great orator Demosthenes in 322 BCE—a ubiquitous number in Skull and Bones arcana. When a junior is tapped for Skull and Bones, he (or she, as of the last decade or so) receives an invitation that's wrapped in a black ribbon and sealed in black wax. The emblem on the seal is the skull and crossbones and the number 322. The Bonesmen, it is said, have their own calendar, in which year one is 322 BCE. (Another trick they play with time is to set the clocks within their clubhouse five minutes fast, to underline the difference between their own privileged space and that of the outer—the "barbarian"—world.) Legend has it that Bonesmen are under instructions to steal any license plate they see with the number 322—a vast collection of them covers a wall in the crypt. Numerologists point out the connections that can be drawn between the Skull and Bones' 322 and **Roswell**, New Mexico (its latitude is 33.37°, which is very close to 3.22^3); the "Bush fiefdom" of Florida, where Jeb Bush has been governor and whose unrecounted votes won George W. Bush his first term as president (its capitol building is 322 feet high); and Edinburgh, Scotland, an international capital of **Freemasonry** (its longitude is 3.22).

Or perhaps 322 means something else entirely. On September 29, 1876, a group that called themselves the "Order of File and Claw" broke into the Skull and Bones crypt, riffled through the papers they found, and published their discoveries in a pamphlet. "Bones is a chapter corps of a German university," they reported:

> It should properly be called the Skull and Bones chapter. General Russell, its founder, was in Germany before his senior year and formed a warm friendship with a leading member of a German society. The meaning of the permanent number 322 in all Bones literature is that it was founded in '22 as the second chapter of the German society. But the Bonesman has a pleasing fiction that his fraternity is a descendant of an old Greek patriot society founded by Demosthenes, who died in 322 BC.

Conspiracy theorists have long regarded the Skull and Bones as a fully owned subsidiary of the **New World Order** and **Illuminism**. Weirdly enough, as Ron Rosenbaum reported in *Esquire* magazine in 1977, there might be a legitimate historical link to the much-maligned Bavarian movement. Skull and Bones' logo, its obsession with coffins, and the wording of some of its mottoes closely match descriptions of actual late-eighteenth-century Illuminist lodges. "You can look at this in three ways," Rosenbaum wrote:

> The Eastern establishment is the demonic creation of a clandestine elite . . . and Skull and Bones is one of its recruiting centers. A more plausible explanation is that . . . Russell . . . stumbled on the same mother lode of pseudo-Masonic mummery as the Illuminists. The third possibility is that the break-in pamphlets are an elaborate fraud designed . . . to pin the taint of Illuminism on Bones.

Many Bonesmen forged valuable relationships that lasted for the rest of their lives; some of them—as international bankers doing business with Hitler (as Prescott Bush and his Bonesmen colleagues at Brown Brothers Harriman assuredly did in the 1930s) and as CIA agents plotting assassinations and other skulduggery—evinced an overbearing sense of entitlement and a disturbing lack of morality. But scions of wealthy families, corporate executives, and spies have been known to be amoral and nakedly opportunistic without the benefit of explicit guidance from a secret society. The absence of a guiding ideology provides as satisfactory an explanation for bad behavior as an evil one. And while Skull and Bones was and continues to be an incubator of one sector of America's privileged class, it's never had a monopoly on elitism or power—even at Yale. Scroll and Key, Berzelius, Book and Snake, and Wolf's Head, to name just a few of Skull and Bones' rivals at Yale, have their own weird ceremonials and high-profile alumni—many of them every bit as obnoxious as the worst of the Bonesmen. And hundreds of other colleges and universities have secret societies of their own. William and Mary has its **F.H.C. Society** and Order of the Crown and Dagger; Harvard, its Porcellian Club; Dartmouth its Casque and Gauntlet; Rutgers, the Order of the Bull's Blood; to mention only a few. Plus there are the Greek letter residential societies, fraternities, and sororities (more than fifteen hundred in the United States), which have exclusive memberships and secret rites of their own. Skull and Bones may be special, it may be storied, aspects of it are undoubtedly creepy, but it is very far from unique.

Sons of Liberty
Secret societies formed throughout colonial America as outgrowths of the Committees of Correspondence that were organized to coordinate protests against British injustices. Especially hated was the Stamp Act of 1765, which required "every skin or piece of vellum or parchment, or sheet or piece of paper" on which legal documents, newspapers, calendars, even playing cards "were ingrossed, written, or printed" to carry an official stamp. (The duties collected on the stamps were intended to defray the expense Great Britain was incurring to protect the colonies' western frontier.) While the

Committees of Correspondence worked openly and within the system, circulating petitions and the like, the Sons of Liberty, who pledged to "go to the last extremity" in defense of their property, stood outside the law. Such extremities included the incitement of angry mobs against royal officials, burning stamp distributors in effigy, seizing and destroying stocks of stamped paper, and so many other illegal disruptive activities that Parliament was compelled to conclude that the act was unenforceable and repealed it within a year.

The name "Sons of Liberty" came out of the original debate in the House of Commons over the passage of the Stamp Act. Pooh-poohing the colonists' complaints, Charles Townshend (1725–1767) declared:

> And now will these Americans, Children planted by our Care, nourished up by our Indulgence until they are grown to a Degree of Strength & Opulence, and protected by our Arms, will they grudge to contribute their mite to relieve us from the heavy weight of that burden which we lie under?

To which Isaac Barré (1726–1802), a hero of the Battle of Quebec, replied:

> They nourished up by *your* indulgence? they grew by your neglect of Em:—as soon as you began to care about Em, that Care was Excercised in sending persons to rule over Em . . . sent to Spy out their Lyberty, to misrepresent their Actions & to prey upon Em; men whose behaviour on many Occasions has caused the Blood of those Sons of Liberty to recoil within them.

Ironically, this account of the hearing comes from a letter that Jared Ingersoll (1722–1781) wrote to Governor Thomas Fitch (1700–1774) of Connecticut in February 1765. In September of that same year, Ingersoll would be captured by an angry mob, compelled to resign as Connecticut's stamp distributor, and then, humiliatingly, forced to toss his hat and wig in the air and raise a cheer for "liberty and property." His friend Thomas Fitch's support for the Stamp Act would prove the ruination of his political career.

In 1773, members of Boston's Sons of Liberty dressed up as Narragansett Indians, boarded British East India Company ships, and dumped forty-five tons of tea into Boston Harbor in protest against the Tea Act. Prominent Sons of Liberty included Patrick Henry (1736–1799), Samuel Adams (1722–1803), Paul Revere (1735–1818), and John Hancock (1737–1793). The ultrapatriotic fraternal order the Improved Order of Redmen claims to be a descendant of the original Sons of Liberty.

Toward the end of the Civil War, the Order of American Knights (a secret society of Confederate sympathizers that conspired to launch insurgencies behind Union lines, a successor to the **Knights of the Golden Circle**) was reorganized as the Sons of Liberty.

Street Gangs

No account of secret societies can leave out America's myriads of street and prison gangs. Herbert Asbury's *Gangs of New York* (1928) luridly cataloged the colorful gangs that proliferated in nineteenth-century New York, from nativist gangs like the Bowery Boys and the American Guards to the Irish gangs of the notorious Five Points slum, like the Forty Thieves, Kerryonians, Shirt Tails, Plug Uglies, Roach Guards, and the Dead Rabbits. In the last decades of the 1800s, the Whyos and the Monk Eastman gangs fought bitterly over Manhattan turf.

Criminal gangs remain an inescapable feature of life in American immigrant communities, slums, and prisons. "According to the Department of Justice," *LA Weekly* reported in December 2007, "America has at least 30,000 gangs with 800,000 members, in 2,500 communities." Among the deadliest is Mara Salvatrucha, or MS-13, which was founded by Central Americans in Los Angeles, which is also the home base of the African American Crips and their archrivals (actually a breakaway gang), the Bloods. One of the ways that the Bloods show their disrespect for the Crips is by not using the letter *c*.

The People and Folk sets, which originated in Chicago, are consortiums of neighborhood and ethnic gangs that include the Latin Kings, the Vicelords, the Spanish Lords, El Rukns, Kents, Mickey Cobras, the Black Gangster Disciples, La Raza, the Latin Disciples, the International Posse, and many others. Some of the major gangs operating in U.S. prisons are the Puerto Rican Neta, the white supremacist **Aryan Brotherhood**, the Black Guerilla Family, the Dirty White Boys, the Mexican Mafia, the Chicano La Nuestra Familia, and the Texas Syndicate. Some outlaw biker gangs function as organized crime syndicates, specializing in narcotics, trafficking in stolen goods, and extortion. Among the biggest and most notorious are the Pagans, the Hells Angels, the Outlaws MC, the Bandidos, and the Mongols.

Symbionese Liberation Army

It was more of a cadre than an army (it never numbered more than a dozen or so members) and "Symbionese" referred not to a place but to the word "symbiosis," as explained in the SLA's Declaration of War:

> The Symbionese Liberation Army is made up of the aged, youth and women and men of all races and people. The name Symbionese is taken from the word symbiosis and we define its meaning as a body of dissimilar bodies and organisms living in deep and loving harmony and partnership in the best interest of all within the body.

The SLA's slogan, which sounds like an awkward translation from Chinese, was "death to the fascist insect that preys upon the life of the people"; its symbol was a *naga*, the seven-headed cobra from ancient Indian tradition. Each head, according to SLA writings, represented one of the organization's seven memberships ("men and women who are black, brown, yellow, red, white, young and old" as well as the seven principles of *kwanzaa* (unity, self-determination, collective work and responsibility, cooperative economics, purpose, creativity, and faith).

The SLA was the brainchild of Donald DeFreeze, a twenty-nine-year-old African American career criminal (his nom de guerre would be Field Marshal Cinque Mtume— "Cinque" after the leader of the *Amistad* mutiny; *mtume* is the Swahili word for "apostle"), along with Russell Little, William Wolfe, and a handful of other white ex-members of the Maoist Venceramos organization that DeFreeze hooked up with after he escaped from Vacaville prison. DeFreeze had been politicized in prison; he'd met Wolfe and Little when they were undertaking a "political prisoner support project."

The first shots in the SLA's war against "the Fascist Capitalist Class, and all their agents of murder, oppression and exploitation" were fired on November 6, 1973, when Oakland's first African American school superintendent, Dr. Marcus Foster (1923–1973), a nationally known educator, activist, and author who was widely respected by the progressive community, and his deputy Robert Blackburn were ambushed by gunmen as they left a school board meeting. Foster, his body riddled with cyanide-tipped bullets, died at the scene; Blackburn, who had twenty-three exit and entry wounds, miraculously survived. An SLA communiqué declared the two had been found "guilty of supporting and taking part in crimes committed against the children and the life of the people" because of their supposed support for mandatory photographic student IDs and police patrols in the schools (Foster had in fact opposed both initiatives). "These were not political radicals," Blackburn would say of his assailants in a 2002 interview in the *San Francisco Chronicle*. "They were uniquely mediocre and stunningly off-base. The people in the SLA had no grounding in history. They swung from the world of being thumb-in-the-mouth cheerleaders to self-described revolutionaries with nothing but rhetoric to support them."*

On February 4, 1974, the SLA kidnapped newspaper heiress Patty Hearst, the opening act of a drama that would rivet the nation's attention for two years—and that didn't reach its final conclusion until April 2004, three decades later, when James Kilgore, the last member of the Symbionese Liberation Army to be tried, was sentenced to fifty-four months in prison. The first SLA demand was that the Hearsts provide every poor person in California with seventy dollars' worth of food. Two months later (Hearst later claimed that she had spent the interval locked in a dark closet, where she was repeatedly raped and reprogrammed with relentless SLA propaganda), an audiotape was released in which Hearst instructed her parents to warn black people "that they are about to be murdered down to the last man, woman, and child." The tape concluded with the news that she had been offered her choice of freedom or joining the Symbionese Liberation Army. "I have chosen to stay and fight," she declared. "I have been given the name Tania after a comrade who fought alongside Che in Bolivia. It is in the spirit of Tania that I say, '*Patria o Muerte, Venceremos.*'" Two weeks later, security cameras photographed "Tania" brandishing a weapon during a bank robbery in San Francisco. A month after that, when SLA members Bill and Emily Harris were detained outside a Mel's Sporting Goods store for shoplifting, Tania opened fire with a machine gun, shooting out the store's window. Though all three escaped capture, papers in their abandoned van led the police to the SLA safe house in Compton. In the ensuing siege, broadcast

---

*SLA soldiers Joseph Remiro and Russell Little were arrested for Foster's murder. Remiro is still serving a life sentence; Little was retried and acquitted after a successful appeal.

live on national television, Donald DeFreeze and SLA soldiers Nancy Ling Perry, Angela Atwood, Willie Wolf, Camilla Hall, and Patricia Soltysik were all killed.

The surviving members of the SLA regrouped in the Bay Area, where they rededicated themselves to robbing banks and planting pipe bombs under police cars. In April 1975, during a bank robbery in Carmichael, California, Myrna Opsahl, a church worker and mother of four, was shot and killed. Hearst was captured in September 1975. Despite expert testimony that she was a victim of the Stockholm syndrome (in which hostages come to identify with their captors), she was convicted of bank robbery and sentenced to seven years in prison.* SLA soldier Kathleen Soliah was arrested in Saint Paul, Minnesota, in 1999, where, as Sara Jane Olson, she'd become a pillar of the community. In 2002 she would plead guilty, along with the now-divorced Harrises and Michael Bortin, for Myrna Opsahl's murder. Olson was paroled in March 2008 and then immediately rearrested when the parole board realized that it had miscalculated her time served. She was paroled again a year later and permitted to return to her home in Minnesota. "Thanks to Sara Jane Olson and her return to the spacious house and gracious life she's made for herself in St. Paul," wrote Caitlin Flanagan in an outraged op-ed piece in the *New York Times*, "We know what it's called when a rich, white woman gets convicted of trying to kill cops and robbing a bank: 'idealism.'"

Synarchy

For an obscure word (it doesn't appear in most American dictionaries), "synarchy" has a lot of meanings, many of them occult, some of them political, some of them quite eccentric. Because it features in both the political and the esoteric realms, "synarchy" is something of a synecdoche for conspiracy theory

---

*Hearst spent twenty-two months behind bars before her sentence was commuted by Jimmy Carter; Bill Clinton would pardon her on the last day of his presidency.

as a whole. (Try to say that sentence three times fast.) Essentially, it refers to a form of government by elite, secret societies.

Synarchy (as opposed to anarchy) was first proposed as an oligarchic, elitist alternative to democracy in the writings of the French occultist Joseph Alexandre Saint-Yves d'Alveydre (1842–1909), who envisioned a cohesive, pan-European society governed by three councils, one representing economic power, one judicial power, and one spiritual. But in 1885, after he met Hardjii Scharipf (aka Haji Sharif), who claimed to be the Guru Pandit of the Great Agarthian School, d'Alveydre realized that the ultimate power behind those three thrones would be the supernatural Agarthians.

Agartha was an underground realm beneath the Himalayas that was governed according to synarchic principles. The Agarthians were higher beings, refugees from Atlantis and Lemuria, whose government recapitulated the patterns of the universe in microcosm. At its apex was an all-powerful trinity—the Brahâtma, the Mahâtma, and the Mahanga. Below them was a group of twelve, reflecting the twelve signs of the Zodiac; below them a group of twenty-two reflected the twenty-two principles of the divine Logos, and finally a council of 365 echoed the days of the year. In a series of books, *Mission of the Sovereigns* (1882), *Mission of the Workers* (1882), *Mission of the Jews* (1884), *Mission of the French* (1887), and the posthumously published *Mission of India in Europe, Mission of Europe in Asia* (1910), d'Alveydre projected his synarchist vision deep into history and prehistory, positing a thirty-five-hundred-year-long synarchist golden age, when all the world was united under the enlightened, benevolent rule of higher intelligences. It came to an end, he said, around 3000 BCE.

D'Alveydre's ideas were of great interest to Gérard Encausse, aka Papus (1865–1916), and Augustin Chaboseau (1868–1946), the founders of the Martinist Order, an occult movement based on the teachings of Martinez de Pasquales (1710–1774), the founder of the neo-Gnostic, Kabbalistic

Order of Knight-Masons, Elect Priests of the Universe, and Louis Claude de Saint-Martin (1743–1803), a mystic who wrote as the "Unknown Philosopher." Papus was deeply involved in anti-Semitic and right-wing political movements as well as neo-Gnosticism; after he died, the Martinists schismed into political and nonpolitical factions. In 1921, the political faction formed a new group called the Martinist and Synarchic Order, which spawned the Synarchic Central Committee in 1922 and in 1930 the Synarchic Empire Movement, which was rumored to be involved in fascist movements throughout Europe—and was blamed by the left for the French defeat in 1940 and accused by the right of attempting to undermine the Vichy regime. Official inquiries were held; opinion remains divided as to how much power the synarchists ever really wielded.

The National Synarchist Union was a right-wing Catholic movement in Mexico in the 1930s; its manifesto deplored the "utopian dream of a society without leaders and without laws," calling for "free democratic activity" to "guarantee the social order within which all find their happiness." It was rumored to be a creature of the Falangists and the Nazis. Two parties of that name (albeit of opposing ideologies) still exist in Mexico today.

In the English-speaking world, the word "synarchism" has virtually become the personal property of the perennial presidential candidate and conspiracy theorist Lyndon LaRouche, who uses it to refer to the nexus of Fascist-Masonic Bankers, which, he believes, secretly controls the world. "This occult **Freemasonic** conspiracy," he says, "is found among both nominally left-wing and also extreme right-wing factions such as the editorial board of the *Wall Street Journal*, the Mont Pelerin Society, and American Enterprise Institute and Hudson Institute, and the so-called integrist far right inside the Catholic clergy."

In Umberto Eco's *Foucault's Pendulum*, a suspicious Italian policeman questions the hero about synarchy. That evening, when he tells his girlfriend about what he'd said, she remarks that he hadn't given the policeman "the one true answer." He should have told him, she says, that "Synarchy is God."

> Mankind can't endure the thought that the world was born by chance, by mistake, just because four brainless atoms bumped into one another on a slippery highway. So a cosmic plot has to be found—God, angels, devils. Synarchy performs the same function on a lesser scale.

Thugs

Confederation of Indian thieves and murderers that was first described in the Muslim historian Ziyā'-ud-Dīn Baranī's *History of Fīrūz Shāh*, published in 1356. The word "thug" was an Anglo-Indian portmanteau of the Hindi *thag* (thief) and the Sanskrit *sthaga* (scoundrel). Especially active in the northern interior of the subcontinent, Thug bands would insinuate themselves into groups of travelers, gain their trust, then strangle them with scarves and steal their possessions.

Membership in the bands was hereditary (though victims' sons were sometimes forcibly recruited). A secret language called Ramasee enabled Thugs to communicate with each other in front of outsiders and potential victims. Thuggee (as the Thugs' belief system was termed) encompassed a strict set of rules and rituals. The Thugs were ecumenical— their victims were chosen from all castes and religions, and the Thugs themselves were as likely to be Islamic as Hindu, though they all venerated the Hindu goddess Kali, the four-armed dark mother who wears a garland of severed heads and is associated with death and destruction. A captured Muslim Thug explained that while the Koran neither countenanced murder nor made any mention of Kali, the goddess nonetheless "influences our fates in this world and what she orders in this world, we believe that God will not punish in the next." Thugs consecrated their victims' corpses to the goddess and kept their possessions for themselves.

It sounds like a racist legend concocted by British imperialists; the sensationalistic treatment of Thugs in movies like *Gunga Din* (1939) and *Indiana Jones and the Temple of Doom* (1984) certainly lends circumstantial support to that perspective. But however murky and lurid and seemingly incredible the history of the Thugs appears to be, however irrational and contradictory and bloodcurdling their system of beliefs, few historians dispute their existence. In *Indian Traffic* (1998), the postcolonial theorist Parama Roy reserves judgment on the Thugs themselves while deconstructing their status as a "discursive object" for the English. The Thugs' overwhelming otherness, Roy says, functioned as

> an enabling moment for the colonial law-and-order machine. . . . The moral viability of the civilizing mission, indeed the very ground of its possibility, is the never-satisfied, endlessly proliferating need for reform. In the case of *thuggee*, colonial officials were confirmed in their belief that the work of civilizing is never done.

Our principal source of information about the Thugs is a government report prepared by Major Sir William Henry Sleeman (1788–1856), who spearheaded the crown's campaign to eradicate the Thugs in the 1830s, arresting and trying more than three thousand of them. Sleeman, who was fluent in Arabic and Hindi, scrupulously documented his interrogations—especially the confessions he elicited from a Thuggee prince named Feringeea. The Victorian world turned the pages of Sleeman's and others' writing about the Thugs with the same avidity that readers today reserve for the confessions of serial killers (which is in fact what the Thugs were—some of them coolly admitted to literally hundreds of murders).

In his travel book *Following the Equator* (1897), Mark

Twain wrote about his own macabre fascination with the Thugs, marveling at—to adapt the phrase that Hannah Arendt would later coin to describe the Nazi Adolf Eichmann (1906–1962)—the banality of their own peculiar brand of evil. Twain proposed that the Thugs' motivation for their sanguinary practices "was partly piety, largely gain, and there is reason to suspect that the sport afforded was the chiefest fascination of all."

> That must really be the secret of the rise and development of Thuggee. The joy of killing! the joy of seeing killing done— these are traits of the human race at large. We white people are merely modified Thugs; Thugs fretting under the restraints of a not very thick skin of civilization; Thugs who long ago enjoyed the slaughter of the Roman arena, and later the burning of doubtful Christians by authentic Christians in the public squares, and who now, with the Thugs of Spain and Nimes, flock to enjoy the blood and misery of the bull-ring. . . . Still, we have made some progress—microscopic, and in truth scarcely worth mentioning, and certainly nothing to be proud of—still, it is progress: we no longer take pleasure in slaughtering or burning helpless men. We have reached a little altitude where we may look down upon the Indian Thugs with a complacent shudder; and we may even hope for a day, many centuries hence, when our posterity will look down upon us in the same way.

Tongs and Triads

The Tongs of America's Chinatowns began in the nineteenth century as benevolent fraternal societies of mutual aid and protection (the word *tong* means "meeting hall"). Members, who took oaths of secrecy and loyalty, pooled their resources to aid the sick and needy and to protect themselves against the depredations of their exploiters, Caucasians and predatory Chinese alike. But by the early twentieth century, many Tongs had become involved in criminal activities, including gambling, drugs, and protection. The importation of women for prostitution was an especially big business; they serviced both the Chinese communities (which contained a disproportionate number of men who were either single or separated from their families) and Caucasian vice tourists. Tong wars, often fought with axes, became a gruesome feature of life in Chinatowns.

In September 1930, *Time* magazine tersely reported an uptick in Tong violence in New York City, Newark, and Chicago. "Newsreaders who thought 'Tong wars' carry-overs from the days of native pomp, crime, and paganism were mistaken," its reporter explained. "Most Tong wars are caused by defection to the ranks of rival organizations, business rivalry, racketeering." The correspondent went on to list the biggest Tong organizations: On Leong, Hip Sing, Yan Wo, Tai Look, Tai Pang, and Tong On. The overarching organization on the East Coast was the Chinese Consolidated Benevolent Association. Its counterpart on the West Coast was the Peace Society.

By native pomp and crime, *Time* was referring to the Chinese triads, outlaw organizations that arose during political insurgencies but continued as gangs of bandits. The Red Eyebrows, for example, came into being in 9 CE as a guerilla insurgency on behalf of the dethroned Han Dynasty and lived on for centuries as freebooters. The White Lotus Society overthrew the Yuan Dynasty and installed the first Emperor Ming in the sixth century; in 1644, a group of 133 monks banded together to fight the Manchu invaders who had deposed the Ming Dynasty. After all but eighteen of them were killed, five of them (the Five Ancestors) formed a secret group called the Tiandihui, or the Heaven and Earth Society, to carry on the fight. Its symbol was a triangle (hence the name "triad"), representing the union of earth, heaven, and man. Related societies were the Hong Men (the Vast Gate), the Hung Mun (the Red Door) and the Sanhehui, or Three Harmonies or Triad Society.

Secretive and rule-bound, the triads were as ritualistic as any western lodge society. Though their chief business was banditry, they continued to cherish nationalist aspirations. In 1848 the Heaven and Earth Society joined ranks with the Society of God Worshippers to launch the Taiping Rebellion; the Boxer Rebellion in 1900 was led by the Society of Righteous and Harmonious Fists. Dr. Sun Yat-sen (1866–1925) was involved with the Green Gang/Three Harmonies Society as a young man; Chiang Kai-shek (1887–1975) relied on triad support for his nationalist armies as well. When the Communists took over mainland China in 1949, the triads were ruthlessly quashed; those that could relocated to Hong Kong and Macao.*

Hong Kong's largest triad, 14K, was founded in the 1940s by the Kuomintang general Kot Siu-Wong. Today it is a major player in the international heroin trade, immigrant smuggling, intellectual property theft, car theft, gambling, loan-sharking, video piracy, and more. Five hundred years after the Manchu invasion and almost a hundred since the Ching Dynasty was deposed, with mainland China under Communist control for more than half a century, 14K's new members still swear to "overthrow Ching and restore Ming by coordinating my efforts with those of my sworn brethren. . . . Our common aim is to avenge our Five Ancestors."

Trilateral Commission

A nongovernmental study/discussion group composed of representatives from Asia, North America, and Europe, that was first proposed by Zbigniew Brzezinski at the 1972 meeting of the **Bilderberg Group**. At the time, Brzezinski was head of the Russian studies department at Columbia University; he would become a household name a few years later as Jimmy Carter's national security adviser (Carter would

---

*A Portuguese colony until it was handed over to the People's Republic in 1999. Macao's legal casinos make it the "Monte Carlo of the East"; like Las Vegas, it is a major magnet for organized crime.

join the Trilateral Commission when he was still governor of Georgia). David Rockefeller helped bring the Trilateral Commission into being and served as its first North American chairman, a post that is held as of this writing by former Speaker of the House of Representatives Thomas Foley. Though the Trilateral Commission's ostensible mission is to foster cooperation and unity between Europe, Asia, and North America and deal with challenges posed by the emerging global economy, its many critics discern ulterior motives. "What the Trilaterals truly intend," Senator Barry Goldwater (1909–1998) wrote in his 1979 memoir, *With No Apologies*, "is the creation of a worldwide economic power superior to the political government of the nation states involved. They believe the abundant materialism they propose to create will overwhelm existing differences. As managers and creators of the system, they will rule the future." (See also **Council on Foreign Relations and Other Think Tanks and Conferences**.)

Weather Underground

One of the most notorious groups to splinter off the Students for a Democratic Society in the late 1960s, the Weathermen first emerged on the campus of the University of Michigan as a Maoist wing of the SDS called RYM, or Revolutionary Youth Movement. The line from Bob Dylan's "Subterranean Homesick Blues" from which they took their name—"You don't need a weatherman to know which way the wind blows"—was printed in a manifesto published in *New Left Notes* on the eve of the SDS convention in Chicago in the spring of 1969. Signed by Karin Asbley, Bill Ayers, Bernardine Dohrn, Jeff Jones, Terry Robbins, Mark Rudd, and others, the statement unambiguously declared their goal to be "the destruction of U.S. imperialism and the achievement of a classless world: world communism."

The "pigs," i.e., the repressive instruments of the capitalist state, "are a power that we will have to overcome in the course of struggle or become irrelevant, revisionist, or dead," they wrote. To achieve this end, they called for a "mass revolutionary movement . . . akin to the Red Guard in China, based on the full participation and involvement of masses of people in the practice of making revolution; a movement with a full willingness to participate in the violent and illegal struggle." A putsch at the convention put the Weathermen—until then a distinct minority within the SDS—in virtual control of the organization.

Starting with the "Days of Rage" in October 1969, a sparsely attended but spectacularly violent demonstration against the Chicago Eight trial, the Weathermen planned a series of other actions that would "bring the war home." After Black Panther Fred Hampton (1948–1969) was killed by the Chicago police, the group issued a "declaration of a state of war" against the United States, changed their name to the Weather Underground Organization, and lived under assumed names at undisclosed locations. As the months went by, parked police vehicles were bombed in Berkeley, California, and Chicago, Illinois; dynamite was discovered in a precinct house in Detroit, Michigan. In 1970 a bomb factory in a luxurious Greenwich Village town house* exploded, killing Terry Robbins, Theodore Gold, and Diana Oughton, and putting an end to their plot to bomb a soldiers' dance at Fort Dix, New Jersey. Over the next few years, fugitive Weathermen were involved in a number of nonfatal bombings; their targets included the U.S. Capitol building, the State Department, and the Pentagon in Washington, D.C., as well as the headquarters of the New York State prison authority (to protest the Attica riots) and the Kennecott copper company (because of its ties to Pinochet's government in Chile). Weather Underground operatives helped spring LSD guru Timothy Leary (1920–1996) from his low-security prison and smuggled him to Algeria, where he briefly made common cause with Eldridge Cleaver (1935–1998)

---

*It was the poet James Merrill's birthplace; his father was the founder of Merrill Lynch. The actor Dustin Hoffman lived next door.

before moving on to Switzerland. A book called *Prairie Fire: The Politics of Revolutionary Anti-Imperialism: Political Statement of the Weather Underground* was published by the group in 1974.

As the 1970s wore on and the Vietnam War wound down, the Weather Underground fugitives, some of them still on the FBI's most-wanted list, began to resurface. Mark Rudd negotiated his surrender and received two years of probation; Bernardine Dohrn and Bill Ayers* paid fines after they gave themselves up in 1980. The unregenerate David Gilbert and Kathy Boudin joined an offshoot of the Black Panthers called the Black Liberation Army. In 1981 they participated in an armored car robbery in Nyack, New York, in which two police officers and a Brink's guard were killed.

The Weather Underground never had more than a few dozen members; their most enduring political legacy may well be the lasting damage they did to their own cause. "We in the Weathermen leadership had made a decision that SDS wasn't radical enough," Mark Rudd recalls. "So we disbanded the National and Regional Offices, dissolved the national organization, and set the chapters adrift. . . . We couldn't have done the FBI's work better for them had we been paid agents." Rudd draws an explicit parallel between religious and political extremism: "You develop your own philosophy and it grows more and more intense, the way a religious cult might develop." The Weather Underground lives on in literature. Educated, tormented upper-middle-class radicals-in-hiding have played significant roles in novels by Philip Roth, Jay Cantor, Russell Banks, Marge Piercy, Neil Gordon, and Dana Spiotta, to name just a few A-list authors who have been drawn to this subject.

During this same period, Germany, Italy, and Japan contended with violent (in fact, much more violent) Marxist-Leninist groups of their own. Citing Lenin in their manifestos,

*Almost three decades later, Ayers, by then a professor of education at the University of Illinois, would become a sideshow in the 2008 presidential election, when Barack Obama was fiercely criticized for their alleged associations.

who "had especially advocated the first goal of armed struggle, that is the liquidation of the individual functionaries of the apparatus of oppression," Germany's Red Army Faction, or Baader-Meinhof Gang—after its founders Andreas Baader (1943–1977) and Ulrike Marie Meinhof (1934–1976)—killed thirty-four people, among them policemen, American soldiers, government officials, and businessmen. When Palestinian Black Septemberists murdered Jewish athletes at the Munich Olympics, Meinhof applauded the action as "simultaneously anti-imperialist, anti-fascist and internationalist."

Italy's Red Brigades carried out kidnappings and murders throughout the 1970s. Their most prominent victim was Aldo Moro (1916–1978), a former prime minister. France's refusal to extradite Marina Petrella, a Red Brigade cell leader who had been sentenced in absentia in Italy to life imprisonment for plotting the murder of a police officer and the kidnapping of a judge, "provoked outrage in Italy and stirred dormant tensions between the countries," the *New York Times* reported in October 2008.

Japan's Red Army, also known as the Anti-Imperialist International Brigade (AIIB), Nippon Sekigun, Holy War Brigade, and the Anti-War Democratic Front, carried out a number of hijackings, kidnappings, and bombings in the 1970s, perhaps most notoriously one that they undertook on behalf of the Popular Front for the Liberation of Palestine. On May 30, 1972, three Japanese commandos arrived at Lod Airport in Tel Aviv, Israel, aboard an Air France jet. When they entered the terminal, they removed automatic weapons from the violin cases they were carrying and opened fire on airport workers, passengers, and other passersby, wounding seventy-eight and killing twenty-four. The attack was said to have been revenge for the victims of the Deir Yassin massacre of April 9, 1948, when commandos from the Jewish Irgun and the Stern Gang murdered between 120 and 250 Palestinian villagers.

Woodmen of the World

The Modern Woodmen of America was founded by Joseph Cullen Root (1844–1913), an insurance salesman and 33-degree **Mason** who also belonged to the **Odd Fellows**, the **Knights of Pythias**, and the **Knights Templar**. He chose the name "woodmen" for the order, he said, because the insurance policies it provided its members would clear away their financial problems as a woodman clears brush. He created Woodmen of the World (and its women's auxiliary Women of Woodcraft) after he had a falling-out with the management of the Modern Woodmen. Tree-shaped cemetery markers, or "treestones," can still be found throughout the Midwest, marking its members' graves. Both insurance companies survive to this day.

Another secret society that seamlessly weds arboreal and actuarial themes is the Ancient Order of Foresters, an outgrowth of the British Royal Order of Foresters, which claims to date back to Robin Hood's day, but was probably founded in the late eighteenth century. The American groups—among them the Catholic Order of Foresters, the Independent Order of Foresters, Foresters of America, and Companions of the Forest, to name a few—mostly came into being in the 1870s; the Catholic Order of Foresters and the Independent Order of Foresters still survive. This excerpt from the Ancient Order of Foresters' initiation oath (circa 1907) shows how the legend of Robin Hood and his Merry Men was co-opted and transformed into a slick sales pitch:

> It has been truthfully said that nothing is more uncertain than the proportion of sickness and death which falls to the lot of the individual, but that nothing is more certain than the percentage of sickness and death among a multitude of men. As a multitude of men, seeking to help each other, and to bear one another's burdens, the Ancient Order of Foresters exists and has existed from time immemorial. It

assumes the individual's inevitable liability for sickness and death, and distributes it among a number of his fellow members, who willingly bear their share, knowing that their own turn will come in time.

This, then, is Benevolence: the refined robbery of Robin Hood. The word "Benevolence" is derived from two Latin words signifying good will, and is synonymous with benignity, humanity, tenderness and kindness. It does not mean charity: for charity, while a worthy virtue, and the corner stone of many societies, has no place in the Forestric vocabulary. We do not dispense charity. Whatsoever our members may receive, they obtain as a matter of right, for which they have paid, and for which they are expected to pay.

World Economic Forum

A nonprofit foundation created by the Swiss economist Klaus Schwab in 1971 whose mission, broadly stated, is "improving the state of the world." The WEF brings together international movers and shakers in commerce, politics, academia, and media at its annual conferences in Davos, Switzerland. Unlike the meetings at **Bilderberg**, virtually all of the WEF's sessions are open to journalists; many of them are also Webcast. One of the sessions at its 2004 meeting was "The Conspiracy Behind Conspiracy Theories: Have Extraterrestrials Made Contact with Government Leaders?" which if nothing else suggests that its organizers have a sense of humor—and an awareness of the conspiracist fringe. Samuel Huntington coined the appellation "Davos Man" to describe those members of the international business and political world who

have little need for national loyalty, view national boundaries as obstacles that thankfully are vanishing, and see national governments as residues from the past whose only useful function is to facilitate the elite's global operations.

Others have called them rootless international financiers—proponents of a One-World **New World Order** in which patriotism is a forgotten relic of a bygone age. (See also **Council on Foreign Relations and Other Think Tanks and Conferences.**)

Yakuza

Japan's heavily tattooed criminal gangs, whose members display their allegiance to their bosses by amputating the joints of their little fingers at their whim. The Yakuza fancy themselves to be descendants of the *machi-yakko*, citizen militias that formed in Japan some three hundred years ago to defend against *kabuki-mono* ("crazy ones"), unemployed samurai who took up marauding. More likely, they're the heirs of the *kabuki-mono* themselves. The name "Yakuza" is a portmanteau of the Japanese words for the numbers eight, nine, and three, which add up to twenty, a losing hand in the popular Japanese card game Oichu-Kabu. The Yakuza, in other words, are "bad hands."

Yakuza soldiers have an *oyabun-kobun* relationship with their bosses (meaning "father-son," or unquestioningly obedient). As in the Italian **Mafia**, there are bosses and there are bosses of bosses. Yoshio Kodama (1911–1984), an ultranationalist with an international reach, brokered treaties between rival gangs and engaged in spectacular acts of corporate extortion (for example, in return for millions of dollars from Lockheed, he arranged to have the president of All Nippon Airways fired and replaced with an executive who was willing to purchase a fleet of Lockheed's new wide-body jets). Kazuo Taoka (1913–1981) ran Tokyo's thirteen-thousand-member Yamaguchi-gumi.

Each Yakuza organization has a *kumicho*, or supreme boss; then a *saiko koman*, a counselor; and a *so-honbucho*, a headquarters chief. The *wakagashira*, or number-two man, oversees a number of local gangs (there are as many as five thousand of them throughout Japan), assisted by a *fuku-honbucho*, who runs a few subordinate gangs of his own. A *shateigashira* and his *shateigashira-hosa* (assistant) are lesser bosses; below them are *shatei* (younger brothers) and *wakashu* (junior leaders). Below them are three kinds of soldiers: *tekiya*, or street hustlers and con men; *bakuto*, or professional gamblers; and *gurentai*, or hoods. *Sokaiya* ("shareholders-meeting men") specialize in corporate extortion: they put executives in compromising positions so they can blackmail them, or shake down whole companies by threatening to expose their dirty laundry at their shareholders' meetings. Or they might ask a corporation to buy ad space in a Yakuza-controlled magazine to forestall a negative story that's slated to appear in the business section, or demand exorbitant sponsorship fees for beauty pageants and golf tournaments.

The Yakuza's other activities, like most organized-crime syndicates, include smuggling, loan-sharking, money laundering, narcotics (especially methamphetamines), stock market manipulation, tourist scams, and gunrunning. Yakuza are deeply involved in the sex trade—they purchase young girls from China and the Philippines and exploit them as prostitutes; produce and distribute pornography; and organize sex tours in cities like Bangkok, Manila, Seoul, and Taipei. The Yakuza are beginning to have a significant presence in America, especially Hawaii, Los Angeles, and Las Vegas, where they are forging alliances with already-established Vietnamese, Korean, Chinese, and Italian crime syndicates.

ALSO BY ARTHUR GOLDWAG

*"As wildly entertaining as it is learned, this engaging book
should prove compulsive for browsers who don't know enough
and have been bluffing for years (in short, everyone)."*
—Phillip Lopate

'ISMS AND 'OLOGIES
*All the Movements, Ideologies, and Doctrines
That Have Shaped Our World*

From fundamentalism to evangelicalism and from
Platonism to New Historicism, we live in a world run
rampant with doctrines, philosophies, concepts, and
creeds. But what do they all mean? Where does post-
modernism stop and poststructuralism begin? Who
practices Wahhabism? What is Locofocoism? When was
modernism actually modern? Finally we have *'Isms and
'Ologies*, the ultimate guide to all the mind-boggling
movements, precocious principles, and tricky theories
that shape the society we live in. It is the answer to our
intellectual prayers and a must-have for the budding
genius in everyone.

Reference/978-0-307-27907-1

VINTAGE BOOKS
Available at your local bookstore, or visit
www.randomhouse.com